P9-CQY-067

CAMDEN MISCELLANY

VOL. XX

CAMDEN MISCELLANY

VOL. XX

CAMDEN THIRD SERIES

VOLUME LXXXIII

LONDON
OFFICES OF THE ROYAL HISTORICAL SOCIETY
96 CHEYNE WALK, S.W.10
1953

Printed in Great Britain by Butler & Tanner Ltd., Frome and London

CONTENTS

A BRIEFE COLLECTION OF THE QUEENES MAJESTIES MOST HIGH AND MOST HONOURABLE COURTES OF RECORDES

BY

RICHARD ROBINSON

EDITED BY

R. L. RICKARD

ASSISTANT LIBRARIAN

NEW COLLEGE, OXFORD

CAMDEN MISCELLANY

VOL. XX

LONDON

OFFICES OF THE ROYAL HISTORICAL SOCIETY

96 CHEYNE WALK, S.W.10

1953

CONTENTS

INTRODUCTION

New College, Oxford, acquired its MS. No. 325 by gift from Thomas Philpott, D.D., Fellow of the College 1609–24, rector of Akeley, Bucks., and of Turweston, Bucks. In the beginning of the Civil War he suffered for his loyalty and good conscience by the loss of his goods and by imprisonment. He died in 1671.

The manuscript, which is in four parts, is written on leaves of paper of folio size, originally numbered A1 to T4, but paginated in pencil on one side only at a recent date. The first part consists of pages A1 to M3, and contains 'A Briefe collection of the Queenes Majesties most High and most Honourable Courtes of Recordes'; pages M4 to P2 contain 'An abstract of the particular Charges defray'd with in divers Courts of Records for H. Majestie at the Common Lawes of the Land very necessarye & needfull for all young practicioners and students at the Lawe, as also for suitors in ye said Courts'; P2 to Q2 contain 'What a Testament or last will is, and how many kinds of testaments ther be'; and pages Q3 to T4 'Cases hors del Curia Wardorum'. Stitched to this is a manuscript written in a different hand, entitled 'A true collection as well of all the Kings majesties offices in any the courts at Westminster, as of all the officers and fees of his majesties honorable howsehold'. The whole is stitched into a parchment cover with the date 1602 on the outside.

MS. No. 125 at All Souls College, Oxford, contains 'A treatise of the severall judiciall courts in England, their jurisdiction, officers, and manner of proceeding therein' and ends with 'Finis Febru. 14. 1593, R. Robinson'. This manuscript consists of 10 folios quarto size, and though similar to the New College manuscript it is very much shorter and less complete.

The present transcript consists of the first part of the New College manuscript. Its author, Richard Robinson (*fl.* 1576–1603), was a freeman of the Leathersellers' Company, as appears from his *Eupolemia*, an account of his works 1576–99, in the passage 'Certain Selected Histories for Christian Recreations with their severall Moralizations brought into English Verse, Dedicated to Mr. Symon Roe, Master of the Company of ye Lethersellers wherof I am a free member who gave mee for his booke 2s vjd and the Company vijs vjd more'.[1] In 1576 he was residing in a chamber at the south side of St. Paul's. In 1585 he is described as 'of Fryers', and in 1595/6 he was living in a house in Harp Alley, Shoe Lane. In 1598 he was a suitor to the Queen for one of the twelve alms-houses in Westminster.[2]

He dedicated *A Second Proceeding in the Harmony of King David's Harp* in 1592 'to the R. Honorable Sr. John Puckering knight Lord Keeper of the Greate seale of England, who gave me for his Booke 2 Angels XXs, his Lady gave mee for her Booke vjs viijd'. 'Of his worthy Patronage and benevolence I may wryte & say O how fayre a thinge ys Mercy in the tyme of anguish, yt ys lyke a Clowde of rayne coming in the tyme of a droughte, Ecclus 35. 10'.[3]

[1] George McGill Vogt, 'Richard Robinson's Eupolemia 1603', *Studies in Philology*, xxi (1924), 637.

[2] *Ibid.*, 643.

[3] *Ibid.*, 637.

A Third Proceeding in the Harmony of King David's Harp was dedicated to Queen Elizabeth in 1595. For this work he received no payment and was obliged to sell his books and the lease of his house in Harp Alley. Robinson gives a long and amusing account of the Queen's acceptance of the gift.[1]

In compiling *A Briefe collection of the Courtes of Recordes* Robinson clearly made use of Alexander Fisher's manuscript *Description of the courts of justice in England*.[2] The Introduction is mainly from Fisher, and though Robinson's account of Parliament is much longer than Fisher's, parts of the two are similar. This is also true of the King's Bench and Chancery, but there is less similarity, for instance, in the Court of Requests. Fisher's order is :—Parliament, Chancery, King's Bench, Common Pleas, Exchequer, Court of Wards, Star Chamber, Court of Requests, Duchy Court; Robinson's order is the same as far as Common Pleas, and then continues Star Chamber, Court of Requests, Exchequer, Court of Wards, Duchy Court. It is a much fuller, and, in view of the addition of the various officers of the courts, a much more interesting document than that of Fisher.

Although the manuscript is dated 10 July 1592 on the title page and 1602 on the cover, it is obvious that the alterations in the list of regnal years (omitted from this transcript) were made by Robinson in 1603, for the regnal years of Queen Elizabeth have been altered over an earlier figure to 45. 4. 15, and 'Jacobus' added, but his regnal years left blank. It would also appear that by the use of 'Her Majesty' in some cases and 'His Majesty' in others that parts of the document were re-written in the same year.

The Editor wishes to thank the Warden and Fellows of New College, Oxford, for their permission to publish this transcript. He also acknowledges with gratitude the kind and expert help given him by Mr. H. E. Bell, M.A., Fellow and Tutor of New College.

[1] *Ibid.*, 637–40.
[2] Fisher, P.R.O., *State Papers Domestic Eliz.*, cx, no. 19.

A BRIEFE COLLECTION OF THE QUEENES MAJESTIES MOST HIGH AND MOST HONOURABLE COURTES OF RECORDES

To The Right Honorable Sir Jo. Puckering: K[t]
Lord Keeper of ye greate Seale of England.
Unto whose honorable Patronage and protection I
humbly submitt mee and this my poore travell
to the publike utilitye of my Prince and Native Countrye.
A Briefe Collection of the Queenes Majesties most
High and most Honourable Courtes of Recordes
wherof Six do concerne ye Administracion
of Justice and Three others her Majesties
Revenues, as how, wheare, and by
what Magistrates, Judges
and other Officers they
are Kepte at West-
minster.

To the Glory of God Honour of Her Maiestie
and utilitye of the Church & Common Wealth
of England more amply discribed
then ever heartofore & perfected
accordinge to the state of
the time now present.

Diligently Collected by R: Robinson
Cittizen of London: Julii: 10[o]
Anno: Dom: 1592:

(*In margin:* Lawes of England Consisting in Practize And Judgment)

The distributive partes of this Booke

The Lawes of England Consisteth in 2 points { Practize / Judgment

In practize are Considered { The persons and their office

The Parsons are { Prothonataries / Soliciters / Atturneys

The Office ys to prepare the matter, and to make it ready for the Judges to determine.
The Prothonataries are the Clarckes in theis Courtes which do record the matters

depending in Judgment, frame their pleadinges, and enter the rules of the Court withe the Verdictes and Judgments there also given.

The Solicitors are or should be Learned in the Lawes of the Realme, who being rightly instructed of the Suitors Case do more skillfully emforme the Serieants and Counsellours at Lawe in the same.

Atturneys are such as have by experience learned and do knowe the orders and manner of proceedinge in every Courte wheare they searve, these purchase out the Writtes and processe belonging to their Clyentes case, there they see their suits that they be not hindered by negligence, they pay the ffees belonging to the Courte and prepare the Cause for Judgment.

In Judgment are considered 4 things { The persons / The place / The matter / The manner } in proceeding to Judgment.

The Parsons in and for Judgment are 1. { The Ho: Judges in ye severall Courtes.
2. The Learned Seriauntes and Councellors at Lawe }

The places for Judgment are the Courts wheare the Sentence is given, and the Lawes are made.

Of which Courts the whole number being Nine, Six therbe servinge for Administracion of Justice, Viz. The most high and most Honorable Court of Parliament. The high and Honorable Courts of Chauncery : Kinges bench : Common Pleas : Starrechamber ; and of Requestes to the Kinges Maiestie : And three other Courts beinge for his Maiesties revennues are theis—

The Honorable Court of the Exchequer : Of the Wards, and Lyveryes : And of the Dutchy or Countye Pallatine of Lancaster. Unto all which in the end of this booke is added ye Court for ye Writt Nisi prius, which may be ether kept in ye Guild hall of London or before the Justices itinerant in their Severall circuits about and thoroughout England.

The matters of all theise Courts and of the Lawe Consist in { Judgment / Justice / Equitie }

The Manner of proceedinge to Judgment in every Court is severall accordinge to the Certaine state and Condicion thereof usuall at this day which in severall forme are orderly thus discribed. viz.

(*In margin :* Parliament.)

Imprimis the Most High and Most Honorable
Court of Parliament.

(*In margin :* Effects.)

In this the Kinges Majesties principall Court of Records and first Court of Justice, Lawes are made, mittigated or abrogated, Subsidies and fifteenes are graunted to his Highnes, States of Dignitye advaunced, and for indignity abased, Guiftes of Offices as well spirituall as temporall vacant at his Majesties disposition, Common wronges not holpen in other Courts are heare amended, and rare or difficult cases ended, heare also are Attainders Confirmed or annulled. Corruption of blood restored, errors Committed in the Kinges Bench or Chauncery Corrected, and all things for the Glorie of god, honour of the Prince and publique benefitt of all his good Subiects, and to the Subversion or Conversion of their adversaries, enacted, ratefied and established.

This Court Consistinge of twoo severall houses, The Higher and the Lower, is kept in the ould Pallace at Westminster neere the Court of Requests and is thus distinctly described.

In the Higher house are these Judges
and occurraunces

(*In margin:* The Kings Matie Supreame head & iudge in this Courte. Writts of Summons at the day & place, *and* His Maties Royall presence & Direccion.)

Imprimis our most gratious Souveraigne Lorde Kinge James by the grace of god, etc. ffirst his Highness sendeth forth his Writtes of Summons at Least 40 dayes before any Sessions of Parliament boath to the Nobylitye Spirituall and Temporall and also to the Sherriffs of every Shire, ffor choice of the Knights, Cittizens and Burgesses, and Spirituall and temporall inferior to come to the Parliament, by a daye, and at a place Limitted in the same Writtes. On which daye his excellent Majestie in his Royall parson, and Robes commeth amongst the states there assembled whearwith prayer unto God by them all generall made for his Majestie, and to the wellfare of his Domminions, his Highnes doth hearuppon (as it weare) open the Doore of their authoritye for their proceedinge unto such things as time and Occasion needfull shall require. There his Highnes sittinge in his Royall Tribunall or Chaire of State separate from all others at the upper end of this house, (after his Maiesties directions unto them, somewhat by the Lord Keeper or Lorde Chauncellor signified) the same day towards ye Evening departethe, leavinge the successe to Godes grace, and their good Consultations in ye same Session of Parliament.

The other Judges in the higher house
are these viz.—

(*In margin:* Other Judges are: The Lordes spirituall.)

Uppon the Right hand of that house do sitt the Lordes Spirituall and they are theis: The most Reverend ffather in God, John by ye Devine providence Archbishopp of Canterburye, Primate and Metropolitane of all England, who hath in his province there present (yf they be living or in Case to come,) Twenty other Bishopps viz: London, Rochester, Winchester, Exeter, Chichester, Bristoll, Bathe and Wells, Oxford, Glocester, Worcester, Norwich, Elie, Lincolne, Peterborough, Salisburye, Lettchfeild and Coventrye, being 16 other Bishopps in England, and iiij other Bishopps in Wales, viz. St Davids in Pembrokeshire, St Asaphe in fflintshire, Bangor in Carnarvanshire, and Landaffe in Glamorganshire. So in all besides himsealfe twenty other Bishopps besides himsealfe in England and Wales; The right Reverend ffather in god, John by Devine providence Primate and Metropolitane of Yorke, who hathe in his province there presente (yf they be Livinge) or in Case to come, 3 other Bishopps viz: Durham, Hereford, Carlile, Chester so that these 2 Archbishopps, sitting uppermost and the other xxiij Bishopps with them according to their Callinge, are in all 25 Spirituall Lordes.

Uppon ye Left side of that house do Sitt all ye temporall Nobylytye in England, in their severall Callinges, as theis weare at the Last Parliament 1589. And yet are of good honour and Reputation: Viz: The Lord Marquesse of Winchester, theis 19 Earles. Viz: Oxford; Northumberland; Shrewsbury; Kent, Darby, Worcester, Ruttland, Cumberland, Sussex, Huntington, Bath, Warwick, Southampton, Bedford, Pembroke, Hartford, Leycester, Essex, Lincolne. 2 Viscounts, Montague, Bindon, Also these Lordes Barrons, 41 of good Honour and Reputacon, viz: Aburgavenay, Audley, Zouch, Barkley, Morley, Dacres, Of ye South, Cobham, Stafford, Gray of Wilton, Scroope, Dudley, Latimer, Lumley, Mountioy, Oagle, Mounteagle, Sands, Vaux, Windsor, Wentworth, Borough, Morden, Crumwel, Evers, Wharton, rich: Willoughby, Sheffeild, Darcye of Cliche, Barron of effingham, North, Shandois, Hunsdon, Lord St John of Bletso, Buckhurst, Delaware, Burhley, Compton, Cheney, Norris, Fytzwaters, in all—one Marquesse, XIX Earles, 2 Viscounts, and 41 Lordes Barrons, do make Three skore and three Lordes of the Nobilytye Temporall sitting on the Left side of the house.

(*In margin:* Lorde Keeper of ye Great Seale of England.)

In the middst of this house some distaince from before his Majestie sitteth by office ye Lord Keeper of the great Seale of england or otherwise the Lord Chauncellor (yf any such be). he was the last parliament, 1589, the right Honorable Sir Chrestopher Hatton, of the most noble order of the garter knight, etc, who deceased the last yeare 1591: and Sir John Puckering created the yeare 1592, and was sometyme speaker of the parliament anno 1586: The Lord Keeper or Lorde Chauncellor (when ther he bee) for all his owne office, for the time beinge during the Parliament; The Orator for the prince for the time, by authoryty useth some Certaine speech from his Majestie to the Lords Spirituall and temporall, the first daye of the Session of Parliament, according as time and occasion offer necessitye, and is all waies after during the same session of parliament, hearing, receavinge, and marking the Consents of boath houses uppon their Bills exhibited from time to time.

(*In margin:* Clearck of the higher House. Certaine Judges at the Common Lawes.)

There sitteth directly under him the Clarcke of the Higher house, who readeth the bills thrice in every 3 severall dayes which are agreed uppon at last in boath houses; And recordeth the Consent of the Lordes Spirituall and temporall by each particular mans severall consent or not consent. But yf they be all agreed for Certainty, then he setteth down the agreement of the Nobylyty Spirituall and temporall thus, the Lordes have agreed and theruppon endorseth this direction. Bee it given to the Commons mening therby to have the agreement also of the Commons therunto Confirmed. And yett all this is not so much to any purpose Materiall, except the Kinges Majestie who is the head in all causes of this Court, and elce wheare in his Majesties Dominions, do as principall Judge returne his good likinge for Confirmacion thereof in theise Words; The Kinge is pleased; or elce reciteth the deliberacion thereof in theis words; The Kinge will advise himsealf. This Clarcke keepeth such roles and recordes of the parliament and also such private Statutes as are not printed which weare Concerning the higher house. Theare do sitt aparte by them selves in this house, also Certaine Judges at the Common Lawes, which have no voice but only shewe their opinion uppon matters then in question betweene ye Lordes propounded, and thus much for the higher House.

In the Lower houses are theise Judges
and occurraunces.

They which are reputed for the Lower house, by name the Commons Consist of theis estates, viz: Knights, Esquires and Gentlemen, as I said before, by his Majesties Writt, 40 daies before any session of Parliament be summoned to appeare, the Sheriffs of every sheere Choosing them thus: out of every Shire 2 Knights: out of every Citty in every Shire, 2 Cittizens: and out of the burroughes, townes hearunder expressed, Twoo burgesses for every burrough towne in england, alsoe out of the 12 shires in Wales out of every shire one Knight, one Cittizen and one Burgesse in manner and forme followinge, and first in England out of sheires, are these Knightes, Cittizens and Burgesses viz: Alphabetically thus described:

1. Barkeshire
   Knightes 2.
   Burgesses of New Windsor, Reddinge, Wallingford, Abington 8.
2. Bedforeshire
   Knightes 2.
   Burgesses of Bedford 2.
3. Buckinghamshire
   Knightes 2.
   Burgesses of Buckingham, Wickham, Alesbury 6.
4. Cambridgshire
   Knightes 2.
   Burgesses of Cambridge 2.
5. Cheshire
   Knightes 2.
   Cittizens of Chester 2.
6. Cornewall
   Knightes 2.
   Burgesses of Launceston als Newporte, Leskarde, Camnellford, Lostwithiell, Portnighsham, Danhenet als Portlowe, Truto, Grampount, Eastlowe, Helston, Prurye, Saltashe, Tregonye, Trebena als Bossin, S[t] Ives, ffowaye, Germin, Michaell, St Maryes 40.
7. Cumberland
   Knightes 2.
   Cittizens of Carleill 2.
8. Darbyshire
   Knightes 2.
   Burgesses of Darbye 2.
9. Devonshire
   Knightes 2.
   Citizens of exeter 2.
   Burgesses of Tottnes, Plimouthe, Barstable als Barnestable, Plimton, Tavestock, Dartmouth, Cliston, Hardnes 16.

10. Dorsetshire	
Knightes	2.
Burgesses of Poole, Dorchester, Lyme, Melcombe, Waymouth, Burport als Brightport, Shaftburye, Warcham [*sic*]	16.
11. Essex	
Knightes	2.
Burgesses of Colchester, Walden als Malden	4.
12. Glostershire	
Knightes	2.
Cittizens of Glocester Burgesses of Cicester	4.
13. Hartfordshire	
Knightes	2.
Burgesses of St Albans	2.
14. Herefordshire	
Knightes	2.
Cittizens of Hereford	2.
Burgesses of Lempster	2.
15. Huntingtonshire	
Knightes	2.
Burgesses of Huntington	2.
16. Kent	
Knightes	2.
Cittizens of Canterbury, Rochester	4.
Burgesses of Maidestone, Quinborow	4.
17. Lancastarshire	
Knightes	2.
Burgesses of Lancaster, Preston in Andernes, Liverpoole, Newton, Wigan, Clythero	12.
18. Leicestershire	
Knightes	2.
Burgesses of Leicester	2.
19. Lincolnshire	
Knightes	2.
Cittizens of Lincolne	2.
Burgesses of Boston, Grimsbye, Stanford, Grantham	8.
20. Middlesex	
Knightes	2.
Cittizens of London	4.
Cittizens of Westminster	2.
21. Monmouthshire	
Knightes	2.
Burgesses of Monmouth	2.
22. Norffolke	
Knightes	2.
Cittizens of Norwich	2.
Burgesses of Lynne, Great Yarmouth, Thetford, Castlerising	8.

23. Northamptonshire
- Knightes 2.
- Cittizens of Peterborough 2.
- Burgesses of Northampton, Barckley, Higham Ferryes 6.

24. Northumberland
- Knightes 2.
- Burgesses of Newcastle uppon Tine, Morpethe, Barwicke 6.

25. Nottinghamshire
- Knightes 2.
- Burgesses of Nottingham, Newarke, East stratford 6.

26. Oxfordshire
- Knightes 2.
- Cittizens of Oxford 2.
- Burgesses of Banborough, Woodstocke 4.

27. Ruttlandshire
- Knightes 2.
- Cittizens and Burgesses 0.

28. Shropshire
- Knightes 2.
- Burgesses of Sallopp, Bruges als Bridgnorth, Ludlowe, Wenlocke 8.

29. Sommersetshire
- Knightes 2.
- Cittizens of Bristowe 2.
- Burgesses of Bathe 2.
- Burgesses of Wells, Taunton, Bridgwater, Minhead 8.

30. Southampton
- Knightes 2.
- Cittizens of Winchester 2.
- Burgesses of South, Portsmouth, Stocbridge, Petersfield, Christcurch 10.

31. Staffordshire
- Knightes 2.
- Cittizens of Leichfeild 2.
- Burgesses of Strattforde, Newcastell under Lyme, Tamworth 6.

32. Suffolke
- Knightes 2.
- Burgesses of Ipswiche, Dunwiche, Orford, Alborough als Alderborough, Sudburye, Eye 12.

33. Surrey
- Knightes 2.
- Burgesses of Southwarke, Blechingley, Ryegate, Guilford, Gatton 10.

34. Sussex
- Knightes 2.
- Cittizens of Chichester 2.
- Burgesses of Horsham, Midhurst, Lewes, Shoreham, Bramber als Brandbro, Steninge, Eastgreenstead, Arundell 16.

35. Warwickshire
  Knightes 0.
  Cittizens of Coventrye 2.
  Burgesses of Warwicke 2.
36. Westmerlande
  Knightes 2.
  Burgesses of Appleby 2.
37. Wiltshire
  Knightes 2.
  Cittizens of New Sarum 2.
  Burgesses of Wilton, Hindon, Westbury, Devizes, Malmsbury, Budwin, Old Sarum, Dounton, Heytsbury, Cayne als Cawne, Chippenham, Cricklade, Ludgsale als Ludgersale, Watton Bassett, Marleborough 30.
38. Worcestershire
  Knightes 2.
  Cittizens of Worcester 2.
  Burgesses of Wich 2.
39. Yorkeshire
  Knightes 2.
  Cittizens of Yourke 2.
  Burgesses of Kingston uppon Hull, Knauesboroughe, Ryppon, Hudon als Hedon, Borrowbridge, Thuske, Aldboroughe, Beverley, Skarboroughe 18.

Barons of the 5 Portes: (Sandwich, Dover, Hastinge, Romney, Rye), Winchelsey, Hithe (twoo auncient Townes) 14.

Somma Totall in theis 39 Shires.

Knights	74
Cittizens	44
Burgesses	288
Barrons of the 5 ports	14
Totall	420

The 12 shires in ye Countryes of Wales.

1. Anglesey
  Knights 1.
  Burgesse of Beawmorris 1.
2. Brecknock
  Knights 1.
  Burgesse of Brecknocke 1.
3. Carmarden
  Knights 1.
  Burgesse 1.
4. Canarvan
  Knights 1.
  Burgesses 1.

5. Cardigan	
Knightes	I.
Burgesse	I.
6. Denbeigh	
Knightes	I.
Burgesse	I.
7. Flintshire	
Knights	I.
Burgesse	I.
8. Glamorgan	
Knightes	I.
Burgesse	I.
9. Merioneth	
Knighte	I.
Burgesse of Hauerford West	I.
10. Montgommery	
Knights	I.
Burgesse	I.
11. Pembroke	
Knightes	I.
Burgesse	I.
12. Radnor	
Knights	I.
Burgesse	I.

The 4 Cittyes.

St Davids, St Asaph, Bangor, Landaph	4 Cittizens

Somm Totall

Knights	12
Burgesses	12
Cittizens	4
In all	28

Which with the Knights, Cittizens and Burgesses together also with ye Barrons of the 5 portes aforesaide do make in all besides the Archdeacons, deanes and other of the Spirituality not heare named, the number of

Knights	86
Cittizens	48
Burgesses	300
Barons	14
In all	448

(*In margin:* Speaker in the Lower house.

Thouse do chuse a Speaker, who is their mouth and meaninge in all matters by them moved; He was ye last Parliament 1589 Mr Thomas Snagge one of the old Seriants at Lawe in Chauncery Lawe; this their Speaker must the Lower house by the Lord Keeper or Lord Chauncellor present unto the Kinges Majestie before the Parliament begin even on the first daye, and his Highnes eyther alloweth or disalloweth of him, as it shall please him, to have liking or disliking of him, by the mouth of the said Lord Keeper or Lord Chauncellor declaringe the same: This Speaker commendeth and preferreth the Bills exhibited from the lower house, to be ratyfied by the Higher house.

(*In margin:* Serieaunt at Mace to the Speaker.)

Upon this Speaker there is an ordinary Serieaunt at Mace, appoynted to be orderly attendinge, riding before him bare headed and beareth the mace before him reverently. This was 1589: Mr Raph bowyer Esq.

(*In margin:* Clerck of the Lower house.)

There is also a Clearcke of the Lower house who sitteth directly under the Speaker; hee Recordeth the Bills propounded by the Higher house, and sent to the Lower house, and keepeth some other of the Rowles Recordes and Statutes not printed for this house. This was one Mr ffulke Anslowe of Bishop streetfeild in Hartfordshire.

(*In margin:* Consent of the Lower house.)

The Consent of the Lower House uppon Bills exhibited is subscribed by the Clearcke of the Lower house thus, The Commons have agreed; and endorseth it with this direction, Be it given to ye Lords; which is done for their Consent or allowance of the same also, but yet all this tendeth to no great effect except the Kinges Majestie as principall Iudge doe allow the same, Confirminge or deliberatinge therof as afore declared.

(*In margin:* Certaine Committies. *and* Boath houses have equall authorytye of making lawes & speaking freely.)

There are Certaine Committies for the Parliament, Chosen eyther by the Lords of the Higher house, or by theis Commons in the Lower house; and they are to frame the Lawe uppon such Bills as are agreed uppon; and afterwards Ratified by boath houses. Note heare that boath houses have equall authority to enact, new Lawes or abrogated ould Lawes as time and occasion shall permitt. They have also freedome of speeche graunted every one of them to speake his minde baudly, so it bee with obsearvinge Decorum of Dutefull Obedience to the Prince and His Supreame Authoritie.

(*In margin:* The Conclusion of the Parliament.)

The last day of every session of Parliament the Kinges Most excellent Majestie commeth againe in heis Royall person and Robes amongst ye whole assemblye, sittinge as aforesaid in his royall Tribunall. And there for Conclusion of that session after prayer and thanks geven generally by the whole assemblye unto allmighty god for the good estate of his Majestie and his Dominions, and for all thinges happely passed and performed that Session. The Lord Keeper or Lord Chauncellour first in the name of the Lords Spirituall and Temporall, And then the Speaker in the name of the Commons do yeeld his Majestie most humble and harty thancks for his Highnes greate and Princely care over the welfare of all his Subiects and Dominions. Lastly againe the Lord Keeper or Lord Chauncellour in the name of his most excellent Highnes, rendringe them all most harty thancks for their painefull diligence and Endevours employed at that session of Parliament. The Bills allowed are read over, Ratefied, and their Contraries are dashed. And so ye Parliament is for that present eyther fully finished or deferred to further tyme of prorogation by advertesemente given and sett downe wheare and whearto appeare againe for Confirmacon of the same.

And this is a Briefe and trewe discription of the order of the Most high and most Honorable Court of Parliament houlden in England, without the which, no forfeyture of Life, Limme or Lands of any inglishman where no lawe is ordained for the same afforehand is avaylable or Can take place amongst us heare in England.

And heare endeth the Court of Parliament which is the first Court of Justice.

(*In margin:* Chauncery.)

Now followeth the Chauncerye.

The high and Honorable Court of Chauncerye.

(*In margin:* Effects.)

In this his Majesties Court of Record, beinge the Second Court for Justice, Called in Lattin Cancellaria of the verbe Cancello, lus, ui, re, to deface or disgrace that which standeth not with integritye and equitie, is also the highe Court of Conscience ordayned to redresse private Causes, such as by extremitie of Lawe, cannot have an agreeable end, by reason of Circumstances hinderinge them.

Out of this Court, as from the person of the Prince Commeth all manner of Writts, and in the Natura Brevium: Also heare hence come most Commonly Commissions, Pattentes, Licences and Inquisitions. This Court is kept on the Left hand at the upper end of Westminster hall nexte unto the Kinges bench Courte.

(*In margin:* Judges in this Courte are. Sir Th: Egerton. Sir Th: Egerton.)

The Judges in this Courte are the Right Honorable now Lord Keeper of the great seale of England being Sir John Puckeringe, knight who was speaker in the Parliament, 1586, and then was Lord Keeper of the great Seale of England 28 May 1592. The right Worshippfull the Master of the Rowles then being Sir Gilbert Garrerd knight. The Worshippfull Eleaven Masters of the Chauncery, then being Mr. Doctor Lawraunce Hussey, Mr Doctor Mathew Carew, Mr Doctor Ed. fford, Mr Doctor Jo. Stanhopp, Mr Doctor Rich. Cosins, Mr Doctor Tho. Binge, Mr Doctor Ri: Swale, Mr Doctor Will: Lewen, Mr Doctor Jo: Hone, Mr Doctor Tho. Legge, and Mr Doctor Tho. Hunt. All which for the most parte have their residence within the Doctors Commons neere St Paules.

(*In margin:* The honorable Lord Keeper of the great Seale.)

The Lord Keeper hathe that name (de Custodiandum [*sic*] magnum sigillum Angliae) of or for keeping the greate Seale of England, which is fixed by his Majesties graunt, unto Lettres Pattentes and writinges of great waight and importance in this Court.

This Seale is borne before the Lord Keeper in a Sumptuous embrodered purse or Sachell for that purpose by an officer hearafter named, with great and due reverence. This Lord Keeper for the tyme beinge is under and for his Majestie the cheife Judge and Patron of Lawe, equitye and Conscience in all Causes of this Courte, so as he is, Vere moderator Summi iuris ad suppremendam quantamcunque summam iniuriam.

(*In margin:* Master of ye Rowles.)

The Master of the Rowles is the keeper of the Records, Judgments and Sentences given in the Court of Chauncery.

(*In margin:* The XI Masters of ye Chauncerye.)

The eleven Masters of the Chauncerye are Learned Doctors of the Civill Lawe assisting this Court, to shew what is the equitye of the Civill Lawe, and what is Conscience in all Causes.

(*In margin:* Officers in this Courte.)

The Officers in this Court are theis, The Kinges Majesties Atturney generall, then being Mr Tho. Egerton Esq: The Kinges Maiesties Solicitor and Recorder then Mr. Ed. Cooke Esq: the Clarcke of the Crowne, then being Mr Tho: Poole Esq: his deputie in the same Mr Watson in Holborne. The 6 Clarcks of the Chauncerye then beinge Mr Tho: Poole afforesaid Esq, Mr Hubberd, Mr Shugborowe, Mr Rotheram, Mr Eavelinge and Mr Kittermaster. The Register Mr Martin James, The Comptroller of the Seale, Mr Tho Poole afforesaid, Twoo Examiners Mr Jones of St Brides parishe, and Mr. Nicholson of St Mary Bowe parishe, The Comptroller of the Hamper, Mr Brond. The Clarcke of the Writts of the statutes Mr. Wm. Paton. Three Clarckes of the petty bagge, Mr Garth, Mr Halley, Mr Standen. Twoo clarckes of the inrollments of the evidences, Mr Baylye and Mr Heard. The Clarcke of the Subpena Mr Grobham in Chauncery Lane. The xxiiij Cursitors, Certaine Common Soliciters. The Serieant at Mace to the Lord Keeper, Mr. Christofer Hamden gent. The Bearer of the Seale, Mr. Wm Smith gent, The Sealer of the Seale, Mr Cuppidge, The Chaffer of the Waxe, Hugh thorneton. The Cryer in the Court, John Cane. Three pursevaunts, Mr. Taylor, Mr Staunton, Mr Carpenter. The Porter of the Courte.

(*In margin:* The Kinges Atturney.)

The Kinges Majesties Atturney generall Learnedly defendeth aswell matters for his Majesties behoofe, as also suites for his subjects, his clyentes in this Courte, asistinge the same with Lawe and Lerned Counsell in Conscience.

(*In margin:* The Kinges Sollicitor.)

The Kinges Majesties Soliciter informeth this Courte Learnedly of Lawe and Conscience touchinge suites for him and his Subiectes, his Clyauntes in his Courte.

(*In margin:* The Clearcke of the Crowne.)

The Clarcke of the Crowne and his Deputie are the Gardians and Writers of all matters of the Crowne in the Chauncerye, what these are, see ye Learned booke of Stanford, intituled pleas of ye Crowne.

(*In margin :* The six Clearcks.)
The Six Clarckes are the Atturneyes as well for the Plaintiffes as the Deffendants suitors in this Courte, and do make out most of the Writtes of this Courte and Seale them.

(*In margin :* The Register.)
The Register is the Keeper and the engrosser of the Decrees, Publications, orders and iniunctions, yssuing out of this Courte.

(*In margin :* The Comptroller of the Seale.)
The Comptroller of the seale, is to see and allowe of all the writtes made and sealed in this Courte.

(*In margin :* The twoo Examiners.)
The twoo examiners do take ye examinacions of the Wittnesses brought to prove and reprove any matter in this Court alleadged, and to put their depositions and annswers made to their interrgatoryes in writinge.

(*In margin :* The Comptroller of the Hamper.)
The Comptroller of the Hamper receaveth the fines, due to every writt sealed in this Court.

(*In margin :* The Clearckes of the petty bagge.)
The Clarckes of the petty bagge receave the offices found in the Court of Wardes and Liveryes.

(*In margin :* The Clercks of ye writtes of the Statutes.)
The Clarcks of the writtes of ye Statutes maketh them out for the suitors to this Courte accordinge as the Case requireth.

(*In margin :* The Clearks of ye inrollments.)
The Clearcks of the inrollments of the evidences do record them, and do make out the writt Called Scire facias.

(*In margin :* The Clearck of Subpena.)
The Clarcke of the Subpena maketh out that writt as the first moste usuall and ordinarye writt to proceed in suit of this Courte.

(*In margin :* The Cursitors.)
The Cursiters are Clarcks for the shires in England and Wales, which write matters of Course belonginge to this Courte, and also make out the originall writts.

(*In margin :* The Common Solicitors.)
The Sollycyters are gentlemen barristers of the Innes of Court which are seene in ye Lawes of this Realme, and by right informacion of their Sutors case, doth the better instruct the Sarieaunts and Counsellours at Lawe therin, for the preferment of the suitors case.

(*In margin:* Serieant at Mace and bearer of the Seale.)

The Serieaunt at Mace, and bearer of the Seale go Nudis Capitibus vinctisque pedibus, with great Reverence before the Lord Keeper, whither soever he goeth, but the Serieaunt at Mace especially is to bringe any man before the Lord Keeper whome his Lordshipp shall nominate and apoynte him.

(*In margin:* The Sealer.)

The Sealer attendeth Certaine dayes in presence of the Lord Keeper to seale such Letters pattentes and other Writinges of importaunce as his Lordshipp delivereth by order of this Courte unto the suitors which are to have them Sealed and Signed.

(*In margin:* The Chafer of ye Waxe.)

The Chafer of the Waxe is then and there ready attendaunt also to further the sealing of the same matters.

(*In margin:* The Cryer.)

The Cryer Calleth the Suitors into the Courte, and attendeth uppon their Causes.

(*In margin:* The Pursephaunts.)

The Pursephauntes are Messengers sent into the places wheare the partyes dwell to serve the Writtes and bringe the parties into the Courte and to carry Proclamations into all the Cheife Sheires Cittyes and Townes of England.

(*In margin:* The matters in this Courte.)

The Matters in this Courte are all causes wherin equitye and extremitie of Lawes do strive, and wher-by the rigor of the Lawe they have no remedy but Conscience and the Moderation of Summum ius; have Sufficient. And hear is to be noted yt Conscience is so to be regarded in this Court that the Lawes are not neglected, but they must needs meete and ioyne in a third, yt is moderacion of extremyty.

(*In margin:* The Usuall processe.)

The usuall Proces first ordenaryly sent forth is a Subpena, out of this Court to call him before the Lord Keeper as uppon paine of 10. 20. 34. 40 or 100[li], after which served, yf he then appeare not, an Attachias is awarded out against him, last of all yf he be disobedient, there goeth out a Writt of Rebellion against him, and the paine yf he will not come in, or in cominge in, yf he will not obeye, the order of this Court is imprisonment at the Lord Keepers pleasure.

(*In margin:* The manner of Proceedinge.)

The Manner of proceedinge in this Court is by Iniunctions, Decrees, and Orders which are to bind the partye, and yf he resist or refuse to stand to the order, his punishment is imprisonment.

To Conclude this Court may well be called Officina iuris civilis Anglorum, because out of the same issue all manner of proces which giveth the partye plaintif his ground of action in other Courtes. And heare endeth the Court of Chauncery, beinge his Majesties second Court of Recordes for Justice.

The highe and Honourable Court
of the Kinges Bench.

(*In margin:* Effects.)

This his Majesties Court of Records being the third in order for Administration of Justice is called the Kinges Bench Courte, Ex Regibus Anglie olim illic sedentibus by reason the Kings of Englande in tymes past sat there in their owne proper parsons, so that his Majestie havinge like rightfull authoryty at this present in the Royall Croune and dignitye of the same Dominions and Subiects, that his noble pro genetors had: This Court by all meanes yeeldeth him the like Soveraignitye and like due obedience according to gods and his owne Lawes by all absolute authoryty of Justice to defend in this Courte the good, and deface the evill subjects and Causes Contrarye or repugnaunt to the same.

It is kept uppon the right hand of ye Chauncery Court in Westminster Hall on this manner.

In this Court are theis Judges.

(*In margin:* Judges in this Court are)

The Lord Cheif Justice of England representinge his Majesties parson, beinge honorable for his place and Callinge, of which in Anno 1592. Sir John Popham knight, sworne and created 28 Maye.

Three other Worshipfull Judges at the Common Lawe, then being Mr Judge Shute, Mr Judge Clynch, and Mr Judge Gawdye, lying at Serieaunts Inne in Chauncery Lane, all three ould Serieauntes.

Certaine new Serieantes at Lawe made that Michaelmas 1589. Mr Yelverton, Mr Drew, Mr Haman, and Mr Owen of Serieaunts Inne in Fleet Streete and are assistantes in iudgment in this Court.

The Councellors at Lawe serving for Judgment in this Court.

(*In margin:* Sentence given.)

The Sentence is given by the Lord Chief Justice, the others all or the greater parte assentinge as it shall appeare to be in other Courtes, But yf the Judges cannott agree, then is the matter referred to a demurre in the Exchequer Chamber before the Justices of boath Benches, viz. the Kinges Bench, the Common Pleas, and the Lord Chiefe Barron of the Exchequer.

In this Court are these Officers.

(*In margin:* Officers in this Court are theise.)
The Kinges Atturnye generall, then Mr Tho: Egerton Esq.
The Kinges Solicitor generall, then Mr Edward Cooke of the Inner Temple.
The Cheif Prothonotary, then beinge Mr Roper Esq and with home is also ioyned his brother Sir Jo: Roper, k[t].
The Clearke of the Crowne, then beinge Mr Myles Sandes of the Inner Temple.

(*In margin:* Officers also)
The Secondary of ye Court, Mr George Kemp, ffleet Street.
The Custos Brevium Mr Rich. Paine Esq. against ely House.

The Custos Sigilli, Mr Wm Anslowe, by the Exchange.
The Clearck of ye exigents, Mr William Paton.
The Clearck of ye Papers, Mr. Jo. Mathew, New Inne.
The Marshall Mr Calesbye, Certaine Common Atturnyes. Twoo Cryers, Rennett and Cuttberd, 3 Pursephaunts Mr Procter, Mr ffedd, and Mr Withrington, ffower Tipstaves, The Marshalls man. The Porter.

(*In margin:* The Kinges Atturney.)

The Kinges Atturney generall defendeth the Right Royall Title and Dignitye of His Majesties Royall Authoryty Dominions Lawes and Causes in this Courte, and is assistant to the Lord Cheife Justice, and other the Judges in Lawe Iustice, and Equitye.

(*In margin:* The Kinges Solicitor.)

The Kinges Solicitor handleth learnedly as well matters for his Majesties behoofe, as other suits for his subiects his Clyents in this Court.

(*In margin:* The cheif Prothonotaries.)

The Cheife Prothonatoryes are they yt record all orders and rules in this Courte, and all verdicts given being not of Crowne matters, their office is kept at Southampton house in highe Holborne every terme tyme.

(*In margin:* The Clearck of the Crowne.)

The Clearcke of the Crowne, (whose deputie was one Mr Tho: Jene, keepinge his office in the Middle Temple by the Watergate) frameth all Indictments of ffellonye, Murder and Treason, and so for all manner of appeales and after to recorde them, to enter the Verdicts, and make and keepe the recordes therof.

(*In margin:* The Secundarye.)

The Secondarye is Prothonatoryes deputye for the said Causes, and is the keeper and the maker up of those Records in Books.

(*In margin:* The Custos Brevium.)

The Custos Brevium fileth up all the Writts, Judicialls, and Originalls after the Sheriff hath returned them, and is Charged with safe keeping of them.

(*In margin:* The Custos Sigilli.)

The Custos Sigilli, keepeth the Seale and sealeth all the Writts, Pattents and Lycences out of this Court taking his dewe fee for them, and is for them accomptant, his Office was within the ffalcon Court over against St Dunstanes church in ye west.

(*In margin:* The Clearck of the Exigents.)

The Clearcke of the Exigents is to frame all manner of processe of Exigi facias, which do issue out of this Courte, to outlawe any man, and Record the Outlawrye.

(*In margin:* The Clerck of the Papers.)

The Clearcke of ye papers keepeth all scripts, roules and pleadinges, with other thinges in writing which are not of record.

(*In margin:* The Marshall of the Kings Bench.)

The Marshalls office is to see the prisoners Committed to his chardge to be safely kept and brought to the barre before the Judges, and to be ordered according to Judgment in the Court awarded.

(*In margin:* Common Atturneys.)

There are Certaine Common Atturneyes belonging to this Courte in Number and Nature such and so many as the Lord Cheife Justice for the time and place shall appoint. Theis are for the plantiffs and defendantes to frame and make their pleadinges and further the Clientes Causes in all thinges as need shall so require.

(*In margin:* The Cryers.)

The Cryers are to attend uppon the Judges and Call the Juryes into Courte.

(*In margin:* The Pursephaunts.)

The Pursephaunts are to serve the processe and bring the parties into Court.

(*In margin:* The 4 Typstaves.)

The foure Typstaves do attend with reverence to go before the Judges, and do make way for them till they are Come to and from the hall unto Serieaunts Inne.

(*In margin:* The Porter.)

The Porter attendeth at the barre to let in and out all persons havinge accesse.

(*In margin:* The Matters of this Courte.)

The matters of this Court are (to speake properly) all matters Criminall, or offensive to ye Crowne and Royall Dignitye of his Majestie what those be see Stanfordes Booke uppon the Pleas of the Crowne afforesaid; some matters in this Court handled are tearmed suits improper, that is when the Prince (as God forbid and defend) hath any losse or hinderaunce; Theis are Conspiracyes, Champerties, Imbrasier, Maintenaunce, Decies tantum, maimes, slanders, and accions sur le Case, Concerning which we see natura brevium.

(*In margin:* The manner of proceedinge.)

The manner of proceedinge in this Court is by indictment, appeale, and Verdict, and the Writtes prosecuted for the same are, Lattitat, arrest and Bill.

(*In margin:* The Latitat.)

The Latitat is to bring in the partye when he hideth himselfe, and would not appeare, and annswer in this Courte.

(*In margin:* The Arrest.)

The arrest is, when the partie is arrested and is then driven to find bale. viz twoo or more sufficient suerties according to the qualytye of the Case.

(*In margin:* The Bill.)

The Bill, is when the partye is in Custodia Mariscalli and is from thence brought (ut fata volentes ducunt trahuntque volentes) to appeare and make answere, wheare he receaveth Lawe, Judgment and Justice, according to the Qualitye of the Case, or nature of his trangression.

And heare endeth the Kings Bench Court,
being the third Court for Justice.

The high and honourable Courte
of Common Pleas.

This His Majesties Court of Records being the fourth Courte for Justice is so called (ex audienda Comunia Placita) of hearinge Common pleas betweene subiect and subiect at the Common Lawes, so as it serveth for the exact and precise administracion of the Lawes. It is kept on your right hand of your entringe into Westminster hall, all dayes on the tearme tyme on this manner.

In this Court are theis Judges.

(*In margin:* 1. Kingsmel. 2. Warberton. Judges in this Court are)

The Lord Chiefe Justice of the Common pleas honorable for his Callinge and place, then being Sir Edward Anderson, knight, and lyeth in tearme tyme in Seriaunts Inne in fleet streete.

Three other Worshipfull Judges: viz Mr Judge Peream, Mr Judge Wyndham, and Mr Judge Walmesley, of the same house, which are asistant unto him in Judgment, shewing what is Lawe, Justice, and Equitye in that Court.

The Serieaunts at Lawe for this Courte are some times more, and some tymes fewer at the Kinges Majesties pleasure, They which then weare are theis, Mr Serieaunt Snagge, Mr Serieaunt ffleetwood, both his Majesties Serieaunts, with Mr Seriaunt fenner, and also Serieants of the same house in fleet street.

Also Mr. Bernard, Mr Harris and Mr. Glanveile, then Serieants made at Michaellmas 1589, of Serieants Inne in Chauncery Lane.

All these Serieants to searve the tearme of the Common Lawes at the Barre, and twoo of them are for the Prince in what Court soever.

In this Court are theise officers.

(*In margin:* Officers in this Court.)

The Custos Brevium then being Mr Thomas Spencer in Aldersgate street.
The Custos Sigilli, Mr Wm. Anslowe in the kinges bench Court.
Three prothonotaries, Mr Scott, Mr Brooker, and Mr Brownelowe.
The Chirografer, Mr Compton.
The Clarck of the Kinges Silver, Mr Udall of Hampshire.
The Clarck of the Warrants, Mr Haman of the Middle temple.
The Clarcke of the Essoynes, Mr ffosters of Clyffords Inne.
The Clarcke of the Outlawries, Mr Antrobus of Lincolnes Inne.
The maker of Pardons and Lycences, Mr Donett in Sir Nicholas Bacons buildings.
Certaine Philizers, at least xx^{tie} for the shires.

The iiij Exigenters for the shires, Mr Drewe, Mr Millington, Mr Gardner, and Mr Parkinges, Certaine Common Atturneys. ffower Cryers, 2 Pursephaunts, The Porter.

(*In margin:* The Custos Brevium.)

The Custos Brevium, beinge the Cheife Office and Clercke of this Courte, hath Custody of all the Writts whatsoever returnable in this Courte, Come they in at the daye of ye returne or after the returne, which is called Post diem.

(*In margin:* The Custos Sigilli.)

The Custos Sigilli is the same Clercke and Officer as in the Kinges bench, and hath his Office within the faulcon Courte over against S[t] Dunstanes in the West.

(*In margin:* The Prothonotaryes.)

The Prothonotaries are they which after the parties have appeareth [*sic*] in Court do enter the matters in suite, make their pleadinges and enter them.

(*In margin:* The Chirographer.)

The Chirographer is hee that hath the writt of Covenaunt with the Concords brought to him, and he maketh Indentures Trypartite; whereof twoo are delivered to the partye for whose use the same is acknowledged, and the Third parte is reserved with him. And all the Proclamations of the same fine accordinge to the Statutes made are endorsed on the third parte remaininge, and it is Commonly called the foote of the fine.

(*In margin:* The Clearcke of the K. Silver.)

The Clarcke of the Kinges Silver is a distinct office of the fines, and is hee who setteth downe the monye, that his Majestie is to have for the fine, accordinge to the yearly value, of the Land Confessed, knowne, deposed or agreed uppon.

(*In margin:* The Cleark of ye warrants.)

The Clearck of the Warraunts taketh ye warrants of an Atturney which shall prosecute for the Plaintiffe and Defendaunt.

(*In margin:* The Clerck of the Essoyne. What the Essoines bee.)

The Clearcke of the Essoynes dothe essoyne the defendaunt in every accion before ye day of appearaunce excusinge his appearaunce. This essoynes is an ordinary delay by Office of Courte in every accion, and the Officer before whome the Clercke is to take theis essoynes is the puny Justice in the Common place, who for that purpose sitteth some tearmes three daies before the same.

(*In margin:* The Clerck of ye Juries.)

The Clarcke of ye Juries is he which maketh the Venire facias, to the Sheriffes to warne the Jurye by.

(*In margin:* The Clerke of ye OutLawries.)

The Clearcke of the Outlawries is hee which maketh out the Writts that go forth of this Courte for the outlawing of any man within this Courte.

(*In margin:* The maker of ye Pardons.)

The maker of the Pardons & Lycenses is hee which for matters of alienacion, dealeth in causes aunswerable to the orders of the Courte.

(*In margin:* The Philizers.)

The Philizers of the Shires are they which gather together and make upp the meane processe uppon the Originall Writts, entering and delivering them to ye Custos brevium, wheare they are put uppon a file or stringe, there to remaine as uppon record.

(*In margin :* The foure Exigenters.)

The foure exigentors do make and [*sic*] out and enter the exigents, writts of Proclamation made in every Countye, where ye parties are that by Capias will not come into the Courte.

(*In margin :* The Common Atturneyes.)

The Common Atturneyes are in nature and number such and so manye, as the Lord Cheif Justice of this Court shall appointe, for the Plaintiffes and Defendaunts, to frame and make their pleadings and further their suites.

(*In margin :* The Cryers.)

The Cryers are to attend on the Judges and Call ye Juries into the Courte.

(*In margin :* The Pursephaunts.)

The Pursephaunts, are to serve ye processe and bring ye parties into the Courte.

(*In margin :* The Porter.)

The Porter at ye Barre attendeth uppon all persons havinge accesse to the Courte.

The matters of this Courte, are all suits of the Common Lawe commenced by any Writt reall or personall, Originall or Judiciall, such as these be.

(*In margin :* Writts of Course Usuall for matters Clauses in this Courte.)

The Reall writte toucheth the inheritaunce or fee of any man.

The Personall writt toucheth transitorye thinges, as goodes, Chattles, and personall wronges.

The Originall writt sayth in ye end thereof in the person of his Majestie. { Teste me ipsa or me ipsa apud Westmonesterium.

The Judiciall writt for ye Kings bench sayth in ye end therof. { Teste Johanne Popham milite Capitali Justiciario de Banco Regis.

The Judiciall writt for this place saith in the end therof. { Teste Edm^{o} Anderson milite Capitali Justiciario de Communio placitibus.

The Order of Processe in this Courte how they followe one another in this Court is first a Summoveas [*sic*] in some accion, then an Attachias, but in most a Capias then alias Capias, then next unto that an alias Capias plures, butt last an exigi facias ; and a Proclamacion unto the County wheare the defendant dwelleth.

(*In margin :* The Summoneas.)

The Summoneas is the Cheife and Originall going out of ye Chauncery, and is directed to the Sheriffe to bringe in the partye by a daye.

(*In margin :* The Seriffes order to serve ye writt.)

The Sheriffs order to serve this Writte is first to go himsealfe, or send his Baylife to his land and there to garnishe the partie by settinge up a sticke in his land. This done the Sheriffe returneth two Common pledges, Johannes Doe and Ricardus Roe an 2 Summoners, Ricardus Den and Henricus fen.

(*In margin :* Ye Attachias.)

After the Summoneas (yf the partie come not in) yssueth out an Attachias in nature of a precept, to authorize the Sheriffe to goe to his land or house, and there to take a pledge for his appearaunce.

(*In margin:* The Plaintiffe outlawing the defendant by order of the said process.)

But yf the Plaintiffe meane to outlaw the Defendant he getteth a Summoneas out of ye Chauncery to warne the partye, who returneth Nihill habet etc, Then the Plaintiffe to take his bodye getteth a Capias; then an alias Capias, and then a plures Capias to all which the Sheriffe returneth in order as they be given unto him, non est inuentus. After that yf the partye appeare not, goeth out to the Sheriffe an exigi facias to proclaime the partye in five severall Counties, uppon the Countye daies; After which proclamation, yf he do not appeare he is then returned quinto exactus, et non Comparuit, et ideo Utlagatus, unlesse he first purchase a Supersedeas to the Court to surcease.

(*In margin:* The Supersedeas.)

The Supersedeas at the suite of the defendant quare placitat out of the Chauncery to cause ye plaintiffe to cease from outlawinge the deffendant: and yet an appearaunce to the suite of the defendant.

(*In margin:* The Plaintiffe declareth & ye Defendant annswereth.)

This done the plaintiffe declareth, the defendant annswereth, yf the annswere by [*sic*] yssuable they proceed to tryall, suggesting to the Courte, that the exigent improvide emanauit, shewing that the defendant was allwayes ready to appeare by his Atturney.

(*In margin:* The Manner of proceeding in this Courte.)

The manner of proceedinge, is eyther to ioyne yssue, and so passe to verdict, or els to demurre.

The triall is by verdict, when the question is de facto, as wheare, what, when and by whome.

The triall is by demurre, that is by argument of the Judges, Serieaunts and Counsellors when the Question is De Jure, whether it be lawe or not.

And heare endeth the Courte of Common Pleas,
being his Majesties iiij^th^ Courte of Justice.

The highe and honourable Courte
of Starre Chamber.

This his Majesties Court of Records being the ffyfth Court for Justice, is so called ye Starrchamber Courte, not as some suppose because it is full of Windoes or for yt all the Roofe therof is decked with Images of Starres guilded, but rather like as ye starres do adorne the ffirmament, and in the darck night do give there light unto the earth, So the Lords of the Nobylytye according to their Callinge, do in this Court shine forth by their Vertues of pietye, wisedome and good Justice, into the Church and Commonwealth extended in tyme of disorder by authoritie from the Prince and his Lawes for preservation of publique peace, and punishing the breakers of ye same; and other misdemeanors hearunder expressed. This Court is kept on the east side of the pallace yard by Westminster hall neare the water side every Wensday and friday in tearme time, and every day next after the Last Day of the Tearme.

The Judges in this Courte are most
usually theis.

(*In margin :* The Judges in this Court then usuall.)
The most reverend ffather in god : John Lord Archbishop of Canterbury.
The Right Honorable the Lord Chauncellor of England.
The Right Honorable the Lord Highe Treasurer of England.
Also Certaine others, the Right Honorable Lordes of his Majesties most Honorable privye Counsell. (viz.)
The Lord Hunsdon : Lord Chamberlaine of her Majesties houshould.
The Lord Howard, Lord high admirall of England.
The Lord Cobham, Barron of ye Cinque portes.
The Right Honorable the Lord Buchurst.
The Right Honorable Sir Tho. Heneage, knight Vice-Chamberlaine.
The Right Honorable Sir Robert Cicill, Knight.
The Right Honorable John Woollye, Secretarye.
and John ffortescue Chauncellor of the exchequer.
The 2 Lord Cheife Justices of boath benches.
The Lord Cheife Barron of thexchequer.
And one of the Clearcks to the Councell, eyther Mr Wade or Mr Ashely whose month it is.

Note that in ye Starrchamber the Honorable Lordes and others of his Majesties most honorable privye Counsell, with theise Judges, as Patrons of trewe Religion, pietye Justice and equitye, do sitt in Consultation, to preserve right, and to punish wronge with proceeding to Judgment, by assent and unitye of voyces, and by open yealding their minds in the Courte, wheare the greater parte is preferred for sentence by declaration of the Lord Keeper who sheweth also the haynousnes of the offence Committed, and the Dewe paine by the Lawes incident to the same, according to the state in every Case ordered by this honorable Courte.

But in the Starrchamber, which is neere unto the Counsell Chamber do most usually sitt theis officers hear under followinge. viz.

(*In margin :* Officers in this Court are theis.)
The Worshipfull her Majesties Atturney generall, then, Mr Tho. Egerton Esq.
The Worshipfull her Majesties Solicitor generall, then, Mr Edward Cooke Esq.
The Clearcke for the Court, Mr William Mills of Grayesinne.
The Register of the Courte, Mr Tho. Milles.
The Examiner in the Courte, Mr Linton.
Three Atturneyes, Mr Hoxt, Mr Grimston, and Mr Writington.
Three Messengers : viz 2 of the Wardens men of the fleete, and one Seriaunt at armes ordinary.
The Keeper of the Starrechamber and ye Courte, Mr Gilpin of Westminster.
The Porter to the Counsell Chamber and to the Court, Mr Humphrey.

(*In margin:* The K: Atturney.)

The Kings Atturney generall, Learnedly handleth as well suits for his Majesties royal prerogative and Learnedly alleadgeth, pro et Contra, as Lawe and Justice alloweth for his Majestie and his subiects.

(*In margin:* The K. Sollicitor.)

The Kings Sollicitor generall, learnedly handleth as well suits for his Majestie as also for his sybiects his Clyentes according to Lawe and Justice.

(*In margin:* The Clerck of ye Courte.)

The Clearcke of the Courte is the keeper of ye recordes, rowles, entries, orders, and decrees, made in this Court and Subscribeth to the Warrants, his Office is at Graise Inne.

(*In margin:* The Register.)

The Register recordeth the matters exhibited and ordered by the Lordes, his Office is within Mr Wm. Milles his office at Graies Inne.

(*In margin:* The Examiner.)

The Examiner taketh the deposition of the wittnesses used on boath sides for the proofe or disproofe of the matter, his office is there alsoe.

(*In margin:* The three Atturneys.)

The 3 Atturneyes are for ye plaintiffe and defendant suitors to the Courte to frame their Complaints and answers and make their matters apt to be heard of the Lordes. Their Lodginges are Mr Hoxt at the Temple, thother 2 at Graies Inne.

(*In margin:* The Messengers.)

The Messengers are to serve the processe, or Warrants out of this Court awarded, and to bringe the parties into Courte.

(*In margin:* The Matters of this Courte.)

The Matters of this Courte, heare usuallye heard and handled are theis, and by statutes published. viz.

Imprimis the takinge of young Maidens, within yeares of age, against the Will of their Parents or Gardiaunts; Anno 4° et 5° Phil: et Mar: Cap. 5°.

All notable forgeries: Anno 5° H. 8. Cap. 8; Anno 5° El. Cap. 14.

All notable periuries. Anno 14° El. Cap. 11.

Counterfaitinge of Lettrs, or privy tokens: Anno. 33. H. 8. Cap. 1.

Sclanderinge of Nobles, and, raising seditious newes. Anno 2. Rich. 2. Cap. 8: Anno 4° et 5° Phil: and M. Cap. 9: Anno 1° Eliz. Cap. 17.

And all the titles of Ryotts, in the Collections or abridgments of the Statutes, made by Rastall, And all notable deceipts or fraudulent delinges wheresoever.

(*In margin:* The manner of proceedinge.)

The Manner of proceedinge being as before declared to iudgment, the usuall proces awarded out of this Court is a Subpena.

(*In margin:* The usuall punishmentes.)

The punishment for the parties so before offendinge, are usuall theise,

Imprisonmentes, Pillorye, ffines, and sometymes boath, according to the qualitye of the Crime.

And heare endeth the Court of Starre Chamber
being his Majesties 5th Courte of Records for Justice.

The high and honourable Courte of Requests.

(*In margin:* Effects.)

This his Majesties Court of Records, beinge the 6th and last Courte for administration of Justice, is yt wherin, all suits, espetially by petitions from poore men exhibited unto the Kings Majestie, are heard, handled, ordered, and ended, neyther indeed should it hould plea of any other Matters then such, and therfore in respect that poore men after longe suits in other Courts and little therin prevailinge, do find in this Court great right for Little Monye, and also speedy redresse in their Causes, it is also called boath the poore mans court and also the Court of Conscyence. It is kept every days of the Tearme, in a wide place upp the staires one way beyound the Kinges bench Court in Westminster hall, and hath a goinge downe an other waye into the old pallace yard, on this manner.

The Judges in this Court are theise.

(*In margin:* The Judges in this Courte.)

The Worshipfull Mr. Jo. Harbert: Doctor civill Lawe.

The Worshipfull Mr. Ralphe Rokesby Counseller of the Common Lawes, who is also Master of St Katherins and theis are boath the Masters of the requests to his Majestie.

Theise Worshipfull Judges skillfully Learned in boath Lawes (as it weare) learned and spetially sollicitors for poore men to his Majestie, and ready meanes for His Highnes to receive, heare, order and end their upright Causes and tedious Causes, with so little Chardge, and as much favour in Conscience & equitie as may bee.

The officers in this Courte are theise.

(*In margin:* The Officers in this Courte.)

The Register, Mr Richard Owseley.

The Examiner, Mr Walgrave.

Three Atturneys, Mr Maddocks, Cox, Vavisor.

Twoo Pursephaunts, No porter to this Court.

(*In margin:* The Register.)

The Register recordeth all matters of Course in this Courte, and Maketh out the processe to bring the parties into the Courte, his office is at the farther staire heade hard by the Courte.

(*In margin:* The Examiner.)

The Examiner opposeth the Wittnesses by oath and recordeth their depositions: his Lodgings and Office is within the New Inne, by the hall dore.

(*In margin:* The three Atturneys.)

The 3 Atturneys serve for the plaintiffs and defendantes to make their Complaints, and frame their answers to a speedy good end, 2 of them, Mr Maddocks and Mr Coats remaine neere the Courte, Mr Vavisor dwelleth in St Giles in the feildses.

(*In margin:* The Pursephaunts.)

The Pursephaunts do serve the processe and bringe the parties into Courte.

(*In margin:* The Matters.)

The matters of this Courte are, as in ye former effectes before specifyed.

(*In margin:* The manner of proceedinge.)

The manner of proceedinge is by petition to his Majestie exhibited and by Clemency from his highnes to the Judges in the suitors behalfe, and the Wisdome and Knowledge of theis Judges in boath Lawes moderatinge the poore mans troble and Chardge and so ordering his Cause to the good and peacable repossession of that, which he before longen and wrongfully was dispossessed of.

The process usuall out of this Courte are a privie Seale, an Attachment, and a proclamation of Rebellion in Case of Disobedience or willfull Stubbornes.

And heare endeth the Court of ye Requests to his Majestie which is the 6th and last Court of his highnes records for administracion of Justice.

Heare endeth the 6 Courts of Justice.

Now followeth ye 3 Honorable Courts of his Majesties Revenues, and first—

The high and honorable Courte of h: Majesties Exchequer.

(*In margin:* Exchequer.)

This h. Majesties Court of Records, and first Court for the Royall Revennues of h. Crowne due unto h. Majestie: is Called in Lattin, fiscus principis, Scaccarium publicum. But now commonly called Scaccarium of the Saxon word Scatz which wee interprete treasure or revennues of the K: as well that which came of the Patrimonye which wee call the Demesnes, as that which comneth of other incidente acquisitions be they Rentes, Customes, Tenthes, Quindecens, Taxes, and Subsidies to be called to accompte in this Courte, which are theise heare under followinge. It is kepte in ye new buildinge upp the staires on the right hand of Westminster hall, in a faire Lardge place, and is devided in manner and forme herunder followinge.

The Judges then usuall in this
Court weare theis.

The Lord high Treasurer of Englande viz Supremus aerarii anglice questor, or tribumus aerarii maximus He was at that tyme ye Right honorable Sir William Cecill Knight of the most noble order of the garter, Barron of Burleigh, and one of her Majesties most honourable privye Counsell, he hath the Chardge and Keepinge of the Queenes treasures, and many offices are at his sole apoyntment and to him accomptaunt: viz as well in the tower and Exchequer Court, as elce wheare in devers places as auditors in the minte, Officers there 5 tellers in the Exchequer, Receavers, Surveyors, Auditors of Lands, Customers of ports and many others etc.

The Lord Cheife Barron of the Exchequer Court hee is honorable for his callinge and place, then being Sir Roger Manwood K[t], in great S[t] Bartholmews, he is called Juridicus rationalis, primus or princeps and is a Learned Judge for Lawe and Counsell, cheifly assistaunte to the Lord Treasurer for Censure to be given in this Courte.

Three other Barrons inferior assistaunts in Lawe and Learned Counsell in the Court, and weare then Mr Barron Gent, Mr Barron Southerton and Mr Barron Clearcke of Serieantes Inne in ffleet Street.

The Chauncellor of the Courte, and by office under Treasurer, supplying the place of the Lord high Treasurer, as governour of this Courte; was then Mr John ffortescue, one of h. Majesties privie Counsell dwelling at the Wardroppe.

The Kings atturney generall, Mr. Tho. Egerton, Esq[r] who is to defend the Kings right, and Royall prerogative in all causes, and to peruse all grauntes particular suites in all causes learnedly alleaginge pro et Cont: for h. Majestie and subiects as ye case require.

The Kings Sollicitor Generall Mr Edward Cooke Esq[r], who handleth Learnedly as well matters for h. Majestie, as suits for his subiects his Clientes in this Courte.

All those do sitt in the Court at ye upper end of the afforesaid new buildinge to heare and handle the Causes of all suitors cominge to the same Courte.

The Officers in this Court usuall are.
Twoo Remembramces [*sic*] so called.

The one beinge Mr Tho: ffanshaw Esq[r] for ye Kings Majestie.
The other Mr. Jo. Osborne gent for ye Lord Treasurer.
The Cheife Clarcke of the pipe: Mr John Morrison Esq[r].
Certaine forreine opposers, Certaine tellers in ye minte.
The Master of the first fruictes and tenths, Sir Ed. Stafford, K[t].
Certaine auditors, Receavers, Rent gatherers, ffeodaries, Tallymakers, Customers, Comptrollers, Searchers, Surveyors, Mintmasters, Monyers.
The foure Tellers of the Receipt in ye Exchequer.
The Gentleman Usher to ye Lord Treasurer, Mr Billsby Esq[r].
Certaine Common Atturneys, Certaine Escheators.
The Serieaunt at mace to the Lord Treasurer, Mr. Jo. Bowyer.
The head Marshall of thExchequer; The under Marshall.
Three Cryers; 2 Pursephaunts; The porter of ye Court.

(*In margin :* The twoo Remembraunces.)

The 2 Remembraunces keepe the Recordes in the exchequer betweene the King and his Subiectes, and their severall Clarckes ; viz Mr ffanshawes in Warwicke Lane, and Mr Osbornes in Ivye Lane in their severall offices, do enter and deliver out the Rules and orders made in thExchequer Courte in Westminster afforesaid, where theire officers are in 2 severall offices there behind the same Courte imployde every tearme tyme.

(*In margin :* The Cheife Clerck of ye Pipe.)

The Cheife Clarcke of ye Pipe, and his inferior Clarckes do make out leases uppon particulars and other Transcripts and Writinges incident to the order of this Courte.

(*In margin :* The forreine apposers.)

The fforreine apposers receave the Sheriffes of every Shires accomptes, and also ye Bonds, tayllyes and other assurances duringe their tyme of Sherifewicke.

(*In margin :* The Sheriffes of ye Shire give up their accompts in this Courte.)

The Sheriffe of every Shire giveth his accomptes upp into this Courte for his tyme, a yeare or more as it is and seeth that ye Kings Justice hath due Course and that processe and writts be duly executed in the shire or Countye, and H. Majesties revenues well answered and brought in by him and his under sheriffe, who do also looke to fines, amerciamentes, and dispatchinge of actions, Criminall and Civill depending in suits of Lawe, which be now come to yssue.

(*In margin :* The Mr of the first fruictes & tenthes.)

The Master of the first fruicts and tenthes as unto K.H. 8 Anno 23 : and K. Ed. 6. Anno 2 : Q. Eliz. Anno 1. by act of parliament Januarii 1559, doth receave them as a dutye payable to H. Majestie in the right of H. Royall Crowne and dignitye answearable from all Bishoppes, Archdeacons, Deacons and other Spirituall persons, by the Auditors, Recevers, Rentgatherers, ffeodaries and Taillymakers.

The Customers, Comptrollers, Searchers, Mint Masters, Tellers in the Minte, Monyers and 4 Tellers in the Exchequer do give their accomptes upp to the Lord Treasurer, or in his absense, to the Chauncellor of thExchequer before nominated.

(*In margin :* The Gent. husher of thexchequer.)

The gentleman Usher to ye Lord Treasurer of thExchequer Courte hath the chardge of lookinge to this Court in due and decent order and attendeth to go before the Lord Treasurer to and from his Courte in tearme tyme daylye, this man also, then had his progenitors had in temporibus Regnorum Regum Ed. 3. Hen. 6. Ed. 4. his pattent of this office Confirmed unto him Anno 4. Eliz. tunc. Regi:

(*In margin :* The Serieant at Mace.)

The Serieant at Mace to the Lord Treasurer goeth on foote bare headed before his Lordshipp, whether so ever he goeth, and is to call any man before him whome he appoynteth.

(*In margin :* Common Atturneis.)

The Common Atturneys are for ye plaintiff and defendant to frame their Common plaintes and answers, and further their suites in the Courte.

(*In margin :* The Escheators.)

The Escheators are they which enquire for tenures of Lands, Tenementes and Hereditamentes and do returne inquisition or offices concerninge the same.

(*In margin :* The 2 Marshalls.)

Boath the Marshalls have the Comittinge Chardge orderinge and disposinge of the prisoners accordinge to the Honorable Decree of this Court.

(*In margin :* The 3 Cryers.)

The 3 Cryers are to attend uppon ye Judges and the Causes in this Courte.

(*In margin :* The Pursephaunts.)

The Pursephaunts are to serve ye processe and bringe the partyes into Courte.

(*In margin :* The Porter.)

The Porter is to attend uppon all persons havinge accesse to and from ye Courte.

(*In margin :* The Matters of this Courte.)

The matters of this Court are all penall punishments All intrusions, alienacions without lycence, and penall forfeictures uppon popular accions ; A popular accion is wheare a parte is given to the informer, the rest to the Prince ; Of this see the whole bodye of the statutes eyther at Lardge or of Rastalls Collection. In this Courte are handled all payments, accompts, receits and expences of ye King Majesties Revenues.

The manner of proceedinge in this Courte is by due forme of Lawe, Justice and Equitye, and the usuall processe of this Courte to prosecute the Cause is a Subpena as in Chauncery aforesaid.

And heare endeth the Exchequer Courte
and first of the Revenues.

The Exchequer Chamber an appendant
to the Exchequer Courte.

(*In margin :* The Exchequer Chamber.)

This is a place adioyninge neer thexchequer Chamber (whearin as I have related in the description of the Kinges bench aforesaid) the Judges then and there not agreeinge, they do hither repaire, referring the matter to a demurrer in this place before ye 2 Lordes Cheife Justices of boath benches, and the Lord Cheife Barron of the Exchequer, And heare by an ould rule, Le Chauncellor et toutes Les Justices (sur diffecullty) suer office par Commission hors de Chauncery Anno 5. Hen. 5. Cap. 2.

The place is also kept by the said Mr William Billsbey. gent. Usher to the Lord Treasurer in the Exchequer Courte, And heere the Judges do use 2 dayes weekly in the forenoone to sitt during every tearme uppon demurres as aforesaid.

The High and Honorable Courte of ye Wardes and Lyveryes.

This her Majesties Court of Recordes and the Second touchinge her highnes Royall Revenewes it [*sic*] that wherin her princely prerogative is mayntayned and advaunced. This taketh name of Pupillus a ward whose father is dead, and of tutor a gardian or governour of the Childe man or woman, taken as it weare into her Majesties most gracious protection, out of this they sue their Liveryes and prove their ages, which are in ward to ye King Majestie because they hould of his excellent highnes. This Courte is kept upp the Stayres on ye right hand in Westminster hall at ye nether end of the Court of requests uppon the left hand, ut seqtur.

The Cheife Judge and Master of the Court of Wardes and Lyveryes.

The Right Honorable Sir William Cecill before named of the most noble order of ye garter K^{t}., Barron of Burleigh, and Master of the Wardes and Lyveries to ye Kings most excellent Majestie. His honour hath the ordering and disposinge, as well of the Wardes and their patrimonyes, Lands, Tenementes and Hereditamentes for His Majesties behoofe duringe their nonage as also, of their goodes, Chattles and proffitts, and the orderinge of all suites and wronges to them happeninge, untill they come to the Lawfull age of XXI yeares, that they may then possesse the same Patrimonies, Landes, Tenementes and Hereditamentes, goodes, Chattles and proffitts unto their owne proper inheritaunce possession and Jurisdiccion.

The officers in the Courte of Wardes and Lyveryes.

(*In margin:* The officers in this Courte.)

The King Majesties Surveyour generall of the Wardes and Lyveryes, then, beinge Mr Richard Kingsmell of Lincolns Inne Esqr.

The King Majesties Atturney of the Wardes and Lyveryes, Mr James Morris of Westminster.

The Auditor, Mr William Tucke in Aldersgate Street.
The Tresurer, Mr Georg Gooring in Whitecross Street.
The Clearcke of the Wardes, Mr John Hare of the inner Temple.
The Clearcke of the Lyveries, Mr John Chickrell in Aldersgate Streete.
Two Common Atturneys, Mr Paule Salmon of the Inner temple, and Mr John Picheringe of Lincolns inne.
The Keeper of the Court house, Mr Marmaduke.
The Gentleman Usher, Mr Goddard.
The Serieaunt at Mace, Mr John Bowyer Esqr.
Twoo Pursephaunts, The Porter.

(*In margin:* The K. Majesties Surveyor.)

The King Majesties Surveyour Generall as he hath the allowinge of every Lyverye that is sued out, so he surveyeth the states of the Patrimonyes, Landes, Tenementes, and Hereditamentes of the Wardes that they may come in good case and condicion to the heires at their yeares at Lawfull age, and that they suing then their Lyveryes may possesse their owne in peace and safetye.

(*In margin:* The K. Majesties Atturney.)

The King Majesties Atturney of ye Wardes and Lyveryes is to defend the Kings right in the wardshipp of the heire till his or her full yeares of age, and is assistant to the Master of the Wardes and Lyveryes in Councell of Lawe, Justice and Equitye.

(*In margin:* The Auditor.)

The auditor taketh and maketh accompts for his Majesties behoofe, and the Wardes of their Patrimonyes, Landes, Tenementes and Hereditamentes as also goods, Chattles, and Proffitts, and procureth processe to be made out against the parties any way iniurious to the same.

(*In margin:* The Tresurer.)

The Tresurer Receaveth Keepeth and payethe monye for his Majesties behalfe, and the wards accordinge to direction and accomptable therfore to the Master of the Wardes and Lyveryes.

(*In margin:* The Clerck of ye wardes.)

The Clarcke of the Wards is Keeper of the Recordes and writer of the decrees and processe to the partie repugnaunt or iniurious as aforesaid.

(*In margin:* The Clerck of ye Lyveries.)

The Clarcke of the Lyveries hath all the dealinge for suing them out, by the heires, and delivering them, as to this Court apertaineth when they are of full age.

(*In margin:* The Common Atturneyes.)

The Common Atturneyes are for ye Plaintiff and Defendant: to frame and make their proceedinges and further their suites in this Courte.

(*In margin:* The Keeper of ye Court House.)

The Keeper of the Court House, looketh to the due decent keepinge therof, and is also attendaunt to the Master of the Wardes and Liveryes when time and occasion servethe.

(*In margin:* The Gentleman Usher.)

The gentleman usher attendeth and goeth before the Master of the Wardes and Lyveryes, to and from the Court barreheaded, and in the Court as tyme and occasion serveth.

(*In margin:* The Sergeant at Mace.)

The Serieaunt at Mace is the same person and office heare, as in the Courtes before named in all respects.

(*In margin:* The Pursephaunts.)

The Pursephauntes do keepe the processe and bringe the partyes into the Court.

(*In margin:* The Porter.)

The Porter attendeth dilligently uppon all persons havinge accesse to and from ye Courte.

(*In margin:* The Matters of this Court.)

The matters of this Court are all benefitts that maye accrue and come to his Majestie by Guarde, Mariadge, Primier [*sic*] seisen, and releife out of this Courte, are ye Liveryes—sued and committed to the Clarckes of ye petty bagge Officers in the Chauncery, but the Ward shal be in ye King Majesties Custodye, till hee or shee sue out the Liverye, although they bee of full age, for it is their follye that they sue it not, when the heire hath proved his or her age, and sued out their Lyverye, they must then do homage to the Master of the Wardes and Lyverye who is the Prince deputye for that purpose, and then must they paye a fine to the Lord privy seale the dealinge whearof was in the hands of the Right Hon. Sir Robert Cecill one of the privye Counsell.

The manner of proceedinge in this Court is by
due forme of Lawe Justice and Equitye.

The Processe wherby the Causes of this Courte are prosecuted are theis: ffirst a generall processe, being a Commission, a precept in forme of a Proclamation or an iniunction warning the partie or parties to appeare before the Master of the Wards and Lyveries at a daye and place Limyted.

The more speciall processe belonging to the Court are theis, a Diem Clausit extremum, a Deuenerunt, a Datum est nobis intelligi, a Melius inquirendum, and a quae plura; Touchinge the nature of theise see Stamfordes booke uppon the Royall prerogative.

And heare endeth the Courts of Wards and Lyveryes, and ye 2nd Court of records for his Majesties revenues.

The Highe and Honourable Court of the Dutchye of Lancaster.

This H. Majesties Court of Records for ye Dutchy or Countie Palentine of Lancaster is that last Court of her Highnes revennues whearin are handled all pleas reall and personall which concerne any the Mannors, Landes, Tenementes, hereditamentes and possessions apertaininge to the said Dutchye now in her Majesties hands and parcell of her Royall Crowne and Dignitye, but severall [*sic*] in Court and Jurisdiction. Yt is kept above the stayres on the right hand of Westminster hall, neere unto the Court of Wards and Lyveryes before written.

(*In margin:* The sole Judge & Cheif Chancellor in this Courte.)

The Sole Judge and cheif Chancellor of this Courte. The Right Honorable Sir Tho. Heneage, Knight of the most noble order of ye garter and one of her Majesties most honorable privye Counsell: Hee seeth that Justice be duly administred betweene the Queen Majestie and her subiects, and betweene partye and partye.

The Vice Chauncellor for Lancashire onely.

(*In margin:* The Vice Chancellor for Lancashire.)

The Right Worshippfull Sir Gilbert Gerrard, knight, Master of the Rowles, in ye Chauncery Court before written, hee seeth that processes be made out for that Countye, to the bringing in of the parties.

(*In margin:* Extraordinary Judges.)

There is in Cases of Difficultye and necessitye or elce not otherwise Certaine Judges at the Common Lawes assistant to this Courte.

There is an ordinary Serieant at Lawe for her Majestie in this Court allwaies asisting, hee was Mr Serieant fleetwood late recorder of London before spoken of.

The officers in the Dutchie Court of Lancaster.

The Queenes Majesties Atturnye for this Court Mr. Jo. Burgrate of Grays inne Esq[r].
Twoo Auditors, Mr Anthony Mildmay, who hathe under him Mr John Harvey.
The other Mr William Purvey, one for the South, thother for the North partes.
The Surveyors Mr. Ed. Stanhop of Graysinne for the Northe, and Mr ffynche for ye South partes.
The Clercke of the Court, Mr W[m] Gerrard, Graysinne.
Twoo Common Atturnyes: Mr Grymstone and Mr. Mathewe.
The Keeper of the Courthouse, Mr. Gylpin: Westminster.
Twoo Pursephauntes, The Porter.

(*In margin:* The Queenes Atturneye.)

The Queenes Atturnye defendeth her Right and Tytle, assistethe ye Chauncellor in Lawe, and learned Counsell, and doth minister right and equitye unto suitors in this Courte.

(*In margin:* The 2 Auditors.)

The 2 Auditors do take and make accompts unto ye Chauncellor of this Court, for her Highnes Revennues, receaved by them, for her Majesties behoofe, from time to time.

(*In margin:* The 2 Surveyors.)

The 2 Surveyors do surveye her Majesties Lands, Mannors, Tenements and Possessions, that they be kept in good estate, and are likewise accomptable to the Chauncellor of this Courte.

(*In margin:* The Clerck of ye Courte.)

The Clarcke of ye Courte, is ye Keeper of the Rowles, and Recordes, setteth downe all orders in this Courte, and maketh out processe into all other Countryes to bring in the parties, his Office is hard by the Chappell at Graysinne.

(*In margin:* The Common Atturneys.)

The 2 Common Atturneyes are for ye plaintiffs and deffendants, suitors, to frame their Complaintes and aunswers and further their suits.

(*In margin:* The Keeper of Courte.)
The Keeper of the Courthouse, lookethe to the due and decent keepinge therof, and is attendant to the Judges as tyme and occasion serveth.

The Pursephaunts are to serve ye processe, and bring in the parties into Court.

The Porter is to attend uppon all persons havinge accesse to and from ye Courte.

The matters of the Court are as in the former effects first above specified.

The manner of proceeding, is by due forme of Lawe, Justice and Equitye, and the usuall and onely processe of this Court is a Subpena.

And heere endeth the Dutchie Court of
Lancaster, being the 3d and last courte
for her Majesties Revennues.
Curiarum Regalium omnium
Recordarum Finis.

A Breife discription of ye Court for the Nisi prius.

(*In margin:* Nisi Prius.)
This writt called in Lattin Nisi prius is an anncient writt used to end matters, eyther in the Guildhall of London, before the Lord Cheife Justice of Common pleas, Or elce before the Justices Itineraunt, in their severall Circuits about and throughout all England.

The Officers in this Courte are theis.

(*In margin:* The Officers in this Courte.)
The Clarcke of the Tresurye Mr Windsor in white heart streete neere the Tower.
The Clearcke of the Juries, Mr Ducumb, as aforesaid.
The Clearcke of ye Nisi Prius, Mr Knight of St Andrewes parishe in Holborne.

(*In margin:* The Manner of Proceedinge.)
The Manner to proceed in this writt, is first to purchase out the effecte, or breife of ye Recorde included in the writt itsealfe inclosed in waxe, this donne by the Clearcke of ye Treasurye.

(*In margin:* The Clerck of ye Juryes after venire facias awardeth a habea [*sic*] Corpora.)
Then the Clearcke of the Juries after ye Venire facias, awardeth an Habeas Corpora, to cause the Jurye to appeare, and nameth the place wheare, and the dayes when of their appearance with this clause Nisi prius Venerat. The same is dated thus: Ad Guildhaldum de London: Anno: die: et mensie [*sic*], and Subscribed thus: Teste Edmundo Anderson milite capitale Justitiario de Comunibus placitus, and for this Cause it is called nisi prius.

(*In margin:* The declaration of Nisi Prius.)
Then the Nisi prius is declared unto the Justice after he commeth to the place appoynted eyther by the plaintiff or by his Atturney, which donne the Cheife Justice

for the time and place, doth open and deliver it, to the Clearcke of that place and Assises.

(*In margin:* The Jurye called & yeild verdict.)

Then the Clearcke of ye Juries, calleth the Jurye, who appeare and yelde their verdicte after some debatinge of the matter; either by their Counsell at Lawe, or by some proofe and wittnes.

(*In margin:* The Verdicts entred.)

This donne the Verdict is entred, then is the same Record remanded into the Common Pleas or Kinges bench, from whence it yssued, and a day given to pronounce the Judgment uppon the verdict before yeilded by a Postea etc. Which is a forme of record recitinge the matter before, and how it was now passed, and sheweth what Costs and Damages, the Jurye gave unto the plaintiff yf hee recovered, and so giveth Iudgment, and this is called the postea. But yf the matter passe by Nisi prius against the plaintiff then is the Judgment entred Querens nihil capiet per breve, sed sit in Misericordia, pro falso Clamore. And so endeth this discription for Nisi prius.

Huius Opusculi Finis.

Deo Laus, Regina Vivat, Valeantque Comuniter Leges.
Vigrant ut boni, mali vilescantque greges per mare, perterras, undique Contignas.

Rom: 5. Verse 3. Is qui Complebit quod Lex perficere nequet.
Rom. 10. Vers. 4. Christus Solus Legis finis sit, salus suique gregis.

Radiantem Solem nemo restringat
per me Richardum Robinson

INDEX

THE HASTINGS JOURNAL
OF THE
PARLIAMENT OF 1621

EDITED BY
LADY DE VILLIERS, B.Litt., M.A.
FELLOW OF SOMERVILLE COLLEGE, OXFORD

CAMDEN MISCELLANY
VOL. XX

LONDON
OFFICES OF THE ROYAL HISTORICAL SOCIETY
96 CHEYNE WALK, S.W.10
1953

D

CONTENTS

INTRODUCTION

In the early seventeenth century many members of the House of Commons made notes of parliamentary proceedings, but their example was very rarely followed in the Upper House. The diary of the Parliament of 1614, published by the Historical Manuscripts Commission in their Report on the Hastings papers at Ashby de la Zouch, is the first complete private journal of the House of Lords to make its appearance in print. The same volume also contains a fragment of a journal of the first session of the Parliament of 1621, too slight to add to our knowledge of the business of the session, but sufficient to show that the diarist of 1614 was again engaged in taking notes.[1]

The Carte collection in the Bodleian includes some papers lent to Thomas Carte by the ninth earl of Huntingdon, and never returned. By this accident they escaped the fate of the rest of the Hastings collection, now in the Huntingdon Library, California, and remain in the country of their origin.[2] One volume of Hastings papers, MS. Carte 77, contains some more pages of the journal of 1621, scattered in haphazard fashion amongst the parliamentary collections of the fifth and seventh earls of Huntingdon. When these pages are put in order and the Ashby fragment is fitted into its context we have an almost complete account of proceedings in the Upper House from the prorogation of 23 January to the afternoon conference at Whitehall on 17 February; part of the proceedings on 16 February alone are missing. By the courtesy of the Director of Publications, H.M. Stationery Office, the Ashby fragment is now reprinted in its place in order that the journal may be read as a continuous narrative. It is followed by a detached account of the proceedings of 10 March and by some more fragmentary notes of parliamentary business up to 29 May.

The Carte manuscript gives supporting evidence of the authorship of Henry, fifth earl of Huntingdon, to whom the 1614 diary is ascribed, and throws some light upon the way in which the journal was put together. The account of proceedings up to 17 February is written as a continuous narrative in a clerical hand and the gatherings are numbered. The pages recording the proceedings of 10 March, also written in a clerical hand, are not numbered. They have a few marginal comments in the earl's own hand and bear his endorsement 'Notes of the Parliament'. The later rough drafts and memoranda here printed are in the earl's own hand and form part of a series of papers numbered O–Z. The first of these is endorsed with the note 'These pages are all to be written over again'. The series includes, in addition to the earl's rough notes, copies of other speeches and documents which have not been reproduced, as they are available elsewhere in print. One of these is endorsed 'For the Earl of Huntingdon: the coppie of the judgement in Parliament against the late Lord Chancelor, Viscount St. Albans.' It seems then that the finished journal was put together by a secretary from the earl's own notes

[1] Historical Manuscripts Commission, *Report on the MSS of the late R. R. Hastings Esq. of the Manor House, Ashby de la Zouch*, ed. Francis Bickley, iv (1947).

[2] For the Hastings papers in the Carte collection, see Sir Maurice Powicke's 'Notes on Hastings MSS.' in the *Huntingdon Library Quarterly*, i. 247–76.

of the Lords' debates supplemented wherever possible by copies of documents obtainable from the Clerk. The preservation of the rough notes awaiting copying suggests that the finished journal may not have been carried much beyond the point at which the narrative now printed breaks off; for once the fair copy had been made the materials from which it was compiled would have served their purpose and would not have been kept. None have survived for the period covered by the completed diary.

Much of the material collected by the earl of Huntingdon reflects his strong interest in matters of parliamentary privilege and procedure, subjects which were beginning to claim almost as much attention from the Lords as from the Commons. It was from the Lower House that the Lords borrowed the idea of a Grand Committee for Privileges, appointed for the first time in this session. The first-fruits of their labours were the 'Remembrances for Order and Decency to be kept in the Upper House of Parliament by the Lords when his Majesty is not there', presented to the House on 6 February and destined to become the basis of all its later Standing Orders.[1] The Committee was further authorized to enquire more generally into the privileges of the peerage and the earl of Huntingdon was named first of the sub-committee appointed to search for precedents.[2] After two cold afternoons spent in unprofitable researches the earl reported 'the labour great and the work intricate' and sought authority to delegate the task to more experienced precedent-hunters. Among the antiquarians consulted were Selden and Hakewill, the results of whose researches were reported by the sub-committee on 27 May.[3] The House directed that a fair copy of their notes should be kept as a permanent record, and returned the originals to Selden for transcription. So it happened that the notes were in Selden's possession during the recess when his papers were seized by the king's order on suspicion of his complicity in the charges against Southampton.[4] On 30 November Lord Haughton reported that although at the urgent request of the sub-committee the papers had been returned, a number of pages were found to be missing.[5] The House took a serious view of this infringement of their liberties. Selden was authorized to make fresh transcripts either from 'the scrybled originall' or from the records themselves, and when he had done so, elaborate precautions were taken to prevent further interference with the text. The receipt given by the sub-committee to Selden on

[1] MS. Carte 77 contains a copy of the 'Remembrances for Order and Decency' at fo. 192.

[2] *Journals of the House of Lords* (hereafter cited as L.J.), iii. 17. The same Lords were authorized to peruse the Journal Book (p. 21). The earl of Huntingdon was also a member of the larger committee appointed for the same purpose on 27 March (p. 73). From time to time he undertook to look for precedents for specific purposes and traces of these enquiries are to be found amongst his papers in MS. Carte 78.

[3] MS. Carte 78 contains a list of doubtful points in connection with the Lords' privileges endorsed 'Memorandum to conferre with Mr. Hackwell and Mr. Selden about in thinges concerning the nobility' (fo. 451v.). The same MS. has an early draft of the heads of the report submitted to the Earl as first of the sub-committees. It is endorsed in his hand 'Mr. Hackwell and Mr. Sheldon's note of priviledges belonginge to peeres and lords of Parliament' (fos. 499–500).

[4] [Sir E. Nicholas], *Proceedings and Debates of the House of Commons in 1621*, ii. Appendix.

[5] L.J., iii. 176. S. R. Gardiner, *Lords Debates in 1621*, pp. 99–101, gives a list of the missing items.

6 December states 'The number of the heads are 7 of one kind and 13 of the other; the number of leaves received are one hundred and thirtie and those words in the preceding pages are a true copy of the preface to the same collection '.[1] The Book of Collections, or Book of Privileges as it was sometimes called,[2] had a table of contents giving the first and last words and the number of leaves under each head. When presented to the House on 15 December it was still in loose quires, but orders were given that it should be bound. It seems uncertain whether these orders were carried out until 1738, when the collection was discovered by the Clerk, William Cowper, and identified as the work long since published under Selden's name with the title *The Priviledges of the Baronage of England when they sit in Parliament.*[3] The original is still preserved in the library of the House of Lords.

The delegation of the sub-committee's powers illustrates the helplessness of the Upper House in matters of this nature. 'On the other side,' said Lord Chancellor Ellesmere of the Commons in 1614, 'they goe both high and lowe and looke of all thinges that concerne their purpose, and we can say nothinge having not seen records. They perhaps will tell us of the lawe of nature and of nations, being learned and able gentlemen who have studied this case long. If any man in this house thinke himself able to dispute with them, lett him do it; for my parte I must desire to be excused.'[4] It is true that the judges were in attendance to inform their Lordships on questions of law, but the debate on 17 February clearly shows that they could not be relied upon to give an opinion in controversial issues. The Lords were thrown back upon the advice of the common lawyers, and the initiative taken by the Lower House in all the major constitutional issues of the time is in part explained by the Lords' conscious dependence upon the professional skill of its legal members. The king in his speech of 10 March rebuked them for their uncritical acceptance of the Commons' legal opinions; 'for though Sir Edward Coke is very busie and be called the father of the law and the Commons' House have divers young lawyers in it, yet all is not law that they say.'

The report of this speech is the most important of the fragments now printed. The *Lords' Journal* for 10 March records the fact of the king's presence and nothing more.[5] The reason for this is explained in a note of Elsing's included in a list of queries presented at the close of the session to the Lords appointed to peruse the Journal. 'And alsoe', he asked, 'what I shall enter for done the 10 of March (the King being then present) which was the last daye my Uncle[6] sate here as Clerke and he was then soe sycke that he dyed very shortly and his scribbled booke soe imperfect that I cannot drawe it up.'[7] This 'scribbled book' is the one discovered by Miss Frances Relf and published for the Camden Society in 1929.[8]

[1] British Museum MS. Stowe 354, fo. 62 v.

[2] J. Hacket, *Scrinia Reserata*, Part ii. 157; L.J., iii. 196–7.

[3] First published in 1642. Reprinted in David Wilkin's edition of Selden's *Works* (1726), vi.

[4] H.M.C. Report, *Hastings*, iv. 286–7.

[5] L.J., iii. 40.

[6] Robert Bowyer.

[7] House of Lords MSS. 'Matters I doubt of which the Lords Subcommittees have not yet perused', 2 June 1621.

[8] *Notes of the Debates in the House of Lords, 1621* (Camden Third Series, xlii). The proceedings on 10 March are on pp. 12–15.

The account there given of the morning's proceedings, valuable as it is, confirms Elsing's view that the full sense of the king's speech could not be recovered from these notes alone. No other first-hand account of the speech has hitherto been available. Gardiner knew of the day's events only from the gossip writers, and based his interpretation of the king's visit upon the misleading account given in Salvetti's news-letter; it is from this source that he quotes the familiar story of the cow and her tail.[1]

The Lords had already had one conference with the Commons on the question of the patents and had reserved their opinion on the proposal that they should co-operate in bringing the patentees to justice. Another meeting had been fixed for the afternoon of Saturday, 10 March, and it was known that the Commons would then raise the question of the referees which, to the dissatisfaction of the House, had been evaded by their spokesmen at the earlier conference. On the Saturday morning, on the spur of the moment, 'it pleased the Kinge to come privately to the upper house',[2] a proceeding so unusual in the middle of a session as to prompt him to borrow one of Coke's precedents to justify it. The Commons were not summoned to the Bar, as Gardiner supposed; for what the king had to say was intended for the Lords alone and it was important that they should hear it before their second meeting with the Lower House. Gardiner thought that the king's urgent intervention at this stage in the discussions was an attempt to save the referees and to stem the tide of impeachment. Yet we find James encouraging the Lords to go ahead without sticking upon precedents, even lecturing them on their unfamiliar role as judges in the revived judicial procedure of impeachment. He was not only content that they should deliver judgement upon Mompesson, but made no effort to save either Bacon or Mandeville. 'As for the things objected against the Chancellor and the Treasurer,' he said, 'I leave them to answer for themselves: for if they cannot justify themselves they are not worthy to hold and enjoy those places they have under me.' There is thus no evidence to suggest that James recognized that 'to allow the Lord Chancellor and Lord Treasurer to be called in question by Parliament would be to sacrifice that claim to sovereignty for which he had always so passionately struggled'.[3] Bacon was perhaps the first of his contemporaries to see the wider implications of 'a beginning to question great counsellors and officers of the Crown by courts and assemblies of estates'. But he was the last person who could offer advice upon this subject. 'Reflexion upon my particular in this,' he said, 'makes me more sparing than perhaps as a counsellor, I ought to be.'[4]

[1] S. R. Gardiner, *History of England*, iv. 48–9. Salvetti says 'Last Saturday the King went into the Upper House of Parliament to see whether by his presence he could quell the ardour of the turbulent spirits in both Houses who were threatening to bring about the downfall not only of the Duke of Buckingham but a great part if not the whole of the royal prerogative.' He recounts the King's objections to the application of precedents of 'ill kings' times' and then goes on to relate the story of the cow and her tail, quoted by Gardiner. The transcript of Salvetti's letter is in the British Museum Add. MS. 27962, A. fo. 422. Briefer but more generally correct impressions of the incident are given by Locke (S.P. 14/120, 15) and by John Chamberlain (*Letters*, ed. N. E. Mclure, ii. 358–9) and in the letter from Woodford to Nethersole quoted below.

[2] Woodford to Nethersole, 15 March (S.P. 81/20, fo. 254).

[3] Gardiner, *op. cit.*, p. 49.

[4] J. Spedding, *Letters and Life of Francis Bacon*, vii. 192.

The king was concerned with more immediate dangers. Elizabeth had seen in the attack upon monopolies an attempt to 'take away her prerogative . . . the chiefest flower of her garden and the principal and head pearl of her crown and diadem'.[1] James could take no other view. He realized that it was no longer possible to postpone judicial action against present offenders or legislative safeguards against future abuses. He sought, none the less, to defend the prerogative by virtue of which the patents had been issued. To this end he drew a distinction between the punishment of the persons and the examination of the legality of the patents. The Lords might with his blessing pass judgement on the former if in the latter they would defer to the opinion of the judges who were already accustomed to determine the legality of patents challenged in the Courts. A still more pressing consideration was the restoration of his personal prestige. It was intolerable to James to find himself cast for the part of tyrant with Lords and Commons united in defence of the subjects' liberties. If grievances were to be redressed in Parliament, he wished to share the credit of the remedy rather than the odium of the disease. Williams advised Buckingham to let the world see 'that the King, who is the Pilot that sits at the Helm, is ready to play the pump, to eject such Filth as grew Noysom in the Nostrils of his people', and James already appears to have been acting on that advice.[2] But it was not enough to throw overboard the monopolists themselves; he must shew himself prepared, if need be, to jettison the referees also. As Cranfield put it to the Lower House, 'If the Referrees be not spoken of, all the Fault of the Grant would lie on the King.'[3]

James believed that if the trials were conducted on the lines laid down by himself, the Crown need have nothing to fear from the revival of the judicial power of the House of Lords, and he was confident that his influence in the House was sufficient to ensure respect for his wishes. His pointed reference to the bishops and to the peers of his own creation shows where his strength lay. By putting himself at the head of the movement and by giving a firm lead to his supporters, he forestalled any attempt at leadership on the part of the younger independent peers whose close association with the leaders of the Commons was beginning to give cause for anxiety. He undoubtedly won a tactical victory. It might seem that in asking the Lords 'to chalk out the way so that the people may know my zeal to justice and my desire to free them from oppression' James was asking too much. For it must have been widely remembered that the abuses now complained of in Parliament had been well known to the king at least since the previous November, when Bacon's advice in favour of withdrawing the most unpopular of the patents had been deliberately rejected.[4] Yet the king's speeches on 10 March and again on 26 March were received with satisfaction and even with emotion.[5]

[1] W. H. Price, *The English Patents of Monopoly* (Harvard Economic Studies; 1906), p. 20.

[2] Hacket, *Scrinia Reserata*, Part i. 49–50. The 'breviate' is undated. Gardiner thought that it must have been presented to Buckingham after 10 March but before 12 March, and attributed what he believed to be a sudden reversal of royal policy to Williams's influence (*op. cit.*, pp. 51–2).

[3] Nicholas, *op. cit.*, i. 137.

[4] D. H. Willson, *Privy Councillors in the House of Commons, 1603–1629*, pp. 40–4; Spedding, *op. cit.*, p. 146.

[5] L.J., iii. 70.

The earl of Huntingdon said of his notes of the latter speech ' my affections were so filled with joy at the hearing of it as they would not give my hand leave to set down the same so largely as I wished I had '.[1] It was moved in the House that the day should for ever be remembered and sermons preached in gratitude for the king's gracious favours to his people. A more extravagant draft of the motion proposed that statues of the king and the prince should be raised in brass to celebrate their justice.[2]

The precarious basis of these harmonious relations is shown by the king's violent reaction to the first suspicion of criticism of the favourite. The reception given to the deputation which waited on the king at Whitehall on 6 May has hitherto been known only from the restrained account of it given to the House on the following day by the archbishop of Canterbury.[3] The name of Buckingham, so carefully excluded from all the earlier proceedings against the monopolists, was recklessly spoken by Yelverton in an attempt to clear his own reputation.[4] In this context James could not ignore the potential dangers of impeachment ; if Buckingham was Despenser, he was Edward II. Yet upon cooler reflection the king decided to leave the examination of Yelverton in the Lords' hands and was rewarded by a judgement which could not have been improved upon had it been delivered by himself.[5]

The homely vigour of James's less formal speech is well retained in the earl of Huntingdon's notes which shed welcome light upon the king's reactions to the events of this critical Parliament. It must therefore be a matter of great regret to the historian that the earl's promising career as a parliamentary reporter was cut short at the end of the first session. Apart from very occasional appearances, when private business rather than public affairs brought him to Westminster, the earl never again attended a Parliamentary session. The care which he took to keep himself informed of the business of Parliament from 1624 to 1626 suggests that his absences did not at first imply any intentional withdrawal from public life. Evidence of his continued interest is supplied by the documents printed in the Appendix. From Sir John Davies's letter of 8 March 1624 (p. 35) it is clear that material was regularly sent to Donington in order to keep the earl abreast of the progress of business in the Upper House. In anticipation of the Parliament of 1625 the earl made brief notes of points which needed watching in drafting legislation (p. 36). The two letters of 26 February and 23 March 1626 (pp. 36–41) suggest that in Francis Staresmore, who doubtless owed his election as knight of the shire for Leicester to Hastings' influence, the earl possessed a reliable channel of information about the daily business of the Commons. The letters add a little to our knowledge of the session. Of greater independent interest is the last letter (pp. 41–3) from Sir John Skeffington, one of the earl's Deputy Lieutenants. Written

[1] H.M.C. Report, *Hastings*, ii. 59 (29 March 1621). The letter is without signature or endorsement, but there seems no reason to doubt that it is a copy of the earl of Huntingdon's reply to Arundel and refers to his notes of the king's speech. These are in MS. Carte 77, fo. 205. They are considerably less full than the printed version (see L.J., iii. 68–70).

[2] L.J., iii. 73 ; Cal. S.P. Dom. 1619–33, p. 238.

[3] L.J., iii. 112.

[4] L.J., iii. 104, 121.

[5] L.J., iii. 114, 124–5.

with greater freedom and intimacy, it throws some new light upon the relations between the two Houses and upon the significance of Arundel's lost leadership in the Lords.

Yet Skeffington's lively account of a critical situation did not suffice to bring the earl to London. Reluctance to leave the country became a habit. To poverty, ill-health and a deep-rooted aversion to the life of a courtier was added a growing sense of alienation from the whole temper of the administration. His Puritan sympathies are shown in the rules established for his household and in his patronage of Arthur Hildersham. His political loyalties are suggested by his choice of Montgomery, Southampton and Pembroke as his proxies; by his support of the petitions against the foreign nobility in 1621 and 1628 and by his refusal of the forced loan in 1626. In later life he became an eccentric recluse.

> 'Despairing to do national good
> he mingled as little as his rank permitted in national affairs.' [1]

These words are borrowed from the epitaph composed by Selina, countess of Huntingdon, for the ninth earl, who inherited many of the characteristics of his great-grandfather. Dying in 1643, the fifth earl himself had no memorial. Neither has he found a place in the *Dictionary of National Biography*.[2]

In editing the text, the original spelling has, so far as possible, been retained, save in the passage reprinted from the *Report* of the Historical Manuscripts Commission, where it had already been modernized. Abbreviations have been expanded and the punctuation occasionally modified to clarify the sense; this has involved some changes in the use of capital letters. Dates in the text have been left in Old Style, though New Style has of course been used in the introduction and notes. Latin phrases have been printed in italics; they are generally so written in the manuscript. There are many passages which suggest careless copying. Sometimes, as in the proceedings of 15 February, the order of the speeches has been confused; often a word has been mis-heard or omitted. But it has seemed better not to try to improve upon the text as it stands; the few additions and emendations of the editor are shown in square brackets. I am grateful to Miss Jean Dawson, B.Litt., for her help in reading the proofs and compiling the index, and I take this opportunity of acknowledging the encouragement and guidance so generously given by Professor Notestein to all students of the period he has made his own.

[1] J. Nichols, *The History and Antiquities of the County of Leicester*, iii, part ii, 622.

[2] Some biographical material may be found in the Hastings papers calendared by the Historical Manuscripts Commission and in the Bodleian.

[JOURNAL OF THE PARLIAMENT OF 1621]
[MS. Carte 77]

[fo. 183] A memoriall of such things as passed in the Parliament begun the xvi day of January 1620 and in the xviii yeare of his Majestie's Raigne of England France and Ireland, and the fifty and forth of Scotland.

There came forth about a fortnight before this day of summons a proclamacion to proroge the Parliament untill the xxiii of the same moneth and then it was prorouged againe by a writ patent untill the xxx^th^ of January.

xxiii of January 1620. [L.J., iii. 6.]

Lord Chancelor Baron Verulam.

My Lords [a] and you the Knights Cittizens and Burgesses of the Commons howse of Parliament, according to his Majestie's writt of summons to the Parliament the xvi of this moneth you assembled at this place where I was glad to see soe fayre an apparance, but then for some resons of State the King's most excelent Majestie was plesed by his writt to command that the Parliament should be prorouged untill this day the xxiii of January, and nowe in regard of his indisposition of body which farr surmounts all matters of State, is plesed to command againe that by his writ patent it should be prorouged againe untill the xxxth day, at which tyme I hope his Majestie wilbe in this howse everyday takinge the fresh ayre abroad which, thankes be to God, he finds very beneficiall for his health. I shall trouble you today rather with matter of ceremony then substance but, aswell in the civill as ecclesiasticall government, ceremony is most necessary for forme gives the essence to things. I have no more to say but to cause his Majestie's writt to be read.[1]

[fo. 183v.] 30 of January 1620. [L.J., iii. 8.]

Lord Chancelor Viscount St. Albones.

My Lords and you the Knights Cittizens and Burgesses of the Commons howse of Parliament: you have heard the King [2] with great admiracion reverence and contentment.

[a] *In margin:* Note that both theis tymes the Lords sate not in their Roabs.

---

[1] Compare Wentworth's summary of this speech in *Commons Debates 1621*, ed. W. Notestein, F. H. Relf and H. Simpson, v. 423.

[2] A version of the king's speech endorsed in the earl's hand 'the briefe of the King's Majesty's speech in Parliament 1620' occurs on fos. 172–5 of MS. Carte 77, but has not been incorporated in the finished Journal. The speech was not printed, as was customary, and the many manuscript versions in circulation differed considerably. See *Commons Debates 1621*, ii. 2, n. 2.

Admiracion in hearing soe excellent a speech as befitts us all to ruminate thereof; it hath not beene usuall for kings to speake in there owne person and seldome read or heare of a kinge to speake like this kinge.

Reverence as I may say I hope you will doe like Mary that was not onely attentive at our Saviour's words but pondered them and layd them up in her hart.

Contentment haveinge receved from the kinge his most excellent Majestie's owne mouth soe great tokens and signes of his love to the people. That excellent kinge Kinge Solomon that the nayles of the words of the wise are driven in by the master of the assemble;[1] soe may I compare his Majestie's words for though they be not prickinge yet I hope they wilbe pearcinge into your memories and affections.

There is noe fittness for me to speake after the kinge, especially after such a kinge in his presence, though in his absence I am his mouth to you; I will only trouble you with one advise not myne owne; I borrowed it from an author, *Nosce teipsum* in modesty to your sovereigne next in your loves and duties to him for there is a great expectation in the beginning of this parliament and I hope there wilbe a happie conclusion in the end thereof soe as it may be of a generative quallitie to beget another Parliament. It is his Majestie's pleasure that you Gentlemen goe together to elect I may rather say select a speaker out of your howse and then it is his Majestie's plesure to give you leave to departe till Satterday.[2]

[fo. 147] Satterday the 3rd of February 1620. [L.J., iii. 9.]

His Majestie came in his Coach and the Lords in theirs, some went to the Parliament howse before and only attended his Majestie the Prince, the Lords of the Counsell and the Kinge's servants in ordinary. The king putt on his robes in his withdrawing chamber, and the Lords theirs in the painted chamber.

Sergeant Richardson's speech who was presently after allowed of his Majestie speaker of the Commons' howse of Parliament.

Most high most mightie and most excellent Majestie: the Knights, Citizens and Burgesses have [with] one voice chosen me their Speaker and theirfore I would willingly doe them any service, but I humbly beseech your Majestie in any place fitt for me, but I am altogether unable to serve in this place. I have (for many yeares) bene an apprentice at lawe and for some yeares a freeman (a course of life painefull and laborious) and I never studied or laboured for eloquence, neither doe I knowe the custome or manner of that howse, and he that should performe this to his credit ought to be a man of that endowment without exception. I doe not accuse that honourable howse but excuse myne owne disabilities, which are soe great that againe I humbly desire to be pardoned to crave that your Majestie would intercede for me and that the Commons howse would proceede to a newe election.

The Lord Chancelor Viscount St. Albons went to knowe his Majestie's pleasure.

[1] Eccles. xii. 11.

[2] A rather fuller account of this speech is printed in Spedding, *Letters and Life of Francis Bacon*, vii. 172–3, and in Nicholas, *Proceedings and Debates*, i. 11–12.

Lord Chancelor.[1]

Mr. Serjeant: The Kinges most excellent Majestie hath heard your modest, wise and learned speech and yet his Majestie will not grant your petition, but commaunds me to tell you that those that are modest are the fittest to be imployed in great actions, for modesty is [fo. 147v.] the condiment of all other vertues, and his Majestie saith that in striving to disenable your selfe you have enabled your selfe, and will not recede from their choice, but doth accept of you as their speaker.

Mr. Speaker Serjeant Richardson.

Most gratious Soveraigne: seeing my humble petition cannot obteyne my desires, I may not in duty strive to withstand it, seing your Majestie hath allowed and confirmed unto me the name of a speaker, I must needs say that such is your Majestie's goodnes which by soe many wayes and great favours holds the affection of your people. Divers nations have embraced severall formes of government, but none soe perfect, soe durable, soe free from corruption as a Monarchie, and as the bodie of a man is the microcosme of a Commonwealth, soe doth this kinde of government resemble the perfectest; for as there is but one God that governes both heaven and earth, soe in the naturall bodie but one head and as in the politique, one man one kingdome. And as all issues from the head, soe all rule and government from the kinge; a kinge is a visible God and God an invisible kinge. To be *sine rege* is to be *sine religione, sine lege, sine ordine*. Your Majestie, not an elective kinge, nor successive, but by the right of inheritance. Your Majestie's wisdome, learning and judgment is such as noe kinge upon this earth is to be parralelled with you. Your Majestie hath brought with you peace at home, peace abroad, and you are soe powerfull as you can where you will make warre, make peace. Your Majestie's religion is famous throughout the Christian world, wryting such excellent Bookes that none before you ever deserved to be stiled as your selfe doth to be *fidei defensor*. Oh what peace have you brought us! Peace of conscience, outward peace, and peace amongest ourselves. Your justice is most admirable, [fo. 148] never kingdome living under a perfecter lawe nor learneder judges, noe judges being freer from corruption or being misled, then theis are, and as in King Henry the third his tyme, it being propounded in Parliament that the lawes of England should be changed, they all rose up, and with one consent said *Nolumus mutare leges Angliae*, and I assure myselfe that all the noble Peeres love soe your lawes as they sitt in the seates of their Ancestors, soe doe they inherit their affections. In all thinges your Majestie showes such favour and grace to your subjects as I want words to expresse it. What an admirable favour was this of yours that where your predecessors did usually call one Parliament as soone as another was ended never staying above two or three yeares without one, your Majestie hath forborne your subjects without craving supplie of them very neere seaven yeares. And nowe the calling of it is that you may receive the juste complaints and be informed of the unjust taxacions of the subject and the petitions of your people; besides, to tye myselfe [to] your Majestie's speech, to make lawes, explaining those that are darke, repealing those that are obsolete and out of use. Another cause of calling the Parliament to supplie your Majestie's wants the which noe doubt but the

[1] For this and the following speech of the Lord Chancellor, see Spedding, *op. cit.*, pp. 173–9.

honourable howse of Commons will doe as much as the abilitie of the people will permitt. The chiefest thinge that we would be humble sutors to your Majestie in is that your Majestie would be pleased that some sharper lawes may be made against the Papists, for never can we forget that bloudie and horrible treason of the Gunpowder Treason which, had not God prevented, would have levelled in a moment Kinge, Queene, Prince, Peeres and the principle parte of the [fo. 148v.] Gentrie of the kingdome, the representative body theirof. As all the Papists, soe especially care would be had to the priests and Jesuites; the lay Papists I may compare to the sea, which though the billows theirof be large and great, yet if the winde of the Jesuites and Priests doe not blow them up we might passe them in a calme, as we may many tymes upon the sea. The chiefest thinge I would humbly recommend unto your Majestie to be considered of this Parliament is the excesse in diet and apparell which is used amongest all persons, in all places and at all tymes in this your kingdome. I could wish that the lawes which amongest the Romans were called *Sumptuariae* were put in use and execution in this kingdome. To conclude, I hope your loyall and faithfull Commons will supplie you. The honourable howse of Commons desire they may enjoy their ancient priviledges during the Parliament, both that themselves and their servants may be free from arreste, for if the howse should loose one of their members it could not be esteemed what a great losse it were, for once in a generall councell one voice did overthrowe a great heresie. Secondly, that they may have freedome of speech, carrying them selves with that regard as is fitt and I assure my selfe they will, both to your Majestie and the State. Thirdly that they may have libertie to come unto your Majestie's person and not to censure them or me untill we have attended your highnes; and if at any time they imploy me to your Majestie, their unworthie speaker, you would pardon me in adding or diminishing of any thinge the honourable howse of Commons shall give me in charge.[1]

[fo. 149] Lord Chancelor.

Mr. Speaker: his Majestie hath heard your large and eloquent speech and comprehended your love. Your speech (Mr. Speaker) I will reduce to fowre parts: first a laudative of monarchies, a large field. Secondly, the manner of his Majestie's government. Thirdly, the institution of princes.[2] Fourthly petitions for your selfe and for the howse of Commons.

It is not fitt for me to speake longe before my Soveraigne, especialy such a Prince that hath soe great abilities, neither will the meanenes of my understanding give me leave. Monarchs shall neede noe dispute especially in the person of such a kinge as our Soveraigne. Monarchie is fitt for growth and continuance.

For the great felicitie we enjoy under his Majestie's government let us offer

[1] The Speaker's oration is only briefly summarized by the diarists of the Lower House, either because they could not hear well as they stood at the Bar or because the formalities of the opening proceedings were beginning to pall. Cf. Locke's letter to Carleton of 5 February: 'My lord of Chichester said there was a right play, what with his [the Speaker's] eloquence to refuse and my Lord Chancellor's to commend, the tyme was spent' (S.P., 14/119/67). The fullest account of the day's proceedings is in Pym's diary (*Commons Debates 1621*, iv. 7–10).

[2] This should read 'the institution of parliaments.'

praises and oblations to our kinge, and he will offer both his and ours unto our God. I must tell you (Mr. Speaker), it is neither in the power of your tongue nor myne to expresse the benefitts we enjoy by his Majestie's happie government. It is tyme, and only the acte of tyme that can do it which was only kept for him, and noe other before him could ever effect. The thinges in number are eight: first the joyning of theis two happie kingdomes together, England and Scotland: Secondly the civilizing of Ireland, like the ancient heroes noe such hath ever beene like it. Thirdly, the plantacions of Virginia and Somers Islands. Fourthly Ireland his Majestie hath made till truth hath actuated.[1] Fifthly, peace hath overcome conquest and although in the Queene's tyme of happie memorie we enjoyed it, yet our peace was mingled with rebellion for twenty yeares. Sixthly, Justice, for his Majestie doth like the good kings of Israel sitt in the gates and judge his people, nay his Majestie is *Lex loquens* and not as some kinges are like statues. [fo. 149v.] Seaventhly mercy, for although the axe were held up and turned toward some Lords, yet never stroke any of his Peeres. Eighthly theis reverend Bishops and the rest of the Clergie the preachers I may say shine in the glory of their functions like starres in the firmament.

Nowe to your third parte; the institutions of Parliament attend inseperably monarchy. The kinge sittes being attended by the Peeres in the exaltation of his orbe and I have some faith that he will like the sunne that shines and gives lustre to the earth, ere the Parliament end, shine in mercy and grace upon us. The fourth parte, the petitions; by the kinges commaund this Parliament is called, either for church, state, lawes and grievances, who in such thinges can followe the Kinge? Of lawes and the multiplicitie theirof are such as you neede not adde very many, make not the heape too great, helpe old lawes and take away the superfluitie of them and (as Mr. Speaker said) sumptuarie lawes are the most necessary to banishe excesse; and thinke not we can doe all thinges nowe and make as perfect a State as the Idea of Plato's Commonwealth. For grievances if you meane to have the real effect of them, you are to represent not to personate the people and therein rather shewe number then waight. The fairest stones have some flawes which are seene more apparently than in those stones that are courser, and as you desire to relieve the people, soe ought you to be carefull not to cast scandal upon the state, the least fault being the soonest apparent in the best Commonwealthes. The manner howe to redresse those thinges amisse, the kinge can better doe than you, for he hath bene longer a Kinge then you Parliament men. For the hill best dis [fo. 150] covereth the vallies *tanquam gemitus Columbae*.

Although His Majestie will give you freedome of speech, yet will noe more either in manner or in matter suffer diminution then he covets vaine glory. His Majestie would have you use your priviledges not to defraud the creditors as also expects from you that due reverence as that you will not overthrowe waightie matter with light carriage. And (Mr. Speaker) I hope will doe your best, rather to prevent mistakinges then to have neede to have them salved. Lastly, I must crave pardon both of the kinge and in some sort of you all, having this comfort

[1] The copyist has gone astray here in writing 'Ireland'. The fourth point made by the Chancellor was that 'His Majesty hath made that truth which was before titulary, in that he hath verified the stile of Defender of the Faith' (Spedding, *op. cit.*, pp. 175–6).

that after this harsh speech of myne there will light uppon you some beames from his Majestie.

The King's Majestie's Speech.

My Maisters: I thinke it fitt for to refresh your memories to remember one word of that that passed the last day; the Parliament is called as I tould you both for the makinge of good lawes, as for to relieve my necessities, the which are not so great but they have beene, soe as I shall not desire any but a moderate summe; where in one of your petitions you desire your ancient libertie for the protectinge of your servants in the Parliament tyme which I am contented you should, but in that I would not have you to trouble and greve honest men in keping from them their dew debt. It hath beene tould me that there are some that have been taken out of gailes and protected which shewes such an indescresion in them as did it as may be being a thing displesing to God, me and the Commonwealth. As our Saviour saith a little leven leveneth the whole lumpe; beware that you put not too much leven in your proceedings which may soure the whole business; your errands are to labour in those thinges that concerne the Glory of God, the honor of your Kinge, and the good of the countryes. So in proceedings there are two wayes, the [fo. 150v.] way of the lion, the way of the fox. If any run the way of the lion I hope you will soone represse them. If any the way of the fox you will soone deserne them; and what you do for my good, doe it quickly and with alacritie, for as the Bishop tould you in his sermon the last day, I must not stand upon thornes. If in any thinge I have said to you that you doubt of you shall understand my mind by your speaker. It were the beasts undertakers that spoyled the last Parliament. In the non Parliament non undertooke for me but as every honest man will doe when I asked them that served and were about me that then durst undertake, my necessities being such, that the Parliament would doe as should befitt every good subject to satisfie my wants and be ready to advise me, when thinges fell out contrary to the veritie. Yet since I must needs say, though I protest to you I knew not soe much before, that I understood some knights put in to the Parliament for that purpose; now all the rubb being taken away that were the impediments and hinderances in the two former Parliaments, I assure myselfe things will succeed hapilie to all our contentments, and I will leave at this tyme these two things for you to remember, my wants and the pressinge estate of the Palatinate, which will breed peace at home such trew friends to this State and I am the likelier to make peace abroad beinge armed with meanes to offend. You knowe that as your Scripture saith, noe king goeth to warr before he hath cast the charge to see how hee may undergoe such a business. And thus I end praying God to give you a good beginninge.

Monday the fift of February 1620. [L.J., iii. 10.]

No bill read which was contrary to the orders of the house beinge the first day of the sittinge, but there were five private bills which the Clarke of the house, though never a member of the house, called upon them to be read.

[fo. 151] Lord Chancelor.

My Lords: as this is the first day of our sitting soe I shall offer two things to your Lordships' consideracion which I understand hath ben the ancient maner of this howse, the one religious worke, the other a dutifull one; the first, that each Earle of the bench of the degrees above or the degree beneath that comes after prayers should give two shillings to the pore; the other, that such Peares that wear not here the last Parliament, may take the oath of Aleigeance.

Thomas Earle of Arondell.

My Lords: besides these things there are many priviliges belonging to us and divers orders which weare anciently observed in this house that by disuse and want of puttinge in practise are now almost lost and therefore if your Lordships be plesed there be a Comittie for priviliges of the house chosen, both these things and many other are considerable to be thought of, which mocion of mine I leave to your Lordships' wisedoms. Uppon this mocion there was a Comittie chosen who went forth presently into the painted Chamber to sitt hearupon.[a]

Duddely Lord North.

My Lords: seing your Lordships hath made a Comitie of priviliges I thinke it fitt to offer to your Lordships' consideracions the wronge that it offers unto us Barons by the partie that made the writs that where heretofore it was the ancient manner to have those words *predilecto et fideli nostro* to be both in the title of the writt and in the labell, in some of the writs it is left out in both places, in other some in the title and in others in the direction. Therfore I beseech your Lordships the partie may be sent for that writte them and if it shalbe thought fitt by your Lordships he may be punished.

[fo. 151v.] Tewsday the sixt of February 1620. [L.J., iii. 11.]

A Bill read the first tyme that no peeces of great Ordnance may be transported out of the King's dominions upon the penalty of a felony.

A Bill read for the first tyme for the making of the Armor of England serviceable and fitt for service.

A Bill read for the first tyme for the naturallizinge Stephen Le Jours [1] borne beyond the seas.

[a] *In margin:* Note that after this the names of the Comittie must be entered.[2]

---

[1] Sir Stephen Leisiver (L.J., iii. 11).

[2] The names are given in H.M.C. Report, *Hastings*, iv. 286. The list is identical with that given in L.J., iii. 10, except for the addition of the Lord Chancellor's name.

Wednesday the seventh of February.

The higher howse sate not being Starr Chamber day.[1]

Thursday the Eight of February 1620. [L.J., iii. 12-13.]

Note that the Prince is called to our howse by writ but sate in the place before the Lord Treasurer's seat, when the King is there beneath the degrees. Before the howse sate and after we were all bare in his presence but sate in the house covered.

. . .[2] That drew the writs was sent for by the Sergeant at Armes.

Lord Chancelor viscount St. Alban.

My Lords: this fellow I before commited unto the Serjeant at Armes. What is your Lordships' plesures to have done with him? It was resolved he should be heard in the howse who therupon kneeled downe at the Barr.

You have committed a very great fault in leavinge out these words *predilecto et fideli nostro* in the lords writs: what have you to say for your selfe?

May it plese your Lordships I have drawne the writs according as I find in the ancient presidents, besides if there be an error [fo. 152] I hope your Lordships will pardon me that have beene in the office but these four yeares and there were no writs granted out for summons of Parliament since *Primo* of the Kinge.

Lord Chancelor.

You have committed a great offence and have but a weake answere to make for your self for there went out writts in the new Parliament in the yeare 1614, soe as this is not soe. You must understand that noblemens' titles are incorporated in to their honours, theire honours into their blood, so as in this default of yours you lose them parte of their right to give them a bare apelacion without these addicions before their names.

For this fault it was ordered that by the howse he should be committed to the Fleete till the howse's plesure weare further knowne.

Edward Earl of Worcester, Lord Privie Seale.

My Lords: the lords that weare Committies have according to your Lordships' plesures mett and comferred about the privileges of the howse and have returned to your Lordships in this paper [3] the some of there proceedings and doe desire to knowe whether they shall now end the Committie or continue duringe the Session of Parliament.

[1] Later in the session, on 24 April, objection was raised to the custom of forbearing to sit on Star Chamber days 'as if this Supreme Courte wear to attend any other inferior courte' (Gardiner, *Lords Debates for 1621*, p. 13).

[2] Richard Cammell, a Clerk under Mr. Ravenscroft, in the Petty Bag (L.J., iii. 12).

[3] The 'Remembrances for Order and Decency'.

Lord Chancelor Viscount St. Alban.

My Lords: I desire to have some things explained before I read theise thinges unto your Lordships which is now read by the Clarke of the howse, Although I would facilitate your Lordships' desires and shalbe very facile yet would I not loose any thinge belongs to my place or to my Master's honour; for though I sitt bare as the speaker of the howse when I speake to it, yet as I am a Peare I am to sitt in my place of a Peare covered.

Robert Rich, Earl of Warwick.

[fo. 152v.] My Lords: I thinke your Lordships were very carefull to make clere this poynt my lord that spoke last makes a question of.

Lord Chancelor.

My Lords: I desire to know your Lordships' plesures whether you would have it put to the question whether these things should be entered as the Act of the howse or as ordered to be observed.

It was ordered by the howse upon the puttinge to the question that these things should stand as ordered but not absolutely as a decree of the howse till the Committies had made a perfect returne of their proceedings.[a]

Lord Shefield.

My Lords: I shall humblie move this to your Lordships whether your Lordships thinke it fitt to put this matter to the question now.

Lord Treasurer.

My Lords: seeinge the judges are left out to attend the Committie I thinke it weare fitt some of them were commanded to attend the Committie.

Lord Hunsdon.

My Lords: It seemes my Lord that spoke last was not present when the Comittie of privileges was apointed for to my Lord Cheife Justice and Mr. Justice Dodridge my Lords of the Committie have referred some things to their consideracions where they desire as soon as may be that my Lords the Judges would declare unto them their opinions, and therfore I hould it in my conceite not fit now to put it to the question untill the Judges have reported to my Lords.

Lord Bishop of Duresme, Dr Neale.

My Lords: I beseech your Lordships, it may be explayned whether we that

[a] *In margin:* Note that these orders of the howse must be entered here.

are Bishopps may put on our hatts beinge no Peares for I conceave we cannot accordinge as the Order is nowe pen'd.

Uppon the view thereof it was found to be so which was presently amended and explayned that the Bishopps may put on their hatts for although [a] bishops be no peers of the realm, yet they be barons of Parliament, having baronies of land granted them when the King makes them bishops.

Lord Chancellor.

My Lords, whether the latitude of these orders are such as they need not be amended but kept inviolable according to the laws of the Medes and Persians I understand not, but rather conceive it is your Lordships' meanings that they may be altered either by adding, diminishing or interpreting till they be fully finished and made an Act of this House, the lords committees sitting for these privileges during this Parliament.

After all this dispute whether it should be put to the question that these orders should be entered or not till the committee had fully perfected the work, it was put to the question and the most voices overruled that these things should be entered as orders but not as yet the Act of the House until that they were fully finished.

The bill of ordnance the second time read and committed.

Lord Chamberlain.

My Lords, I observe two things in this bill which for my own part I must tell your Lordships truly I like not, the one that it makes the punishment as great for him as carries over ordnance or is privy or witting thereunto as in high treason, and for my part I would have the punishment agreeable to the offence; the other that the punishment is taken from the High Admiral and given to the King's Bench or to the Judges of the circuits to inflict punishment.

Lord Treasurer.

My Lords, I never since I knew Parliaments read of such a bill. Since I had the honour and trust from his Majesty of this staff I have looked into the merchants sending over both of ships and ordnance, but to limit the King in this manner, which makes it seem strange unto me, many other errors there are in it and therefore I think fit it be committed.

Thereupon it was committed.

The bill of reforming unserviceable arms second time read and committed unto the same committee as the former, saving the addition of all the Lords Lieutenants.

[a] *With this word begins the fragment printed in H.M.C. Report,* Hastings, iv. 286–9.

A bill for the naturalizing of Sir Francis Stuart, William Stuart, James Maxwell, gentleman of the Order of the Garter, and William Cave.

Friday Star Chamber day.

Saturday the 10th of February 1620. [L.J., iii. 14.]

A bill read the first time for the confirmation of the sale of some of the lands of Edward Walgrave.

Walgrave's petition,[1] one of the Petty Bag Office that drew the writs and left out the style of the Barons, viz., *predilecto et fideli nostro*, read and upon his submission and penitency the House was contented to release his imprisonment.

Note.—The House was called to see who were present and who absent that it might be seen who had proxies.[a]

Monday the 12th of February 1620. [L.J., iii. 15–16.]

The bill of making the arms of England more serviceable brought in by the committees and the senior of the committee made the report; the amendments were twice read.

Lord Chancellor.

My Lords, I understand it hath been the manner of this House that when a bill hath been committed and brought in with the amendments my predecessors[b] had wont to open it thus: Betwixt the word 'of' in the 10th line and the word 'and' put out all the words and put in the words 'and all'; thus, my Lords, here was nothing but chopping and changing of words which sounded harshly and not the sense set down, so as I have caused it to be written, which if your Lordships like the words before and after that you may [understand] the sense of the place.

This was better liked of and the amendments[c] in a paper joined to the bill so written and read.

Lord Chancellor.

My Lords; I conceive this bill hath a large scope and good intention for the making of the arms of England more serviceable, which I doubt not but are reasonable good already, so many addresses having been from the Council Board to the

[a] *In margin:* Note that the Prince sat in the House this day and was called and answered to his name as a peer.

[b] *In margin:* Note that where my Lord Chancellor had wont to read those amendments to save his trouble and pains the Clerk of the House now reads them.

[c] *In margin:* Note the amendments are never interlined in the bill but only marked where it shall come in but written in a paper by itself pinned to the bill.

---

[1] An error for Cammell's petition (L.J., iii. 14).

Lieutenants in each several shire. I hope this Parliament will yield to the King both for the regaining of the Palatinate and the relief of his Majesty's necessities a good crop and therefore I would not have the ground worn out with other payments, for the fertilest ground will be made barren with often tilling; therefore I could wish that where these arms are commanded to be made perfect by Michaelmas next, the fruit of the people's love and duty might not be reaped for this crop till Michaelmas come twelvemonth.

Earl of Arondell.

My Lords; I think your Lordship hath moved very well, but this is not to make new arms until the old be out of use and unserviceable, but my lords the committees did consider hereof and what arms is thought fit to be allowed is left unto the Lords Lieutenants.

Lord Treasurer.

My Lords, I think as my Lord that spoke first it were best to have time given until Michaelmas come twelvemonth to have the new arms to be bought, for the people at this time have many charges upon them, and the rate of their cattle and corn bears a very small price. I conceive there are diverse statutes already made for the supply of the defect of arms and for the former causes aforesaid I wish that as many of them as may be may be made serviceable and answerable to such as have been allowed in former times.

Lord Steward, Earl of Richmond.

My Lords, I am of opinion that this bill is well as it is, and better it were a new bill were put in to the House than to clog this with any other matter or to express the repeal of the former Acts in this.

After this dispute it was put to the question whether this bill should go as it is to be engrossed for the third reading or recommitted. It was put to the question and there were 43 that gave their contents to have it recommitted and but 23 that said not content and that would not have it recommitted.[1]

My Lord of Essex counted the not contents that sat and I the contents that stood up.

A bill read the second time for the naturalizing of [sic] Leiours.

The bill of Charles Walgrave for the confirmation of the sale of the Manor of Pinhowe in the County of Devon second time read.

Lord Archbishop of Canterbury.

My Lords, I think in a bill of this nature it were good to have it committed; that if there be any in remainder or can challenge any title in this land they may be heard with their counsel.

[1] The Clerk gives the division as Contents 40, Non-Contents 22 (F. H. Relf, *Lords Debates in 1621*, p. 2).

Lord Chancellor.

May it please your Lordships, this bill hath been so thoroughly scanned that I think all parties are agreed, for this is but to put a new piece in an old garment, for the former Act in *septimo* of the King gave him leave to sell this land and this is but to confirm those sales and to explain the former bill.

Tuesday the 13th of February Star Chamber day, being the day next after the end of the term.

Wednesday the 14th of February 1620. [L.J., iii. 17.]

My Lord Chancellor excused my Lord Chamberlain's absence by reason of his attending the King late yesterday night at the mask at Court.[a] [fo. 268] My Lord Chancelor likewise excused my Lord Bishop of Duresme by reason of his preaching this afternoone before the Kinge.

A message was brought from the lower howse by Sir Edward Coke Kt., wherein they desired conference with the lords and that the Lords would joyne with them in petition to his Majestie about the banishinge the popish preistes. Jesuits and Papists ten miles from the cittie of London.

After that he had delivered the message wee desired them to retire themselves.

After they were gone forth we consulted what to doe and agreed to joyne with them in peticion to his Majestie, and seing they desired the tyme might be as soone as may be, we sent for them presently in againe and tould them we were content to conferr with them presently, the place the Painted Chamber, the number 40 of our howse.

Earl of Arondell.

My Lords: I thinke my Lord Chancelor may doe well if your lordships soe plese to knowe whether they meane to have a Committie of the whole howse or but a certen number of the Comittie.

Earl of Southampton.

My Lords: It is the ancient manner of our howse first to agree when to meete, the number and the place, and then to send for them in againe for stayinge of them too longe and in the meane tyme whilst they are goinge, to make report to the howse to name and chuse our Comittie.[1]

[a] *Here ends the fragment printed in H.M.C. Reports.*

---

[1] The earl of Huntingdon was not a member of this Committee (L.J., iii. 17). The 'Remembrances for Order and Decency' make it clear, however, that 'either at any committee of ours, or any committee or conference with the Lower House, any member of our House though not of the Committee, is not excluded from coming in and speaking, but he must not vote; as also he shall gyve place to all that are of the committee, though of lower degree, and shall sitt behynde them' (MS. Carte 77, fo. 200).

Sir Edward Coke at ye Conferrence.

May it plese your Lordships: the knights, cittizens and burgesses of the Commons' howse of Parliament doe send to your Lordships of the higher howse, humbly to desire your Lordships to joyne with them in Peticion to his Majestie, in these things followinge. The peticion we have devided into these five parts: first that his Majestie wilbe plesed to send forth a Proclamacion that all papists [fo. 268v.] with all convenient speede retire from the Cittie of London and 10 miles there from and presume never to come to the Court ether of his most excellent Majestie, or of the Prince his Highness's Court and that they be not suffred to goe further then 5 miles from their howse or usuall aboad. The love, dewty and zeale we beare to his Majestie hath begot this presumption to be suitors to him for they grow and increase exceedingly and never weare more presumptuous and bould then they are. Secondly that his Majestie wilbe pleased to give charge both to the Justices of Peace and as well to the ecclesiasticall Judges to take away the Armes and Gunpowder from every Recusant leavinge them no more then shall be necessary for the gard of their howses. The third article that his Majestie will forbid all his subjects to heare Masse ether in their owne howses, the howses of their frends, in private conventicles or corners or in the howses of any forraine Embassadors, for upon Sondays and holidays they swarme and flock thither in very great numbers: Forthly that his Majestie would cawse the lawes to be put in execution with all celeritie against Jesuites and Popish Priests and that in the meane tyme his Majestie would be pleased to give command to have them kept streight. Fifthly and lastly that his Majestie would be pleased to command both the Judges and others to see the lawes duly executed against them and that all their licences may be taken away. All these things to be declared by his Majestie's most gratious Proclamacion. All these things, my Lords, are grounded uppon the Statute made in the third yeare of the Kinge soe as nether in the matter nor manner doe offer to your Lordships any new thinge, nether do we meane. Besides this Statute divers of your Lordships that are Lords of the Privye Counsell did about some 4 or 5 yeares since from the Councell Board address your letters to the Justices of Peace in all the severall shires in England for the puttinge in execution some of these things, the coppie of which letters I have here to show your Lordships.

After this speeche ended we retired ourselves to resolve whether we would joyne with them in peticion to [fo. 269] his Majestie; we stayed not in our howse above a quarter of an hower before with one consent and voyce we resolved in the howse to joyne with them in Peticion to his Majestie.

My Lord Chancelor made report to our howse of Sir Edward Cokes speech.

Lord Chancelor at the Conferrence deliverd his answere as from the howse.

My Lords doe commend you the Knights Citizens and Burgesses of the Commons' howse of Parliament for your exceedinge love and dewty to his Majestie and your zeale in regardinge this in the principall place which of all other things is the hart of Oake, their Lordships are willinge according to your desire to be peticioners to his Majestie with you for these things and give you no other argument of the affection they bere to your howse then their rediness to joyne with you herin, for those things wherin the will affects moves spedilie, where it doth not, the contrary, soe as ther remaines nothing now to be done for the present but to tell you that some of my Lords of the Committie will knowe his Majestie's plesure whether he will give us leave to attend him hearin and the tyme when, which we will signifie to you to morrow morninge.

After this wee presently went againe and sate in the howse about other businesses.

The Lord Archbishop of Canterbury made report unto our howse what was done in the morninge at the Committie about the privileges of the howse.

May it please your Lordships: my Lords of the Comitties have met and sate about the priveleges of the howse and demanding of those judges that their lordships referred the consideracion of some poynts that they desired to be resolved in, receaved not that satisfaction from them as they expected and therfore they have, if your Lordships so like, named a sub-committie who they have desired to looke of the records and presidents in those things; if it please your lordships to give them warrant that they may have recourse to all his Majestie's offices for the viewinge and seeinge of the same.[1]

My Lord Chancelor reported this to the howse, who liked well of the motion and gave order accordingly sayinge, your Lordships have done wisely and discreetly; I remember that Tacitus hath this sayinge that Precedents are the best Doctors.

Thursday the 15th of February 1620. [L.J., iii. 18.]

My Lords; we that weare authorised from the howse have wayted [f. 269 v.] uppon his Majestie and his Majestie doth well resent both the howses' peticion and hath appoynted the tyme for you to waite upon him, Satterday next, at two of the clocke in the afternoone; his Majestie is pleased to hasten it soe soone because it is a busines that conduceth to so good an end.

Lord Chancelor.

My Lords: to avoyd confusednesse, especially cominge before soe great a person as the kinge our master, it would be thought of now amongst us who shall speake, and what, and who shall begin, whether we or they; if they use their speaker then your Lordships may use yours; if not, you may be pleased to use some other lord.

Lord Chamberlain.

May it please your Lordships: it hath beene the manner of this howse, as

[1] The names of the sub-committee are given in L.J., iii. 17, and in H.M.C. Report, *Hastings*, iv. 286. The earl of Huntingdon is the first. Their warrant is given below, p. 21.

I doe remember it, in the case of wardshipps, both the howses meetinge in conference and afterward attendinge his Majestie, my Lord Chancelor spoke for both.

Lord Wentworth.

My Lords: seeing there is not above 4 or 5 of the Earles bench more then were before of this Committie I humbly offer it to your Lordships whether you please to add them to it.

Lord Chancelor.

My Lords: my Lord Admirall beinge not here yesterday when the Committie were chosen I thinke it now well if he weare added to it.

Lord Darcy.

May it please your Lordships: if so be you add any that then you would be plesed to add my lord of Oxford the lord Steward and the lord Chamberlaine.

Earl of Southampton.

My Lords: the Comittie beinge chosen allreadie it hath not beene the manner of the howse to add any, but if you doe theise, then to make a Comittie of all the whole howse shall doe well for our number is not great.

Earl of Dorsett.

My Lords: as I take it the addinge of one alters the forme of the howse as well as all and therefore it comes all to one to add them all.

[fo. 266] Lord Chamberlaine.

My Lords: I pray your Lordships that my Lord Chancelor may be suitor for us to the Prince that his highness would doe the howse the honour to be one of the Committie.

The Prince desired he might not seeinge it was not the maner of the howse to have any added after the Comittie were sett downe; yet uppon all the lords standing up and moving him he was pleased to yeild to be one of the Committie.

George Villiers, Marquess of Buckingham.

My Lords: I pray your Lordships thinke not to have any of us of the Committee but his highness, for methinkes we have spent more tyme hearin then such a business as this is requireth, for it deserveth not such dispute it beinge of no greater moment.

John Egerton, Earl of Bridgewater.

My Lords: I desire to knowe your Lordships plesure whether your meaning is that at our attendance uppon the Kinge the whole howse be made a Comittie or onely the Committie that wear made at first.

After divers other speeches all to this purpose whether the whole howse should be made the Comittie or onely the Prince, the lord Admirall, the lord Steward, and the lord Chamberlaine, it was ordered by the howse none should be added but the Prince, who was pleased to doe us this honour.

The bill for makinge of the Armes of England more serviceable the third tyme read and passed.

Lord Tresurer.

My Lords: Seing all the life of lawes are in the execution of them and that as this act for the makinge of the Armes more serviceable can not be unless the trade of makinge Armes be norished and maintained which is now much decayed, for the Armorers' better furnishing of themselves the king my master is pleased that the Armorers shall have 1000 pounds a moneth for the setting of them on worke and pay it back againe with Armes, and for the payment of them this money I had yesterday his Majestie's warrant.

[fo. 266v.] Earl of Arondell.

My Lords: when both the howses peticion together to the kinge my Lord Chancellor had wont to be the person to speake to his Majestie for both the howses.

Lord Chancelor.

My Lords, and you the knights Cittizens and Burgesses of the Commons' howse of Parliament, although I doe desire to be excused from this ymployment yet next unto the interest of my Master's service I shalbe willinge to doe service to your howse the other or to both.

Sir Edward Coke.

My Lords: The knights, cittizens and burgesses did much rejoyce in your Lordships' speedie answere, for Religion is the foundacion of vertue and the principalest consideracion of staite and now we have heard your Lordships answere we must report it to our howse having noe power given us to treate with your Lordships.

The bill of Levours the third tyme read and passed.

The bill of Viscount Falkland first tyme read.

Lord Chancelor.

My Lords: the message brought from the lower howse consisteth of those two fould questions: first, whether they should use the mouth of one or two to speake. Second, who should begin. They resolved both the questions thus sayinge they intended to use but one and that should be if I could intreat your Lordships my Lord Chancelor who they soe much desire to have you doe it as they assented to it *una voce* for in the very same busines in *septimo* of the King both the howses used my Lord Chancelor Elesmere and we had a happie and gratious answere from his Majestie and all their peticions graunted.

After this we returned to the howse.

Lord Chancelor.

My Lords: Seeing both this howse and the other do lay the charge uppon me which is rather *onus* than *honor* for my owne warrant and that I may understand your Lordships' and the Lower howse's mind the better I beseech your Lordships to send to them to desire a conferrence tomorrow morn [fo. 267] inge by nine of the clocke that I may receve in charge from both the howses what to say to his Majestie.

Lord North.

My Lords: I think your Lordships are satisfied alreadye what they and we desire to be moved to his Majestie and therfore I see no cawse that we should crave a conferrence with them, but I submitt my humble motion to your Lordships' wisdoms.

But for all this the howse resolved to desire a conferrence with them tomorrow morning about nine of the clock.

The message was sent downe to them by Sergeant Crewe and Sergeant Finch and they sent us word by the same messengers they would give us meting at the hour apointed.

Lord Bishop of Duresme.[1]

My Lords. This bill your Lordships hath sent downe about making the Armes of England more serviceable I thought fitt to offer theise three things to your Lordships' wisdoms the which I should have moved your Lordships in but that I was absent yesterday by reason of my preaching before his Majestie. First, that those preists that take the oath of allegeance, may not be kept so streight and close prisoners as those that refuse the oath. Secondly that the licence granted to the Papists for the keping their Armes in their owne hands may be all of them taken away. Third that those popish Preists that are not Jesuits or Jesuitically affected may be allowed better meanes in the prison. If their be no distinction

[1] The bishop's intervention on behalf of the Catholics who had taken the Oath of Allegiance caused great offence in the Commons. Locke wrote to Carleton on 24 February: 'The Bishop of Duresme was their frend in the upper house, for which he had as much thancke as for that he did the last Parlament. Their fingers did itch at him in the lower house' (S.P.D., 14/119/106).

made betwixt those that conforme themselves and show their aleageance to the Kinge it may be it will make both of them to fall off and fall from those degrees and steps they have runne and make others carlesse to take the oath of aleageance. Nay I knowe both by the Pope and the Court of Rome howe hardly these are censured, being thought though they [fo. 267v.] be Catholiques almost as though they were revolted from their Religion. In the Northerne parts there are divers papists that have licences under the great seale for the kepinge of their Armes in their owne custodie so as if your Lordships think good it were well that those and all other licences were called in and so specified in the Act. Lastly those preists that have taken the oath of Aleageance are so villified by the rest as may be and have scarce any foode but bread and water whear the other Jesuites and Preists have dayly sent them the best meat in any of the papists howses or money to buy as good meat as can be gotten. I hope your Lordships meane that there be a distinction made betwixt these and the other and that these pore soles may have better allowance and not be kept so strict and close prisoners as the other.

Earl of Bridgewater.

My Lords. I have bene so little while a Parliament man as fitter for me to ask questions then to speak. Those things that my Lord that spoke last offered to your Lordships' consideracion I think are worthy of your Lordships to advise of. And for this bill of serviceable Armes if your Lordships please I think that this of taking away licences from . . .

end of 267 (b).

[Friday 16 February.] [L.J., iii. 20.]

[fo. 153] and [a] there were 45 voyces that gave content for his [1] close imprisonment and but 31 that said not content.

My Lord of Barks was sent for in by the Gentleman Usher to come to the Barr and having his sword our sentence being past was willed to put it of and that Maxwell [2] should have the keping of it. My Lord cominge up to the Barr without his Congies was willed to goe to the dore againe at the lower end of the Parliament howse and come upp with three curtesies and to kneele downe at the Barr beinge a delinquent.

The sentence pronounced by my Lord Chancelor which was the decree of the whole house.

My Lord of Barkshire, my lords have in there grete judgments wayed your offence in the ballance of their justice and doe thus sentence you. They find the greatness of your fault to overway the weakenesse of your answeres and your fault soe much the greater being done in the presence of his highnes and therfore you

[a] *This folio is marked 9, gatherings 7 and 8 being missing.*

---

[1] The earl of Berkshire.

[2] The Gentleman Usher.

are to goe imediately from heare with the gentleman usher of this howse to the Fleete there to remaine close prisoner until their Lordships be pleased to realese you.

My Lord Scrope was afterwards caled in and willed to goe to take his place.

Lord Chancelor.

My Lord Scroope, my Lords do commend your wise and discreet cariage, and doe find you have not offended by any act of commission, but that which they find fault with you is an omission in that you did not make knowne this to the howse of yourselfe which, if it had not beene by some other meanes then by yourself, they had not come to the knowledge of this greate offence committed to the howse in generall and unto your self in particular but they hope that this shalbe a warninge both to your selfe and to any of my lords hereafter that if any such like occasion happen they will make it knowne to the howse.

February Satterday the 17th 1620. [L.J., iii. 21.]

[fo. 153v.] The bill for the explaination of a former bill for ye cutinge of the river of Thames to and beyond the Cittie of Oxford first time read.

Earl of Huntingdon.

May it please your Lordships, whereas my lords the Committees for the customes and orders of this howse and the privileges belonging to the Peares of this kingdome and lords of Parliament were pleased to appoint a sub committie of some others and my self, requiringe to search all such records as should be needfull for this end, their Lordships with my selfe spent two whole afternoones in making search in divers places and their Lordships findinge the labour great and the worke intricate doe humbly offer this to your Lordships consideracion that you would be pleased to give them comission by their warrants under three or foure of their hands at least to authorise and depute whome they shall thinke fitt for this purpose to make search for their Lordships greater ease and then they will goe and view the records themselves before they present them to you and give your Lordships accompt of their imployments.

Hereuppon the motion was graunted and an order made to that end which is here under written.

Satterday the 17th of February 1620.

It was this day ordered by the whole howse with generall consent the Earle of Huntingdon, the Earle of Dorsett, the Earle of Warwick, the Lord Scroope, the Lord Wentworth, the Lord North, the Lord Hunsdon, the Lord Russell and the Lord Haughton, who by the Lords Committees formerly appointed by this house to take consideration of the customes and privileges of the Lords of Parliament were chosen by [a] the house named as a Sub-committie to expedite and facilitate that business and were so approved and allowed by this house, shall for the said cawse and busines have free access unto all or any his Majestie's Records of any Court or others where soever remaining at all convenient tymes whensoever the said Lords Subcommittees shall require without charge to any of their Lordships or fees therefor to be demanded. And that their Lordships shall herein be obayed, assisted and attended by all and every the officers, clerks and ministers of all and any his Majestie's Courts and by all persons whatsoever, having the custodie of all or any the said records, and what coppies the said Lords Subcommittees shall require of any thinge or matter touchynge the premises so beinge of Record shall write or coppie forth and certifie under his or their hands or, being written forth or coppied, shall examine, signe and subscribe with his or their hand as shall appertaine.

[fo. 154.] Afterwards *videlicet die Sabbathi 17 Februarii* upon mocion made by the Earle of Huntingdon one of the Subcommittees aforesaid it was by the Court ordered that the said Lords Committees for their more ease and better dispatch of the busines aforesaid shall and may under the hands of three more of them or more nominate and appoint severall persons to the number of fower or fewer to search and have view for the cawse and matter aforesaid of and in any his Majestie's Records before mentioned and touchinge the same matters to have such notes and coppies as shall touchinge the premisses be necessary and appertaining.

Robert Bowyer.
Cler. Parl.

Lord Hunsdon.

My Lords: now my Lord that spoke last hath made a motion to your Lordshipps I shall make another by reason of some things that happened at our meetinge at the great Committie of Privileges when we came to demand to know the judges resolution instead of giving us an answere they would give us no satisfaction therin but said that it was a matter of prerogative so as they desired pardon to deliver their opinions untill they knew his Majesties plesure, which thing semes to me very strange that, movinge no new matter, they should not resolve us in theis thinges which are and have been our ancient privileges and, my lords, the intituling the king hearunto as a matter of prerogative they show their endeavour to possess the Kinge with an ill opinion of us as though we would not be as carefull of his Majesties prerogative as the Judges and therfore I besech your Lordships that you will declare whether we in fault that were the Lords Comitties in makinge this demaund or the Judges in not delivering their opinions as we required them.[1]

[a] *MS.* and.

[1] The question on which the Judges refused to answer was the Lords' claim to answer in the Courts upon protestation of honour instead of oath. On 10 March a Committee referred the dispute to the King who was 'satisfied with our intention and doings' and confirmed the privilege. (Relf, *Lords Debates in 1621*, p. 16, n. 1).

Lord Haughton.

My Lords: as both my lord that spoke first and my lord that spoke last spoke for the Privileges of the howse soe for the first the lords graunted the mocion being pleased to give us warrant to depute such as we shall think fitt to make search and prepare such things for us that we may be the better able to give your Lordships accompt of our proceedings, for the latter mocion I have looked into the writs by which the Judges sit [fo. 154v.] and I find they ought to give advise being asked and required to doe by your Lordships; yet contrary to their duties they would not speak and therefore I humbly beseech your Lordships this howse would resolve whether they ought to speak and give us advise and not to evade as they doe when they have no will to speak and that now they may be enjoyned to speake to give us satisfaction why they were silent the other day.

Earl of Arondell

My Lords: this latter mocion is new to me and I knew not of any intention to make it, but for the matter of fact I can declare to your Lordships that I was present when they were required by my Lords to speake and they would not, but because there is but one of those two heare that were required to declare theire opinions I would humbly offer this to your Lordships that you would give them tyme till Satterday morninge to give us satisfaction in those things we required.

Uppon this mocion of my lord of Arondell the howse consented to it and soe ordered it.

A bill read the 1 time to give libertie to Edward Earl of Bedford and Francis Lord Russell to make sale of some lands in County of Devon.

The bill of the Lord Viscount Falkland for the confirminge of a letter patent of a mannor which he bought of his Majestie for 10 thousand pounds second tyme read.

Lord Tresurer.

My Lords: I have noe reson to speake against this Bill in respecte of any of myselfe. I dislike of it, but in regard of my place which doth privilege me to stand up and speake when I here any thing that toucheth my master's profitt as I conceave it. As the bill is now drawne his Majestie shall loose both a tenure and a tenant; besides, it may be the grant is not good, for his Majestie may be deceaved in his grant or many other defects there may be in it and therfore I offer it to your Lordships' consideracion desiringe it may be comitted and that Mr. Atturney Generall may have the pattent sent to him to view.

Here uppon it was committed.

Lord Scroope.

[fo. 155] May it please your Lordships, whereas you were plesed to committ a Peare of this Realme for some unfittinge carriage in this howse, no question but that my Lord is sory for the same and I beseech your Lordships to release his imprisonment.

Lord Chancelor Viscount St. Albans.

My Lords: this lord that spoke last in his mocion hath spoke most nobly and like himselfe and therfore if it plese your Lordships to consider thereof that that Lord that gave this howse such just cause of offence may now he hath receved some imprisonment may be released of parte of his punishment, that is of his close imprisonment. I think your Lordships shall do a threefould act of nobleness to the Lord that spoke last, the Lord that is in prison and make knowne your mercies.

Lord North

My Lords: although your Lordships ware pleased to commit my Lord of Berkshire close prisoner yet I doe imagine your Lordships' ententions were that he be alowed one or two servants to waite uppon him such as he think most necessary for him.

It was consented to that they should be alowed him.

Earl of Arondell.

My Lords: if it please your Lordships to give my Lord of Berkshire some inlargement, I think you shall doe a favour to that Lord that spoke first, but although you are plesed to relese his close imprisonment yet I thinke your Lordships shall do well accordinge to your order to observe that rule not to give my Lord more then the freedome and libertye of the Fleete till he do peticion to the Howse which no question but he will doe very shortly for I assure myselfe by this tyme he sees his owne errour.

It was ordered that the Gentleman Usher of the howse Mr. James Maxwell should lett my Lord of Berkshire understand of the howses favour to him to release his close imprisonment.

At the conferrence at Whitehall before his Majestie upon Satterday in the afternoone at 2 of the clocke the 18th February 1620.[1]

Lord Chancelor.

May it plese your most sacred Majestie, the Lords Spirituall and Temporall and the Knights, Cittizens and Burgesses of the Commons' house of Parliament have intrusted me to present unto your Majestie their humble and affectionate petition. [fo. 155v.] But before I present their humble suit and desires I must make a peticion to your Majestie for my owne imperfections which are so great as I am unworthy to speake unto a Kinge and for soe great a bodie as a howse of

[1] *Sic.* The date should be 17 February. The best account of this conference is Pym's in *Commons Debates 1621*, iv. 69–75.

Parliament, especially to such a kinge, soe judicious and wise a kinge as your Majestie, and for soe learned a howse as this howse of Parliament: but this is my comfort that your Majestie regards not the tinklinge of words but substance, and waight of matter needs no Art, for let downe with the softest hands never so lightly a ponderous thinge, it will find his centure. To use that reverend Prelate's speech in his sermon the first day of the Parliament this Assembly is *magna sinagoga* and therefore as the Assembly is great the matter must be suteable, and as your Majestie was gratiously plesed to say you called this Parliament principally though not solely for these ends, the good of Religion and for the makinge of lawes for the politique government.

Our peticion to your Majestie is like to our peticions to God which is to commend to God his owne cawse, soe doe we to your Majestie which is to commend to you your owne good and safetie. Your safetie is the principall, our feare the accessory, soe as we doubt not but we shall receve from your Majestie a gratious answere and this way and in this manner even for the same things your Majestie beinge pleased to graunt the howse of Parliament's humble peticion, they nothinge doubt but they shall receve the like grace. It is nether fitt for my place nor age to presume to speake longe before your Majestie nor to trust my memory in this waighty busines and therfore I beseech your Majestie give me leave to resort to my memoriall.

Now having gone through with the particulers according to the commands I receved from both the howses, there remaines nothinge but to expect your benigne answere and gratious plesure.[a]

The King's Majestie's speech.

My Lords Spirituall and Temporall and you the knights, cittizens and burgesses of the Commons house of Parliament, I wish my voyce were soe loud or I could extend it soe much as you could all heare me. I thanke you all for your great care of my safetie and for your peticioninge to me in this maine poynt the matter of Religion which I thanke God I have beene alwayes carefull in, and as I have tould you *a Jove principium* soe must you receve the matter and manner of proceeding from me, and as heretofore soe shall I still be most carefull in things that concerne the good of the Church.

[fo. 156] I heare its generally rumoured abroad that I should connive at Papists and that I grow could in my Religion. I am sure both my Lords the Judges and other my inferiour ministers can wittness that I never stayed the execution against Papists; but as I have said before that as the foundation of our Church is not laid and simented with blood, soe doe I hould it a great honour to our Religion that none is put to death for it unless they be traytours to my person or the State. If I that have found soe great a blessinge of God in professing his trew Religion should not love and maintaine it I were much to blame knowinge that without that blessing of God nothing can prosper and I wish the world may know I need noe spurs to put my lawes in execution in matter of Religion, which may be thought

[a] *In margin:* Note I omit to set downe the 5 severall things in the Peticion, havinge done it before.

by both the houses' petition. But I assure my selfe and judge charitably that you doubt not I would goe on without this for if it be not my constant government as well out of as in tyme of Parliament it will doe little good, and as there hath been no care wanting nether shall there be any fault in me for the plantinge of trew Religion in my other kingdoms as well as this. And nowe I must excuse my selfe that I declare my selfe no larger by reason my many affayres I have had lately. My Lords and gentlemen, as my Lord Chancellor did, soe for the helpe of my memory I doe crave to have the note read againe and I will give you answeres to the five perticulers in your peticion. For the two first Articles you doe desire my plesure may be declared by Proclamacion, but for the manner of doinge it you must leave it unto me that am your kinge who knowes best how to order in matters of State. Now Bohemia is lost and all most all the Palatinate. The Valtaline being as it is, Fraunce standing upon so ticke poynts and the Protestants upon their gard and in soe great feares. I thinke it is a very unseasonable tyme to send forth a Proclamacion [fo. 156v.] against Papists for you may be sure what measure we show to them heare the same wilbe meted . . .[1]

[fo. 177] The effect of the Kinge's Majestie's speach unto the Lords in the higher house of Parliament upon Satterday in the morning the 10th of March 1620.

My Lords: I had not come hither this day, being unusuall but at the beginning and ending of a Session, but that I heard that it was told you by Sir Edward Coke at the conference with the lower howse that I alwayes sitt in this place amongst you by representacion, and theirfore I conceive I may much more come personally when I will. The errand because I heard that some were called into question, yea some of my servants, about some Patents or grants they had from me. Seing all Patents come from me being the fountaine theirof and soe consequently the execution theirof reverting to me, I hold it fitt to declare myselfe herein; but before I descend into the particulers (I speake without flattery) never a Lower howse shewed more respect unto their kinge, than the Commons howse this Parliament have done unto me. But, my Lords, you that are neerer to me than they, unto you, theirfore, did I thinke good to declare my selfe never doing any actions but such as I am not ashamed to speake of. Being not present I could receive that which passed but by relation; theirfore I would have you, my Lord Chancelor, make report unto me what passed at the conference.

Lord Chancelor.

May it please your Majestie: My yeares being many and my memorie weake and decayed, I beseech you give me leave to resort to my papers, for it is a dangerous thing to speake to a kinge, especially to soe judicious and learned a kinge as your Majestie. For truly, Sir, it was soe longe and branched into soe many partes, as I should make an abrupt relation to you otherwise. Hereupon the King gave him leave to read his papers.

[1] The rest of this folio is blank.

The Kinge.

My Lords: As I told you before, as I have bene alwayes a hater of projects and projectors, as those of my privie counsell both upon their honors and consciences can tell you howe often I have consulted with them about theis thinges, and shewed my dislike and distaste of them. They have bene soe troublesome to me that neither my selfe nor those about me could rest in their beddes quiet for projectors, as the greate backe gallery, if it had a voice, could tell. Theis kinde of people and Patents makes me odious to my people for they cannot judge of me that heare me not, but by my actions. I am contented (as Sir Edward Coke moved) there should be a lawe made against theis thinges. My Lord Treasurer that sitts there knowes howe I have bene cousened by this Patent of [fo. 177v.] concealments of three of my forests. And although I hate theis projects, yet before Sir Gyles Mompesson had this Patent of gold and silver thread my Lady of Bedford had this patent. It is noe injury to name the person for she did it for myne as well as her owne good; but Mompesson regarded not me, but gott it only for him selfe. Buckingham hath moved me many tymes in things of this kind, beinge informed that they were not prejudiciall to my people and would redound much to my proffitt; but alwayes with this protestacion, sayinge if they be good, it is fitt for your Majestie, but for my selfe, I will have none of them. After Mompesson had moved me for theise Patents I referred the consideracion of them unto 4 of my Judges, my Atturny and Solicitor, who all can witness that they tould me that I might graunt them by law, and that there was nothing hurtfull in them to the prejudice of my people. But if by the execution an evill event have proceded I wish they should be extinguished.[a]

Sir Henry Yelverton can tell that I have ben moved in that I refused to graunt many Patents least they should be hurtfull, although none can tell whether they be ill at the first till they be seene by experience for there is none of them but have fayre faces and pretences. Yelverton acquainted me how prejudiciall the Patent of Innes was, Sir Gyles Mompesson having sent out 300 Corantoes[1] and how hee would not confess the ples of them beinge soe much complained of by the subjects. I tould Sir Gyles he should have graunted licences for Innes, not at once but by little and little it should have been done; but he was soe farr from redressinge the abuse of Alehowses as from fayre Inns hee converted them to base Alehouses. I was soe troubled with complaints in this kind at Newmarket as they were brought unto me when I was in my bed. Mompesson being there, I sent for him, and Buckingham in my presence tould him that sure by the many complaints that were brought to me these licences were unfitt to be graunted and if there were a Parliament he might be sure he should heare of it, but for his owne parte let him beare it as hee could, hee would quite his hands of it. Mompesson replied that if there were a Parliament he was sure he should be of it and he would justifie him selfe well enough, and for those that lately complained to me about Royston, there was

[a] *In margin:* The King had comanded his Attorney to enter a clause that if the Patent were inconvenient to be voyde. Yelverton's fault if not inserted.

[1] Compare Wentworth: 'he [Sir Giles Mompesson] had taken forth 3500 and odd writs of *quo warranto*'. *Commons Debates 1621*, v. 488.

two Justices of Peace nere that place that certified of the sufficiencie and fittingness of them.

The lower howse have showed great modestye in there proceedings and in their places have proceeded as farr as they can in the informacion for they are noe Court of Record nether can give oath ; it is you that have the power of Judicature. As for the thinges objected against the Chancelor and the Treasurer, I leave them to answere for themselves and to stand and fall as they aquitt them selves, for if they cannot justifie [fo. 178] themselves they are not worthie to hould and enjoy those places they have under me.

All this while I have been tellinge you of my desire to have my people righted ; but now I desire you to doe your kinge justice. For though Sir Edward Coke be very busie and be called the father of the Law and the Commons' howse have divers yonge lawyers in it, yet all is not law that they say, and I could wish, nay I have tould Sir Edward Coke, that he would bringe presidents of good kings' tymes such as my Grandfather King Henry the 7th, or King Henry the 8th, a wicked man but a good king, the late Queene Elizabeth of ever livinge memory, the wonder of her sex and the admirablest Prince that ever rayned since Augustus tyme, or presidents of my tyme and not ether of Henry the 6th, a poore weake Prince governed by his counsell or of Richard the 2, who was murthered, and such like Princes and tymes when one house was up today and another to morrow and the Crowne tossed upp and downe like a tennis ball. I hope in his vouchinge presidents to compare my actions [1] to usurpers or tyrants tymes you will punish him, for the Starr Chamber which is an inferior Court to this will punish *pro falso clamore*. After you have examined this matter and heard all the proofes, I pray you referr this patent for poynt of lawe to the Judges, for the legalitie of it I wish you to proceede this way by the Judges, who must judge of triall of lands betwixt you and mee and of lands betwixt your selves, nay of mens' lyves.

For the second patent that of gould thread where it is aledged it is a monopoly it is therefore fitt for the Judges to deliver their opinions. This matter should have beene brought unto my Privy Counsell, for Sir Edward Villiers that is Master of my Mint came and tould me that this allowance of makinge of gould and silver thread did hurt the Bullion, but in regard of my many businesses and his imployment in my affayres abroad I could not heare the exceptions against the Patent. The Proclamacion came forth to back my right and not to back them in their unjust execucion and therefore Sir Edward Coke is mistaken ; the Proclamacion was not sent forth for private ends. I will say nothinge of Sir Gyles Mompesson having wronged me and himselfe in the execution of these Patents, but I conceave he laboured for my profitt and soe few have I about me that doe trewly regard it as I must not discourage nor give creaditt untill I find just cause against those I ymploy, for then should I have no good servants. I will not rest, which is no greevance, untill I ridd my selfe of a great many inutile servants who doe gaine

[1] Here the copyist has made an insertion which should perhaps replace rather than expand the sentence as first written. The passage might then read ' To compare my actions to usurpers' or tyrants' tymes is a wrong to you all. I hope you will rather punish the partie that aledgeth them then ruile your judgments by him, for the Starr Chamber which is an inferior Court to this will punish *pro falso clamore*. I leave it to you to heare and examine me.'

me nothinge, but eate and spend my estate. I doe owe thanks unto the lower house for informinge me how that in the last Patent, that of Concealments, there should be some things past they know I would soe much dislike of.

[fo. 178v.] Havinge spoken of the two former Patents, that of Innes and that of Gould and Silver Thread, both which concerne soe much the good of my people, I will say but a little in this latter of the Patent of Concealments which onely concernes my selfe, for those things that are prejudiciall to my subjects I cannot, beinge their Prince that am bound by my kingly office, suffer them to indure wronge ever remitt but that which concernes my selfe I thank God hee hath given me the Charitie to forgive as I forgave two severall persons in Gowrie's Conspracie that committed Treason against my owne person; whereas Mompesson had passed away in his grant divers hospitales I will promise never to graunt the like patents heereafter. I shall say no more of this; the two first Patents were both put in execution; for this latter it was onely in intencion some things being contracted for but nothinge past.

Now my Lords, I have somewhat to say to you: you neede not search presidents whether you may deale in this business without the lower howse for there is no question yours is a house and a court of Record. You neede not stick uppon it, for the lower howse, they are but a howse of customes and orders and their house hath come from yours, for though heretofore a long tyme since you were but all one house, yett uppon the division all the power of judicature went with your howse.

Now to speake as a Judge these things are necessary for you to observe: first the partie accused; secondly the accusers; thirdly the matter of the accusation; fourthly witnesses and proofes. That is (1) Sir Gyles Mompesson (2) the Lower howse (3) Patents (4) Matters of Record and the parties that are to be sworne. In your judgment learne not of accusers how to judge but judge as you see cause, for things must be judged by real proofes, and in questions of lawe judges are to speake if it concerne any particular partie much more to heare them when the matter is upon a question of lawe and that it concernes me. Lawes are not to loke backward and forward; for the prevention of abuses of things to come make as seveare lawes as you will find, for those things that are prejudiciall for the present shalbe taken away. I will joyne with you as I say leavinge me that latitude that is fitting for you to leave to your kinge. I honour Parliament but more veritie. In former tymes kings sate not in the Parliament by representacion but person, as I doe now, both houses makinge then but one. I know not the misteries of the omnipotencie of a Parliament. I thinke him an enemie to monarchy and a traytor to me that menciones my actions with such kings as I have tould you.

[fo. 179] I am accomptable to none but to God and my people for my Government. If I had knowne theise abuses I would have seene a reformacion, but they come to my knowledge now in Parliament as though nothing could be done but in Parliament. I hope both my lords the Bishops, you, my Lords that are made by me and other that are of the ancient nobilitie will do me right against theise tongues that wronge me both for the love you beare to me and your owne honors; for Buckingham since he came to me beinge so neare to me hath beene more troubled then ever any that served me that I may say his tyme hath beene a purgatory to him and that he hath had more ease this Parliament then he hath had of a long tyme before, for now he is not pestered and troubled at his chamber with projects or projectors. I will tell you a tale of a cow which tale when I was a youth my tutor tould me. There was a cow in the spring tyme was weary of her tayle and fisked and kept a stir that she could eate no meat untill it was cut of, but after the heat of the yeare in the winter, the wether beginning to be could, she was desirous and would faine not onely to have had her tayle but her clicket againe that grew under her tayle. So nowe everybody would be glad to be ridd of their patents and envay and speake much against patents and courtiers, but after the Parliament is ended, like the Cowe then they will come againe and be glad to regard those neare about me and then Buckingham shalbe troubled again, some coming to begg something of me, but I must answeare as the Apostle said monny have I none [1] some to receave favour and furtherance in their suits and some ambitious and desirous of honour.

For my Lord Chancelor and my Lord Treasurer let them hould up their owne heads and for Buckingham I heare nothing spoke in the generall of complaints against him, but in Innes and Alehouses, their like Raskalls doe they speake of him. But my Lords, I desire you not to looke of him as adorned with theise honours as Marquess of Buckingham, Admirall of England, Master of my Horse, Gentleman of my Bed Chamber, a Privie Counsellor and Knight of the Garter, but as he was when he came to me as pore George Villiers and if he prove not himselfe a white crow he shalbe called a black crow.

My Lord of Buckingham answered uppon his knees.

Sir, if I cannot cleare myselfe of any aspercion or imputacion cast uppon me I am contented to abide your Majesty's censure and be called the Black Crow.

[fo. 179v.] The Kinge againe.

For the Judges they are men of great understandinge and gravitie, but for Common Lawyers they are wind instruments their tonge beinge their pipe. A Bagpipe is a greater noyse then a viole although a viole hath better musique and hevier. This is now a tyme of bringing all things to proofe, nay a day of judgment. I feare not to apeare before sun and moone when I come to triall, such hath ben all my actions in my tyme. I pray you excuse me I have troubled you soe longe, but I determined not to come till this morninge, and after I have heard my Lord Chancelor and my Lord Treasurer speake againe.

Lord Chancelor stood in his place as a Peere.

May it please your most Sacred Majestie to give me leave to speake a few words. Ever since I came to your Majestie's service in being trusted with the custodie

[1] The reference is to Acts iii. 6. The sentence appears to have been transposed in copying and should read: 'Some coming to begg something of me, some to receave favour and furtherance in their suits and some ambitious and desirous of honour. But I must answere as the Apostle said monny have I none.'

of your great seale I have beene so farr from sufferinge things to pass hands over heads that I have taken the bouldness to stay many patents at the seale untill I have attended your Majestie to know your gratious pleasure; and may it please your Majestie, for all my Lord Coke hath said, I hope in futuer ages my acts and honestie shall well apeare before his and my honesty over ballance and waigh his and be found hevier in that scale. I doe not speake to theise Lords as my associates but as my Peares and Judges to judge of me in their honours; but I humbly beseech your Majestie that I may have tyme to looke over my memorialls and then I am readie to put my self to triall of my honestie.

Lord Treasurer.

May it please your Majestie: you have alreadie pronounced sentence upon me, soe as if I cannot cleare my selfe and satisfie your Majestie of my inocencie I am not worthie to be your Officer nor to carry this staff, soe as there remaines nothing then but the execution thereof. I must confess unto your Majestie that I have receaved more and more graces from you and have had the honour and hapiness to be your servant and imployed in your affayres this sixteene yeares, in all which tyme if I have abused your favours or done any one thinge unworthilie I desire never to aproach againe in your presence. I must confess I was privie to all the 3 patents both that of Innes, Gould and Silver Thread and of Concealments, and I hope in all I have done nothing unworthie of the trust reposed in me by your Majestie. For at that tyme theise patents [fo. 180] were graunted unto Sir Gyles Mompesson I served your Majestie in the place of your Serjeant and fore of your principall Judges, your Atturney Generall and Solicitor had the perusall of them and they were liked well of them all, and my selfe doe thinke as I did then that the Patents are not ill in themselves. What the execution may make them I know not and for the warrant dormant when it was brought to me (for I never saw any more but one) I refused to signe it, saying I would rather have this hand cut off then my name should be sett to yt. I will presume to say no more hopinge that it doth evidently apeare to your Majestie that I have done no more then becomes your servant.

Marquesse of Buckingham.

May it please your Majestie, it is unfitt for me to speake in this great assembly and especially before your Majestie that is soe great a scholler, without premeditacion and therefore should have been silent but that I must crave your Majestie's pardon to declare my innocencie. I had thought never to have changed or altered my Religion but I must be a Papiste in this perticuler to thinke their is a purgatory and that all men's actions must be purged, and for my selfe I desire to be purged by your Majestie's gracious declaracion whether since I had the honour to serve you I have solicited you in any thinge that is hurtfull to your people; if I have not I beseech your Majestie I may still live in your gratious opinion.

The Kinge againe.

My Lords: I pray you give me pacience to make a conclusion and take this with you. The lower house desires you to judge this man which, for the execution, goe on as the Starr Chamber doth judge of Riots and other things; but as the Judges out of Parliament are to judge of the legalitie of Patents, soe would I have you heare them now for the legalitie of Patents. And for such things you are to judge looke to the presidents of the best tymes and this is all I crave. I meane not to debarr you to try any thinge you have presidents for, in the tyme of lawful governments, and that I have given you libertie soe to doe enter my being here this day. [fo. 180v.] For the convenience of theise Patents I thinke you will not judge of them at this tyme. I thinke you conceave you have a good Kinge. I beseech you, my Lords spirituall and temporall, soe to chalke out the way that my people may know my zeale to justice and my desire to free them of opression. I pray you consider how longe the lower house both night and day for divers weeks together have taken paynes in the examination of this business and have used all the care and diligence that might be to search this matter to the bottom. Therefore I conceave it will not stand with your gravitie and judgments to give sentence within a few houres of that they have ben soe longe about.

Consider how the season of the yeare growes on that there may be no wastfull spending and consumtion of tyme, but that the same may be spent in doing that to which end the Parliament was called, which was for the releefe of my necessitie to furnish me with monny to recover my grandchildren's ancient inheritance, and for the making of such good lawes as shalbe for the wellfare of my people. For I would not have you endevour to be thought gratious lords to the people, but let my honour be seene and how willinge I am to doe any thinge for the punishment of Sir Gyles Mompesson. Consider you cannot resume patents without me and the execution of your sentence must come from me. Consult of the way of punishinge Mompesson and I will joyne with you, but consume not millions of dayes in those things which have enterveyned since the Parliament began, and were not the cawses of calling of it. You see the disease and as you bend your cares to salve the sore, soe leave it not forth of your cares to save the King's honour as much as you can, who hath alwayes hated all things that may any way be vexatious unto his people.[a]

[Notes of later proceedings.]

21 March 1621. [L.J., iii. 58.]

[fo. 239] The [b] names of the Lords Commitys for the examination of witnesses in My Lord Chancellor the Lord Viscount St. Alban's cause whoe devided themselves into 3 partes.

1.	2.	3.
E. of Arundell	E. of Huntingdon	E. of Southampton
B. of Duresme	B. of Winton	B. of Covent. et Lichf.
Lo. North	Lo. Wentworth	Lo. Spencer
Lo. Hunsdon	Lo. Haughton	Lo. Say.

[a] *Endorsed at foot of fo. 180:* Notes of the Parliament.
[b] *This fragment is marked* O.

The interrogatoryes set downe by the Lords Committys to examine the deponents.

1. Whether they by themselves or any other parson have given mony or other gratuity unto my Lord Chancellor or to any other servant frend or follower of his.
2. Whether they have advised or directed any soe to doe or knowe of any that have soe done.
3. Whether they or the partyes which they advised so to do or have hard soe to have done had then any cause or sute dependinge before him or intended to have any.
4. Whether they have attempted or knowne others have attempted or contracted for any gratuity soe to be given thoughe not performed.[1]

17 April. [L.J., iii. 75.]

[fo. 231] Against[a] the Lord Chancellor

His person and place might have given him that favoure[2] yet under tryall of this house the Councell durst not advise him,[b] but his Majestie suddenly lighted on such a course as all the worlde coulde not advise a better, that was that his Majestie would speake privately with the Lord Chancellor, which he did yester, beinge Monday

1. To stand upon his innoceency if his answeres were fayre and cleare to those things objected against him.
2. To admitt him to the extenuation of the charge where his answeres were not soe fayre and cleare.
3. Where the proofes are[c] undeniable he would ingeniously confesse and put himsealfe upon the mercy of the Lords.

The King commanded the Lord Treasurer to make report hereof.

[fo. 210] Archbishop[d] of Canterbury's Speach to his Majestie at Whitehall as mouth of the Lords the 6th of May 1622.[3]

May it please your Majestie: my Lords hearinge from your gracious mouth that your Majestie conceaved that in Sir Henry Yelvertons speach in the higher house your Majestie conceaved your honor was touched, and since by my Lord Treasurer perceavinge it was your pleasure that you would not have my Lords

[a] *This fragment is marked* P.
[b] *In margin:* E. of Huntingdon. B. of Bath & Wells. Lo. Hunsdon.
[c] *MS.* and.
[d] *This fragment is marked* Y.

---

[1] A report of the examination of the witnesses was made to the House on 19 April by the earls of Arundel, Huntingdon and Southampton (Gardiner, *Lords Debates in 1621*, pp. 8–9).

[2] Bacon had asked for an audience with the king.

[3] The House had been divided in their opinion of Yelverton's meaning. Some thought the king's honour was touched and that the case should be withdrawn. After considerable debate it was decided to ask the king for an audience (Gardiner, *Lords Debates in 1621*, pp. 49–53).

meddle with that, their Lords, not a few but all the whoale body and assembly of the higher house doe by me humbly beseech your Majestie that as he was put into their hands by your Majestie soe you would not take him out their hands which they conceave breakes the liberty and priviledges of ther house and which will exceedingly trouble them, make them imagine your Majestie mistrusteth them to doe you justice against Sir Henry Yelverton, which their Lordships all protest that as they have soe will they allwayes shew them sealves lovinge and dutiefull subjects and most tender in those thinges toucheth your Majestie in point of honor.

The Kinge.

My Lords: for this message delivered by my Lord of Canterbury from you I will give you the like answere as a great Prince my predecessor did, a Prince worthy of all memory, and as I have said in some of my writings a Prince worthy to be compared unto the Emperor Augustus, a Queene happy in her government at the cominge to her raigne, happy in the progresse of it and happy at the end of it at her death; that is an answere answereles. But before I tell you my reasons of sendinge the message by my Lord Treasuror I marvayle that in this concernes me you make not him [1] the messenger seinge I have soe honored you in lettinge him sitt in your house; but in his brother's tyme he called him the Archbishop of Yorke soe now you come neare it sendinge it me by the Archbishop of Canterbury. As I sayd you shall have an answer answerles but the reasons are theise. First, I saw by your not makeinge him a cloase prisoner which if you have done well in it I am sure I have done ill for many in my tyme have I committed [fo. 210v.] cloase prisoner and the partys afterwards acquitted them sealves for that is but to keepe them from the helpe of others. I doe not say I will put him to you for whoe can judge of me but God and none is fitt to judge a Kinge but himsealfe. If you sensure him you doe well, but if you doe not you judge me and never any Monarch will be judged by his Nobility; noe more will I. For if you may judge of my honor you may depose me. Not to sentence Yelverton is to judge me and makes good what he sayes; if Yelverton be Mordecai [2] Buckingham must be Haman and be hanged. If he Spencer,[3] I Edward 2, for theise are relatives, King and people, Master and servant, Father and sonne, and to reckon me with such a Prince is to esteeme me a weeke man and I had rather be noe kinge then such a one as Kinge Edward the 2nd. My Lords, I like not as the Lower House you to stand upon reason and precedents. For the other part of my Lord of Canterbury's speach that you woulde thinke I mistrusted your

[1] Prince Charles. When Charles was duke of York Prince Henry would 'taunt him till he made him weep telling him he should be a Bishop' (T. Birch, *The Life of Henry Prince of Wales*, p. 302). The prince's services had been in demand as an intermediary between the Lords and the king. On this occasion he had opposed the approach to the king and excused himself from the Committee.

[2] Yelverton had said 'I resolved in this to be as stubborn as Mordecay' (L.J., iii. 121; see also Gardiner, *Lords Debates in 1621*, p. 47).

[3] Yelverton's words were: 'If my Lord Buckingham had but read the Articles exhibited in this place against Hugh Spencer and had known the danger of placing and displacing officers about the King, he would not have pursued me with such bitterness' (*Ibid.*).

affections to me, for that I dislike not, but for your priviledges you have them and your honor from me.[a] I pray you regard my honor for it concerns you being the Peares of my kingdome, for the wronginge of me concearns you all. For what regard when you come into your Cuntrys would the Clownes make of you if you be not graced by me? Noe more than of Jacke Cade. I say you now shall have an answere answereles but to morrowe in the afternoon you shall in writinge, havinge a little tyme to consider of what you have sayed, receave my answere.

Tuesday morninge 29th of May 1622.

[fo. 208] Sir [b] Edward Coke.[1]

My Lords: Your Lordships very nobly granted to give us a free conference.

A prorogation is a settinge of a session but an adjornament is but a continuation.

The bills of continuance will within a few dayes will be readie. The King passinge 4 or 5 bills is noe determination of the session.

In *primo Hexrici septimi* bills passed for the restitution of divers noblemen and gentlemen.

The message from his Majestie by a noble parson.

1. the longe sittinge.
2. the heate of the yeare.
3. the King goinge his progresse.
4. the course of justice havinge binne hindered.
5. the Lieutenants and Deputy Lieutenants.
6. the King's owne busines.
7. foreigne busines abroade.

Wee desire a session and a generall pardon.

My reasons:

1. In sittinge 26 weekes a schandall to doe nothinge.
2. Havinge given the King 2 subsdies never were given without the pasinge of bills.
3. Never soe good intendment as this Parliament if it have a good end for the honor, safety, profitt of the King and the benefitt of the Commonwealth.
4. In the Statute of Marlborow both houses are called *Commune Consilium*.

[a] *In margin:* Though I can take no notice what you say yet beinge a Record I may.
[b] *This fragment is marked* Z.

[1] A fuller report of Coke's speech at the Conference is given by Pym, *Commons Debates 1621*, iv. 386–7.

APPENDIX

1. Letter from Sir John Davies [1] to the earl of Huntingdon.

[MS. Carte 62, fo. 584.]

Charing Cross,
8 March 1623 [1624].

Right Honourable,

It may please your Lordship: the Lord Archbishop of Canterbury this morning brought into the house of the lords a Report of the King's answer in writing, made to the Committees of both Houses, who presented their Resolution and Advise for the absolute breach of the long continued Treaties, both touching the Match and the restitution of the Palatinate. The Report in writing was delivered to the Clark of the Parliament to the end that every man that would might take a copy thereof. So as your Lordship shall receave a perfect and entire copy of that answer by the hands of Mr. Newton, who spends this afternoone in procuring other notes from the Clark according to your Lordship's commandment.

This great matter of Advise did so take up all the tyme in both Houses as that there came upp no bills from the house of Commons, till within these 3 dayes, when 5 publick bills and one private bill was presented, the titles whereof your Lordship will receave by Mr. Newton. These bills have had one Reading; and 3 or 4 other bills originally preferred in this house have been twice read and are in the hands of the Committees; but these acts (as I conceave) will have but a slow proceeding untill the maine business bee reduced to more certenty. There are divers Lords absent, and 4 which appeared doe retire themselves, refusing to take the oath of alleageance, namely, the Lord Viscount Montagu, the Lord Vaux, the Lord Evers, the Lord Roper: [2] but my Lord Morley hath taken the oath very willingly and so (I take it) the Lord Winsor and Lord Sturton have donne: for they remayne in the house and are present at prayers every day. There is a bill passing in the house of Commons, that no man shall take above eight in the hundred for loane of money. They have the same committees for greevances and for abuses in Courts of Justice as they had the last Parliament, but little dispatcht, by reason of the great transcendant busines. I think your Lordship hath no cause to repent that you have not been present at this first meeting, which (I doubt) will scarce prove a session before Easter. In the mean tyme I shall not omitt to advertise your Lordship of the ordinary passages. Thus presenting my best service to your Lordship I remayne your Lordship's humble and faithfull servant

John Davys.

This Tuesday morning (for Mr. Newton is not yet dispatcht) I attended in the upper house but there hath been *altum silentium* touching the great business. Wee

[1] In 1623 the earl of Huntingdon's son Ferdinando had married the daughter of Sir John Davies, Attorney General for Ireland and later Chief Justice of the King's Bench. Other letters from Sir John keeping the earl in touch with Parliamentary business in 1624–5 are printed in H.M.C. Report, *Hastings*, ii. 63–9.

[2] Baron Teynham.

spent the tyme in reading of our bill for my Lord the Earle of Oxford to confirme a decree made for him and his tenants of many tenements in White-chappell which in tyme will prove a great inheritance. My Lord of Suffolk did publickly oppose the bill: but the affection of the house was strong to my Lord of Oxford and the bill is committed.

Endorsed: The Rt. Hon. my very good Lord the Earl of Huntingdon. Donington Park. Leicestershire.

[MS. Carte 77, fo. 272.]

2. Remembrances against the Parliament made the 13th of October 1624.

To conferre with some Lords and the Bishops that the overture for the increasinge of ministers' livinges be moved.

To remember that if the bill for Hospitalls and Schooles goe on that the fines may be devided amongst the whoale Society and that all may not goe to the Master as in Wigston's Hospitall of Leycester it doth.

To remember that where ther are divers feofments for charitable uses none of the feoffees may be tenants to the lands or howses as in Ashby they be, for that hinders the charitable uses 3 parts in 4 of the true valew of the lands.

To remember that if the bill of the Saboath goe on that none may be arrested that day or upon a holy day either goinge to the Church, stayinge ther or returninge from the Church.

Endorsed: Remembrances against the Parliament in February next 1624.

3. Letter from Francis Staresmore [1] to the earl of Huntingdon.

[MS. Carte 77, fo. 280.]

London, at the signe of the Plow
neare Charing Cross.
26 February 1625 [1626].

Right Honourable,

In the first place I humbly crave your Lordship's pardon, that I have addressed no letters unto you since the beginning of the Parliament. My excuse must be this, that as yet it hath not produced any thinge which is come to a conclusion.

The admittance of Sir Edward Cooke or his discharge is not determined; much dispute hath beene about that matter and records look'd up and brought into the house and there read concerning the restraint of electing a sheriffe to be a knight of the shire. That clause in the writ is as ancient as 46th Edward 3rd, interrupted from the 8th of Henrie 4th till the 14th, and since continued in the *Nolumus* or Prohibition. The best opinions are that he shall neyther be admitted nor any writte sent out for a new election, but onely left to attend his office in the country. What resolution wilbe taken therein till it be reported to the house is uncertaine. Hitherto it hath beene thrise deferred.

[1] Francis Staresmore sat as second knight of the shire for Leicester.

Divers bills have received 2 readings both private and publike bills; as yet none sent up to the Lords. The publike bills are these:

A Bill to account for the countryes' money for bridges or any other receipts.
A Bill against concealments.
A Bill against simony.
A Bill for due election and free choyce of knights and burgesses.
A Bill to restraine transportation of ordinance.
A Bill for reliefe of creditors, and to reforme abuses in under-sheriffes.
A Bill against secret offices and inquisitions taken by sheriffs escheators etc.
A Bill against scandalous ministers, which I feare will not passe in the lower house. It is upon the 2 reading and report's recommitted.
A Bill against exportation of wools and woolfels.
A Bill for free fishing.
A Bill against bribery in courts and obtaining of places of judicature.
A Bill against Edmund Nicholson for his patent of praetermitted customes.
A Bill for subscription.
A Bill for breeding and bringing up of recusants' children.
A Bill against muster masters.
A Bill against the abuses of false measure in sea cole.
A Bill for reliefe of market townes about cottages and inmates.
A Bill touching the graunting administration of the intestates' goods.

These are the publike bills that have beene read, but not one of them sent up as yet to the upper house.

By an order in the house of Commons all grievances *a primo Jacobi* together with the answers heretofore given are to be examined.

The English merchants trading in wines petitioned the house against the imposition layed upon wines by the Earle of Middlesex, complayned how their goods, bills, obligacions to the valew of 700,000 pounds are arrested in Fraunce and 11 of their ships. The cause is, as they informed, for that the French merchants could have no justice in the Admiralty of England for their goods which were seysed here, especially for the 2nd arrest of a shippe called the Peter of Newhaven and making sale of the goods after the king had commaunded shee should be released, and a decree by the judge of the Admiralty passed for her discharge, and that upon that decree shee was fallen downe to Gravesend, but being windbound, lay almost a fortnight there after her discharge and [fo. 280v.] before her second arrest. Sir Henry Martin, the judge of the Admiralty, being a member of the house was required to give an account of her 2nd stay and whether he did commaund it. He denyed that he had done any more in it then what was done by the decree for her discharge: more then this, being asked whether if that shippe did colour any Spanish goods, shee might not, notwithstanding the decree, be stayed again upon supplementall proofe and good witnesses, to which his answer was shee might, but the proofes were to be without exception, adding further, that neyther proofe nor witnesse was offered to him after her release till her 2nd arrest, and so layed the blame upon the Lieutenants of the Tower and Dover for that which was done therein, saying moreover that he was sure if this 2nd arrest of that shippe had not beene, there would have beene an imbargo of all our merchants' goods in Fraunce, but gave no reason of his knowledge in any particuler.

Sir Allan Apsley came the next day to his answer and so did Sir John Hippesley, the 2 Lieutenants. Hippesley sayd he knew nothing of that matter. Sir Allan Apsley answered he did nothing but by commaund, and that Sir. Henry Martin had councelled to make the 2nd arrest which was affirmed by Secretary Cooke. But Sir Henry Martin on Friday last in the afternoone at the Committee with great asseveracion sayd he gave no councell for the 2nd. arrest made after his decree of release, but being asked whether she might not be stayed upon further supplementall proofe, he should say there could be noe stay in justice, but onely *Regia manu*, which the King would by noe meanes give way to. So the contest when it comes next to be debated will rest betwixt the judge of the Admiralty and Secretary Cooke.

We are now come to take into consideracion the necessary defence of the kingdome in generall, and to take some course about the revenues of the crowne, and it is now resolved upon the question that the evills, the causes and the remedies are to be thought on in the first place.

I heare nothing of Sir Henrie Hastings [1] coming up, so that I am wholly alone and shall have no assistance from him. Sir Edwine Sands is this day come into the house. Mr. Segraves his hast of going out of the towne inforces me to runne on confusedly in this relacion. On Saterday there was some vehement dispute amongst the Lords about proxies; the Duke was earnest that they might give voyces for as many as they had beene trusted with, but it was resolved and ordered they should give their vote but for 2. When time produceth any thing worthy your Lordship's view, I will presume to trouble you therewith. In the meane time, craving your Lordship's pardon for this my boldness with all humblenes recommending my duty and service to your Lordship and my honorable Lady, I take leave and rest ever

your Lordship's most affectionate servant to be commaunded
Francis Staresmore.

post script

I humbly desire I may receive a particuler of the charge and expence for imprest and conduct money that I may make demaund of it in the behalfe of the country, because it was promised by the Lords of the Counsell it should be restored.

Endorsed: To the right honourable and my very good Lord Henry Earle of Huntingdon at Dunnington Parke, give these.

4. Letter from Francis Staresmore to the earl of Huntingdon.

[MS. Carte 77, fo. 274.]

London.
23 March 1625 [1626].

Right Honourable,

Much time and debate hath beene spent in Parliament about the search and examinacion of the evills (which oppresse us) the causes and the remedies. The

[1] Sir Henry Hastings was the first knight of the shire for Leicester.

causes (I thinke) are generative, every day producing new, so that they cease not to multiply and increase in number. To redresse them or how to provide remedyes proper and fitt for so desperate a disease wilbe an high point of skill. I know your Lordship hath heard of Doctor Turner's 6 heads, presented to the house upon Saterday was sevenight, late at night, by way of queries brought to him by common fame, wherein he labouring to search out (as he tearmed it) *causa generalissima*, instanced my Lord Admirall, in his questions demaunding whether those things might be charged upon him; as first, whether the King since he was admirall have lost the regality of the narrow seas; 2nd, the exorbitant wasting and misimployment of the King's estate and revenue, much of it being bestowed upon the mainteynance of him and his friends; 3rd, the engrossing the great offices of the kingdome into his hands; 4th the countenancing and dependances of papists upon him, his mother and father in law being the head of that faction. 5th, the selling of places of judicatiure, bishopricks and church livings, offices and honor and placing men in commaund and authority that are unfit; and 6thy, whether the ill successe of the last sea voyage may not be imputed to him for that he went not in person, but appointed others, himselfe being both generall and admirall in that service.

On Munday following a message came from the King by the Chancelor of thexchequer requiring justice to be done by the house upon 2 of the members, Mr. Cooke and Doctor Turner, which if it were not done by them he would use his regall power against Cooke for using these words in the house (who having heard from Sir Richard Weston that the enemy was in readines to put forth by the latter end of this moneth) said that he had rather dye by the hand of an enemy then at home by a countryman. It was aggravated the words were seditiously spoken. I confes some rash speeches fell from him which sounded ill; but the house cleared him that those were not the words which he spake, neyther were they seditious. Yet, if the whole frame of his speech were not observed, some words passed from him which might beare an ill construction, whereupon it was referred to a committee, who adjudged him (there being 2 voyces more against him then those that would have cleered him) to acknowledge his unadvisednes at the barre upon his knees. It is not yet reported to the house and what wilbe the end of it I cannot tell.

Doctor Turner, the matter was urged against him that he had not onely scandalously injured that great Lord, but in him had layed an aspersion upon his Majestie's government and his father's. This day sevenight Turner came into the house, having beene absent (thorough sickness as he pretended) from Saterday till then. He made a defence by a way of apologie, saying he tooke it to be a Parlamentary way to offer accusations against great persons by the voyce of fame, instancing the like to be done in Parliament against Edmund Duke of Suffolke in the time of Henrie the 6th and that by the Roman and Imperiall lawes it was an usuall course, not dissenting from the Decrees and Canons of the Church. [fo. 274v.] Because the words were not the same, Saterday last was given for him to set downe his queries and answer them. That day he sent a letter and came not, wherein he confessed that they were the same which Mr. Wainsford had taken who was in the chayre when he spake them, alleadging sicknes for his not coming, and withall submitted himselfe to the censure of the house, desiring them to take it so, that he did nothing but what as an honest Englishman he thought himselfe bound to doe for his countrie's service, without scandalizing the Lord Admirall, and further, that if they cleared him upon question and that his sicknes brought him to his grave, he might goe to it with the reputacion of an honest man. Stay was given till Wednesday to search records whether there was president for the like course and that the roles of Parliament should then be brought into the house. Other business of weight intervening, it was againe deferred till tomorrow.

On Munday the 20 of March the King sent to the house to quicken them for supply in his urgent affaires requiring a present answer what they would doe. The copye of the letter I have sent your Lordship herein inclosed. It was answered they could not tell how to proportion the supply without they did know his Majestie's revenue and how his estate stood and desired they might be informed of that this day and prepare what to answer upon Munday. In generall they had intimated they would give asmuch as should secure him at home and making him feared abroad, so that they might have redresse of their grievances. This day the King sent againe to let us know that when we had signifyed what we would doe, he would then give remedy for our just complaints. And today likewise Mr. Secretary Cooke tould us of the principall occasion of assembling the Parliament and the charge his Majestie must be at to maintaine a warre offensive and defensive. He gave it in particulars by speech, what necessarily must be done, the somme for one yeare amounting in grosse to 1,067,221*l.* 13*s.* 3*d.*, the particulars these.

		l s d
Spent already in 3 offices for Cales voyage		313,547. 13. 3
The charge for victualing 40 ships at this present		170,306*l.*
For Ireland . . .		2000*l* a moneth
Composicion with the King of Denmark	30,000*l.* a moneth for 6 moneths.	
Count Mansfield	20,000*l.* a moneth for the same time.	
Low Countries.	8,900*l.* a moneth	

besides the mainteynance of 10,000 men for the defence of the sea coasts which will stand in 80,000*l.* for 10 moneths, so that the charge wilbe very great and insupportable.

He likewise layd downe the power of the King of Spaine and his present preparacion and forces viz. 50,000 foote and 5000 horse in the Low Countries.

Under the Emperor's title and the Catholike League in Germany 30,000 foote 8000 horse.

In Hungary under the conduct of Count de Monte Negro 15,000 foote 3000 horse. His forces in Italy 15,000 foote and 3000 horse and in Valtolin and Millan 10,000 foote.

He hath made peace with France so that the forces of Italy are like to fall downe upon us.

Spinola provides strongly for sea, and all the power Spaine can make at home is prepared.

Complaints come in daylie against the Duke, but the King shewes him all favour, having himselfe warned the house not to meddle with his deare and neare servant; yet some thinke he will not breake with the house for any occasion. All Turner's heads upon question in the generall are resolved to be causes of our evill, so that now nothing more remaines then to personate that great man, which I suppose wilbe within these 2 dayes.

[fo. 275] I would be more large but that I have beene over tedious already and intend to write again very shortly unto your Lordship. In the meane while while craving pardon of your Lordship for my boldnes, I humbly take leave and rest

your Lordship's humble servant

Francis Staresmore.

My Lord of Oxford this day hath judgment in Parliament that the Earldome belonged to him, but the place of Lord High Chamberlain is not cleared, so that my Lord Willoughby fayled of his purpose.

My Lord of Arundell remaynes still in the Tower. Bristoll peticions to have his writ sent downe for him and that he may come into the house.

Endorsed: To the right honourable and my very good Lord Henry Earle of Huntingdon at Dunnington Parke, give these.

5. Letter from Sir John Skeffington [1] to the earl of Huntingdon.

[MS. Carte 77, fo. 437]

17 May 1626

Right Honorable,

In my last letter I mentioned the several endictments intended to be preferrd in the King's Bench against the Lords of [Buckingham] [2] and Bristol, it being then so resolved in the Upper [House] whereof, since the day following produced a soddaine al[teration] I must also yeald your Lordship some account of the pro-[cess] of that readvise and change of counsel. First it was [thought] derogatory to the honour of that House to take cogn[isance] of things from any other Court, during theyr owne [sitting.] Secondly the King himselfe being to yeald testimony of the passages, the King's Bench could not well [heare] him both as a judge and witnesse. Lastly bec[ause] those Lords having flowne to so high a pitch of acc[usation] against each other, the one being arrested of h[igh] treason by the attorney, and the other equally by his opposite, it was rather thought [fit] to retaine the cause within those walls. [If] when the charge of either part should appeare [to be] more slight or heavy then the nature of the ev[idence] could well support, it might be either retracted [or] aggravated according to the discretion and vote [of the] House.

Those articles of greevance whereof I sent your Lordship a coppy we[re] long since put into forme and presented to the L[ords] from the Lower House. Eight of our ablest memb[ers were] selected to deliver them up, and although the [charge]

[1] Sir John Skeffington sat as member for Newcastle-under-Lyme, a seat previously held by Sir John Davies. He was one of the Deputy Lieutenants for Leicestershire.

[2] The outer margin of the first page has perished and the last word of almost every line is missing in whole or in part. They have been supplied and are given in brackets.

itselfe were of no smal content and volume, yet it was [allowed] by the house to those 8 reporters to aug[ment] and illustrate theyr several relacions and parts wh[ich they] had undertaken. Wherein some of the orators w[ere so] curious to shew theyr malicious learning that w[ithin] 2 or 3 daies the King sent the prologue and the epil[ogue, Sir] Dudly Diggs and Sir John Elliot, to give hansel [1] to the Lieutenant of the Tower, Sir Anthony Ashly, who [by the] remooval of Sir Allen Apsley was at the same h[our] of this commitment ready to meete with these new g[uests.] Upon this imprisonment all buisnesse began to be diver[ted.] The House of Commons after some recollection of theyr amaze[ment] [fo. 437v.] thought upon nothing but remonstrance and petiticion to the King that he would either be pleased to restore theyr imprisoned members or dissolve the Parliament. Within three days Sir Dudly was sent backe again having attended the Counsel Board and kist the King's hand: but the other gentleman that had beene more satyrical, the King sent a message to the house to let them know that he was detained for some other causes which he called extra-judicial; whereof, when some further explanation was required, it was answered to be for some other offences preceeding the parlament, and the house was presently desired to go on in their buisness. (which is intended) to be the passing of the bills of subsidie. But this buisnesse is yet in agitation and I make a question whether the King will obtaine any proceedinge at theyr hands to yield him satisfaction except he be first pleased to redresse them in those violated privileges and after in the reparacion of greevances.

The Lords call as fast for my Lord of Arundel but the King insists upon the resentiment of his injury and came himselfe to the house upon Thursday the 10th of May where he let them know as much for the reason of his detention and for answere to theyr remonstrance. But they redouble theyr impatience and theyr demands and being now upon a readinesse and willingnesse to go to censure the Duke, it seems they want only the company of such a Lord whose example and courage would give animation and boldnesse to some such as dare not wel looke out of theyr cold neutralities. I had forgotten to tel you, my Lord, that when our House of Commons had presented theyr bill of greevances and ympeachment against the Duke it was added as an unanimous request from the house that the Duke might be committed during the search and disquisition of his offences; and the same request was formerly made by Bristol but could not passe in the Lords' House.

The world discourse diversly of the fortunes and affaires of this great Lord. Some say he hath past the climacterical of his dangers, that he is very wel able to render an honest and faire account of himselfe against all his accusations, that if his owne innocence could not preserve him the King's affection and favour would; whereof I may wel assure your Lordship there have past many remarquable testimonies in this parlament. Others say that this parlament wil make him a less Duke, that the King begins to yeald something to the inclination of the Lords and that the Lords hold a neerer correspondence with the lower house then in former parlaments where it hath beene ever esteemed a stratagem [fo. 438] of state to preserve a little discrepancy and emulacion of the 2 houses; that all forren princes concurr in a desire of seeing his subversion, that the King of Denmark hath lately

[1] I.e. a house-warming present to celebrate his new appointment.

written letters of advice to the King to expose him to his meritts and to abandon so pernicious a counsellor and minister. Many opinions of this and of the other kind might be collected, but since the greatest part have had theyr ground from mens' distempered affections, I wil the more sparingly present them to your grave and honourable judgment, desiring only to find therein a faire interpretation for mine owne imperfections which cannot stand invisible though they be shrowded amongst the faire pretences of your commands and my dutye and whatsoever else drawes any relacion from your Lordship to me that am

your humble and affectionate servant

John Skeffington.

I desire to present my dutiful respects to my most honourable Lady and my best endeavours to her favourable opinion.

INDEX

THE MINUTE BOOK OF JAMES COURTHOPE

EDITED BY

ORLO CYPRIAN WILLIAMS, C.B., M.C., D.C.L.

CAMDEN MISCELLANY

VOL. XX

LONDON

OFFICES OF THE ROYAL HISTORICAL SOCIETY

96 CHEYNE WALK, S.W.10

1953

CONTENTS

INTRODUCTION[1]

I

MS. Rawlinson A. 86 in the Bodleian Library at Oxford is a manuscript minute book kept by a committee clerk, James Courthope, during two sessions in the reign of William III, the first being that of December 1697–July 1698 and the second that of December 1698–May 1699. The period which it covers is therefore exactly co-extensive with Vol. 12 of the Commons Journals. It contains the minutes of proceedings, hardly ever quite complete, of 64 select committees,[2] of which 16 were on matters of public interest, 14 on public bills, 31 on private bills, two of the remaining three being committees appointed to draw up reasons for disagreeing with Lords amendments to Commons bills, and the other being a committee appointed to draft an address in answer to a speech from the king.

The survival of such a book in a collection of manuscripts is a singular phenomenon. The minute book of a committee clerk was never an official document, to be preserved with any other documents relating to particular committees. It was simply a record from which the report of the committee was compiled, after which it must usually have been destroyed. Moreover, it is only since 1852 that the minutes of proceedings of select committees have regularly been reported to the House together with the minutes of evidence, with which they have usually been ordered to be printed. The minutes of proceedings of private bill committees, since these were differentiated from select committees, have never been ordered to be printed, though they are now laid on the table of the House. Previous to 1852, therefore, the day-to-day minutes of a select committee's proceedings are unrecorded; and before 1801, when, after the union with Ireland, it became the practice of the House to order the reports of select committees to be printed, the only information as to the reports of such committees was that recorded in the Journals, except where printing was ordered in particular instances, as was increasingly done towards the end of the eighteenth century.

Every student of the earlier Journals knows that there are lamentable *lacunae* in the entries, especially of documents presented, including the reports of select committees handed in at the table by the chairman of the committee after formal

[1] I should like here to express my gratitude to the Leverhulme Trustees for the grant which made it possible for me to carry out the work involved in this publication.

[2] Only one of the 64 was specifically termed a select committee in the Journal, but they were all of the nature of select committees, there being at that time, and for long afterwards, no distinction between committees on public matters or bills and those on private bills. In Courthope's day the term 'select' or 'particular' committee was rarely applied, though it will be observed that the latter term appears written by some later hand on the first folio in the book. It was not till well into the eighteenth century that committees nominated of a limited number of members were regularly termed select committees in the Journals. As regards the special development of private bill committees, I refer readers to my *Historical Development of Private Bill Procedure &c. in the House of Commons*, vol. i (H.M.S.O.).

reading. One finds some of the petitions, reports of committees, and other documents set out in full, but often there is a blank where the Clerk had intended to annex a document, but had presumably lost or mislaid it. It is true that all such documents were supposed to be preserved by the Clerk among the papers of the session; and Journal entries are to be seen which record that certain documents, e.g. plans, put in with a committee's report, were being so preserved: unfortunately for the historian, the fire of 1834 completely destroyed this irreplaceable collection of papers, so that there is no remedy for the imperfections of the earlier Journals. This fact renders immeasurably more precious than they might otherwise have been any documents that amplify Journal entries. Such a document is James Courthope's minute book, which covers only two sessions of Parliament and eighteen months of time. When one reflects that he was a committee clerk for at least twenty-four years, and that three other clerks, his colleagues, were engaged on the same service, presumably filling some sixty such minute books between them over the period, regret that more of them were not preserved is attended with wonder that even this one has survived.

It is a folio volume measuring 210 × 330 mm. in a contemporary binding of vellum on boards. On the spine is written 'Dec. 1697 anno 9° Will. 3^{tij} Regis'. The silk ties have been broken off. It is obviously an example of the 'one committee book' included in the list of stores issued sessionally to the Clerks without Doors as recorded in an unpublished manuscript [1] in the House of Lords Record Office. On the first leaf (fo. i) is written in a large formal round hand: 'At the Sessions begun ye 3^{d} day of Dec. 1697 Anno 9° Gulielmi 3^{tij}', and in the right-hand top corner is the signature 'J. Courthop(e)', the final 'e' having been worn away. The other contents of this folio were plainly added by a later owner. The folios are only occasionally numbered in the right-hand corner of the *recto*, the only visible numbers being 1, 5, 10, 20, 30, 40, 50, 60, 70 and 71. Only 71 folios have been effectively used, and there are several blanks, even of more than one folio, in the series 1–71: the last twenty folios, except for a very short entry on the last but two, are blank, and on the inside of the back cover are two calculations of fees. For purposes of reference I have given every folio its correct numbering.

As will be seen, James Courthope made his entries in a more or less chronological sequence, but they are by no means consecutive. His practice was sometimes to enter the first meeting of a committee at the top of a page and to add later meetings below, and sometimes to continue the page with minutes of another committee of about the same date, often without specifying what committee it was. In cases of committees which sat for some time one finds the continuation of the minutes separated from those on the first page of entry by a number of folios containing minutes of other committees, with no references backwards or forwards. The dates are not always accurately given, and at times no date at all is entered. Courthope seems to have been indifferent whether he began a new committee on a *recto* or a *verso*, but where he had left a *verso* blank, he often filled it in with the

[1] This consists of the report and appendices of the select committee of the Commons on Fees of 1732, copied out by some clerk in the Lords in a small notebook—another lucky find filling a deplorable lacuna in the Commons Journal, for calling my attention to which I am much indebted to Mr. M. Bond, the Records Officer of the House of Lords.

minutes of a committee of much later date than that of the entry upon the next *recto*. On the other hand, whereas fo. 15v. ends with proceedings of 19 April, the next entry on fo. 19r. (with nothing but blanks in between) bears the date 8 February (an error for March) of the same year.

The manuscript is, on the whole, remarkably good and clear and written mostly in a clerkly round hand which is the same throughout, except for three intrusions by another hand on fos. 10v., 13v. and 57v. Courthope's writing, however, varies considerably in size and regularity. The majority of the entries are so neat, regular, and free from corrections that they must have copied from a rough draft; but in other instances, when he was actually entering proceedings, especially amendments, or taking down heads of evidence, while the committee was sitting, his writing became more hurried, the most extreme contrast in this respect being noticeable on fo. 27v. between the well-written entry for 28 April and the very hasty scribble recording part of Newton's evidence on 30 April (see p. 38, note *a*). It is interesting to note that, in proportion as he was hurried, Courthope slipped more into the secretary hand, which his master, Paul Jodrell, seems invariably to have used.

The pages have been ruled with a line down the left-hand side, leaving a margin of about one inch. This margin has been used for such things as the titles of bills, the name (where entered) of the chairman, the names of counsel or witnesses, and the folio and line of the bill to which a particular amendment was made: but this use is irregular, other items overrun the margins, and any of above headings may appear in the centre of the page. In my transcription of text I have not thought it worth while to adhere absolutely to the distinction between margin and text, except where a series of amendments to a bill is recorded. Likewise, I give no indication of the end of lines or of the ornamental flourish with which a clerk in those days ended a line of his manuscript. The only indication given of the size of the handwriting is that, where the formal words 'Ordered' and 'Resolved' occur in the minutes, always written in a larger hand, I have followed modern practice in printing them in italics.

The order of the entries in the manuscript has been preserved, and the text has been reproduced essentially as it stands. Erasures and other textual particularities have been entered in the italic footnotes, but where any word or words written above the line, the place of insertion being marked by a caret, clearly belong to the text intended, I have not called attention to this. The punctuation and use of capitals have been modernized to some extent, and the brackets [1] enclosing words to be left out or inserted (in amendments made to bills) have been inserted where Courthope often omitted them or placed them wrongly. The apostrophe in the possessive case has been inserted in accordance with modern usage. Vagaries and inconsistencies of spelling have been scrupulously reproduced: so have the abbreviations.

[1] The practice of enclosing such words in brackets and of registering the date of sitting in Latin is still adhered to in the House of Lords: the Commons have long since substituted inverted commas and dates in English.

II

So much for the visible features of this manuscript, of which a transcription cannot reproduce the variety. As for its author, his features have not been preserved, but his parentage, given one probable assumption, is not obscure. The assumption is that the James Courthope whose name disappears in 1720 from the Treasury records of payments to clerks to the House of Commons was identical with the James Courthope the administration of whose goods was granted in London to his widow Anne on 31 January 1721.[1] There is no direct evidence to prove this identity, but the common year of death, 1720, furnishes a strong presumption in its favour. If it is correct, then James Courthope was the son of George Courthope of the Middle Temple and of Moseham in Wadhurst, Sussex, 1613–91, by his wife Anne Bryan; and he himself was sometime of Wharton Court, near Chancery Lane, and afterwards of St. Dunstan's in the West—a parish just off Fleet Street. He was one of the new Company of East India Merchants incorporated by charter in 1698, and in 1714 his name appears as one of the clerks in the Transfer Office of the Lottery of 1710.[2] More than one of the Commons clerks, including Paul Jodrell, the Clerk of the House, lived in the neighbourhood of Chancery Lane at that period; and Courthope's taking the opportunity to join a new trading company, which was much canvassed in Parliament, and to get an extra clerkly job when it offered would have been thoroughly in keeping with the incumbency of an under-clerkship in the House. It is only a little strange that the genealogist who gathered the above facts did not also gather that for at least twenty-four years James Courthope held an identifiable position in the House of Commons.

Be that as it may, there is no uncertainty whatsoever as to the parliamentary identity of the James Courthope who wrote the minutes in this committee book. In or about 1711 the four under-clerks without doors submitted a petition to the Lord High Treasurer for further recompense. The original document, bearing the signatures of John Hookes, George Cole, James Courthope and H. [Hicks] Burrough, has been preserved among the Treasury records.[3] Courthope's signature to the petition is in the same hand as the 'James Courthop(e)' at the top of fo. i of the minute book. The four under-clerks attending the House of Commons make a sudden and unheralded appearance in the Treasury Money Books in the year 1696: but thereafter, for well over a century, their sessional salary, charged as a single sum for the quartet and with no variation after 1701, was paid from the Civil List. In 1696 the Treasury warrant for £110 (i.e. 100 guineas at the then value of 22*s.*) was made out to John Hookes, George Coles (always wrongly spelt by the Treasury), James Courthope and Hicks Burrough, 'four Under-clerks attending the House of Commons in reward and satisfaction for their services and pains in writing, copying

[1] Admin. Acts Book (Pinfold), 1721, fo. 11.

[2] For the above details I am indebted to my friend Mr. Anthony Wagner, C.V.O., Richmond Herald, who informs me that in the Royal College of Arms there is a voluminous genealogy of the Courthope family, compiled by a former Herald of that name, in which further details of James Courthope's descent and connections are to be found.

[3] P.R.O., Treasury In Letters, T. 1/160, fo. 103.

and ingrossing several bills, writings & other papers for his Majesty's service '.[1] These words, repeated in the following year, became the stereotyped formula for this payment, even when, at a much later date, the four under-clerks without doors were generally known to be the principal clerks of committees and, as such, holders of sinecures on which deserving senior clerks were retired. They then took two-thirds of the committee fees on private bills, while the work was done by deputies and assistant deputies, one of each to a principal clerk's ' desk ', for one-third of the fees, committees appointed by the House being allotted in strict rotation, as entered in the Votes, to the four ' desks '. The system was abolished in 1833 pursuant to the report of the Select Committee on House of Commons Offices (H.C. (1833) 648) in which its working at that date was fully described.[2] In this connection, it is interesting to note that, on a rough computation from the Journal, Courthope's minute book shows that he was allotted about one-quarter of the total number of committees appointed in the two sessions which it covers, though the allotment was not regularly every fourth committee appointed ; and, in the second session, he had rather less than his share of private bill committees.

However, although the development of the four under-clerks without doors into the principal committee clerks was clear enough, and the Treasury books reveal that they received an official salary from 1696 onwards, the Treasury formula to describe the services for which they were paid left it to be inferred that they were originally copying and ingrossing clerks, not committee clerks. The important fact established by Courthope's minute book is that the Treasury formula was always a travesty of the true position, since the duty of John Hookes and his three colleagues, from the first, was to attend committees. Moreover, the appointment of regular clerks for this purpose must have been, in 1696, a fairly recent innovation. In Elizabethan days, when the committee system first began in the House of Commons, there was no staff to attend committees. Both then and in the Stuart Parliaments such under-clerks as existed were mainly occupied in copying and ingrossing. This is even true of the Restoration Parliaments, when William Goldesbrough and his son were successively Clerks of the House of Commons.[3]

There is the further consideration that, until Parliament succeeded in meeting every year, as it did after the Revolution, there could be little inducement for a clerkly person to give up any other more certain occupation in order to attend the House of Commons at unpredictable intervals. Moreover, although in earlier times casual scribes or lower Chancery clerks may have been called in occasionally to attend committees, they could only have been paid, on public matters, by contributions from the members : and, as regards private bills, though the Clerk's chief ' man ' sometimes received a gratuity in Elizabethan times from wealthy promoters of private business in the Commons, there is no mention of any fees payable to clerks attending committees on private bills in the Tables of Fees of 1649 and 1653.[4]

[1] P.R.O., Treasury Money Books, T. 53/13, fo. 141 for 1696 ; *ibid.*, fo. 270 for 1697.

[2] See O. C. Williams, *The Officials of the House of Commons* (1909, J. B. Nichols), in part ii of which monograph the evidence taken before that committee is summarized. This monograph will be replaced by my complete work on the Clerks of the House of Commons to be published (I hope in 1954) by the Clarendon Press.

[3] I cannot burden this introduction with the evidence for these statements : but see the petition of William Brerewood in *Cal. S.P. Dom., Charles II, 1678*, p. 601.

[4] 6 C.J. 287 ; 7 C.J. 291–2.

Such fees were first included in the Table of Fees between 1690 and 1700.[1] From these various indications, and from the fact that there is no trace before 1696 of any quartet of regular under-clerks, I conclude that the institution of regular committee clerks was due to Paul Jodrell, Clerk of the House from 1693 to 1726, who made other reforms in his still exiguous department.[2] He must have seen to it that fees were sanctioned for their attendance on private bill committees, and also have been instrumental in securing for them from the Treasury a sessional salary for their attendance on committees appointed to consider public matters or bills. No fees were chargeable in respect of these latter committees, and Courthope's minute book shows that they took a good deal of his time.

Until the publication of the *Court and City Register* began to give the names of the chief officers of the two Houses (my earliest reference being 1743), the Treasury books are the only authority for the names of the four under-clerks without doors. The quartet Hookes, Cole, Courthope and Burrough continued unchanged till 1718 when Hookes departed, followed by Cole and Courthope two years later. I have little doubt that they were the first four under-clerks without doors to be appointed, and that their chief function from the first was to attend committees. An additional indication that their appointment was a new departure is the wording of petitions submitted by the clerks in 1698 and 1701 which suggests that they had been disappointed in their expectations, whereas, if they had had predecessors, they would have known what these expectations were. Thus, in 1698, Hookes and his three colleagues complained that:

> They had faithfully discharged their duties, but their incomes were barely sufficient to support them during the sessions, and in the intervals they had to live on their private fortunes; they pray for a grant of some employment which would support them.[3]

In 1701 it was represented in a petition to the House [4] that the four clerks had 'totally for many years quitted their employments to apply themselves to their attendance upon the House', that they had no other consideration for public business but what the king was pleased to bestow on them, and that the profits on private business had not afforded them £30 apiece. This latter petition was effective in securing an increase in the Treasury payment from £110 to £200 for the four under-clerks without doors. James Courthope, therefore, in 1698 was receiving a salary of 25 guineas from the Treasury and about £30 in fees for attendance on private bill committees: and, by the end of his time, his salary was £50 and his

[1] The Table of Fees reported by a committee on the subject in 1700 (13 C.J. 356–7) contains a list of the fees to be taken by clerks attending committees on private bills. The Table of 1690 was lost, but that of 1695, though not entered in the Journal, was extant at least as late as 1731, when another committee reported a new Table of Fees. I have evidence that the table of 1695 differed little from that of 1700. Two bills of costs from solicitors for the passing of private acts in 1695 and 1698, of which I have copies, show that the committee clerks were then receiving the same fees as those established in 1700.

[2] E.g. he appointed and maintained in his own house at his own expense a clerk to keep the papers in order, and to assist members who wished to consult them at any time (see the Clerks' petition of 1713, P.R.O., T. 1/60, fos. 97–102).

[3] *Cal. T.P., 1697–1701/2*, p. 190.

[4] 13 C.J. 640.

fees may have amounted to about £90,[1] besides any extra gratuities that he may have earned from promoters of private bills for special assistance in their business.[2]

III

I now turn to the contents of this minute book, and begin by giving a complete list of the committees the minutes of whose proceedings, complete or incomplete, are entered therein. The figures in brackets show the folio or folios on which the proceedings of each committee appear: the necessary references to the Journal will, in every case, be found in the notes.

Session 3 December 1697–5 July 1698

Matters of Public Interest

To examine the states, estimates and accounts presented to the House, relating to deficiencies of revenue and arrears of pay (1r. and v., 92v.).

Oldershaw's petition (arrears of pay to Irish regiments) and other similar petitions (5v., 6r.).

Sufferers by the Londonderry siege (petition of Londonderry) (8r., 10r. and v., 42v.).

Challoner's petition (unjust imprisonment) (19r.).

Claims on Lottery Tickets, etc. (petition of persons who held lottery tickets for payment, and petition of persons who had advanced money on the credit of certain rates on marriages, births and burials (20v.–22r., 25r. and v., 26v., 27r.).

Servants of Charles II (petition for payment) (24r. and v.).

Hammered Money (petition of Perrott and others complaining of non-payment for hammered money by the mint at York) (27v., 28r., 29r. and v., 34r. and v., 36v., 37r.).

Clifford's petition (29r.).

Privilege: Unconstitutional Pamphlet (complaint of passages in an Irish pamphlet denying the authority of the English Parliament) (39r., 42r., 43r.).

Victualling Office Arrears (petition by various tradesmen of the Victualling Office for payment of wages due) (39v., 40r.).

Procedural

Suppressing Profaneness, etc., Bill. To draw up reasons for disagreeing with Lords amendment (36r.).

[1] In a petition from all the clerks presented in 1711 (T.1/160, fos. 99–101), it was represented that the expectation of fees for private bill committees amounted to £90 for each of the 4 clerks until the passing of the General Naturalization Act of 1709 caused them the loss of £50 annually owing to the cessation of private naturalization bills. They finally received an extra year's salary in compensation, and the Naturalization Act was repealed in 1712 (see Treasury Order Book, viii. 362).

[2] Certain bills of costs put in to the Court of Aldermen of the City of London by the City Remembrancer in 1709 and 1711 show payments to Courthope for services in connection with the City's parliamentary business, which were not committee fees (MSS. in Corporation of London Record Office).

Public Bills

Undue Marriages of Infants (*Lords*) (2v.).
Preventing Throwing Squibs, etc. (3r.).
Assize of Bread (4r., 5v., 11 v., 12r.).
Militia (to prepare and bring in bill) (4v., 5r.).
Salt to be sold by weight (5v.).
Malt (15r.).
Exporting Wool and Fullers' Earth (15v., 32r. and v.).
Improving Woollen Manufactures (19v.).
Better Payment of Lottery Tickets (30r.).
Exporting Watches, Swordhilts, etc. (36r.).

Private Bills

Knott's Estate (2v.).
Lascells' Estate (*Lords*) (4r.).
Fitzharris' Estate (petition for leave) (6v., 7r.).
Aire and Calder Navigation (7r. and v.).
Crediton Workhouses (8r.–9v.).
Newcastle-upon-Tyne Waterworks (12v.).
Houghton's Estate (13r.).
Turner's Estate (13v.–14v.).
Hall's Estate (*Lords*) (15r.).
Whitbourne Rectory (*Lords*) (15v.).
Hawkes' Estate (*Lords*) (19v.).
Hare's Estate (*Lords*) (23v.).
Jenkin's Estate (23v., 31v.).
Kingston-upon-Hull Workhouse (30v.).
Mascall's Debts (30v.).
Churchill's Estate (*Lords*) (31v.).
Rogers' Estate (*Lords*) (40v.).
Trafford's Estate (41v.).

Session 6 December 1698–4 May 1699

Matters of Public Interest

Exporting Wool (petitions from Taunton and other centres of the clothing industry) (46v., 51r.–53r., 57v.–58v., 60r.).
Election Fees, etc., to Clerk of the Crown (Chute's petition) (49v., 50r.).
Militia, to bring in bill (54r.).
Hereditary Excise Patentees (petition) (66r. and v.).
Forestallers of Corn (Barton's petition) (67v., 68r.).

Procedural

To draw up address in answer to King's Speech (53v.).
Supply Bill, Duty on Paper: to draw up reasons for disagreeing with Lords amendment (71r.).

Public Bills

Elections, Preventing Irregularities (50v., 59v.).
Writs of Error (60v.).
Augmenting Vicarages (60v.).
Newfoundland Trade (63v., 64r. and v., 67r., 68v., 69v.).

Private Bills

Yarmouth Harbour (46r. and v.).
Tone Navigation (47v.–49v.).
Price's Estate (54v.).
Aire and Calder Navigation (55r.–57r.).
Darcy's Estate (59r.).
Trent Navigation (61r. and v.).
Methwold's Estate (62v.).
Aldworth's Estate (62v.).
Hough's Estate (63r.).
Lascells' Estate (*Lords*) (63v.).
Wake's Estate (*Lords*) (65r.).
Byde's Estate (*Lords*) (65v.).
Westlyd's Estate (*Lords*) (69r.).

IV

Finally, without wishing to distend this introduction by the discussion of purely technical points, I am bound to notice the light thrown by this manuscript upon the committee procedure of the House at the end of the seventeenth century. It would, of course, be idle to compare Courthope's minutes with those kept by a clerk of today, for the form and content of minutes of proceedings has now for a long time been settled, both for select and for private bill committees, and certain standing orders lay down the matters which must be reported to the House. Moreover, the introduction of the shorthand note of evidence and the printing of evidence and other matter for the use of the committee, while relieving the committee clerk of those reporter's duties which Courthope and his colleagues obviously undertook, have imposed on him other duties which were unknown to these earlier predecessors. It so happens that none of the evidence noted by Courthope, e.g. from the cloth-merchants as to the smuggling of wool out of the country, was reported to the House and entered in the Journal; but the twelfth volume of the Journals contains many instances where similar evidence was so reported and entered at length.[1] It is difficult to believe that the committee could have relied upon the clerk alone to produce such précis of evidence: it is more probable that the more assiduous members of the committee also kept notes, and that the final document presented to the House was really the work of the chairman. This probability is increased

[1] E.g. from the committee on Ledginghams's Ships Pumps (12 C.J. 257–8), from that on Woollen Manufactures (*ibid.*, 275–6), and the very long report (*ibid.*, 210–34) on Foreign Lustrings and Clandestine Trade.

by the elaborate account, written out by a shorthand clerk specially employed, of the inquiry by the Select Committee upon the State of the Gaols in 1730 into the charges against Sir Robert Eyre, Lord Chief Justice of the Court of Common Pleas. This account,[1] which has never been edited, gives a very striking illustration of the manner in which statements from witnesses were taken and recorded at that time, and of the part played in such matters by the chairman and leading members of the committee.

Turning to other points, and remembering that Courthope's minutes were not meant for publication, it is none the less curious that he so frequently omits the name of the chairman, and that only in two instances [2] does he note that the chairman was chosen. No record is kept of the attendance of members, nor is there any mention of questions being formally put or of any division in the committee. As regards the report, Courthope is most casual, often omitting any record of its being formally presented and agreed to. This is particularly noticeable in the first session, when the committee's report is only mentioned in the minutes of committees on public matters in two out of a possible eleven cases. Where bills, both public and private, are concerned, the order to report the bill is omitted in about half the possible cases. Again, one often finds Courthope entering the adjournment of a committee to a certain day and then omitting any entry of a meeting on that day: nor is it unusual to find that what must have been the final meeting of a committee is not entered at all. It is also interesting to observe that the practice of disregarding the order of the House for the committee to meet at five o'clock on the afternoon of the day of appointment, which was rather sadly noticed by the author of *The Liverpool Tractate*,[3] already prevailed in Courthope's day, for it is only in a minority of instances that in his minutes the day of a committee's first meeting coincides with the date of the order of the House.

As regards committees on private bills, it is obvious that in those days there were no parliamentary agents for a bill or for an opposing petitioner. The member who brought in the bill was usually, though not invariably, the chairman of the committee, and counsel appeared without an agent to brief them. The chairman of the committee usually reported the bill, but in one or two instances recorded by Courthope [4] the reporter was not the chairman. Only in two instances is any reference made to consideration of the preamble of the bill, and in neither is it stated that the allegations of the preamble were proved; [5] in one case it was agreed

[1] MS. Stowe 373 in the British Museum.

[2] In the second session, the committees on the Exportation of Wool and on the Newfoundland Trade Bill.

[3] The anonymous treatise on procedure (*c.* 1760), which is among the Liverpool papers in the British Museum (Add. MS. 38456), and has been edited under the title *The Liverpool Tractate* (Columbia University Press, 1937) by Catherine Strateman, of which edition see p. 25. The practice then was, as regards a bill or petition, that the member in charge came out and told the clerk the day on which the committee was to meet, with which notice, wrote the author of the treatise, the clerk was very well satisfied, provided that he might charge the adjournment or attendance 'without the trouble of crowding against the House up into the Speaker's Chamber'.

[4] Aire and Calder Navigation Bill (2nd session) and Newcastle Waterworks Bill.

[5] After a standing order first made in 1699 examination of the allegations was the first business of a committee on a private bill.

to stand part of the bill, and in the other it was simply agreed to.[1] The hearing of opposing petitioners by counsel was, generally, consequent upon the reference to the committee by the House of a petition praying to be heard, but there are one or two curious exceptions to this. In the proceedings on Turner's Estate Bill three petitions were so referred and counsel were heard on them, but three other opponents appear to have also been heard though no petition in their names is recorded. Again, in the committee on the Newcastle Waterworks Bill (see p. 22, n. 2) counsel for a Lady Gerrard obtained a saving clause, though she had not petitioned. On the other hand, in the proceedings on Knott's Estate Bill the petition of George Manwaring, which had been referred to the committee, is not alluded to in the minutes. Nevertheless, it is clear from this minute book that, although practice was still very much in the making, proceedings in committee on private bills were already conducted with a considerable degree of formality and precision.[2]

[1] Tone Navigation Bill (fo. 47v.) and Methwold's Estate Bill (fo. 62v.).

[2] I refer any interested reader who wishes to compare Courthope's minutes of private bill committees with the stage of formality which such proceedings had reached by 1760 to my *Historical Development of Private Bill Procedure &c. in the House of Commons*, i. 27–40.

[THE MINUTE BOOK OF JAMES COURTHOPE]

[fo. ir.]

J. Courthop(e) [a]
I suppose to be the Clerk
attending the Comees [b]

At the Sessions begun ye 3d day of Dec. 1697
Anno 9o Gulielmi 3tij [c]
The .... Minute Book
of the Committees of the
House of Commons for
the years 1697
1698 & 1699.
for some partlar [1]
Committees.[d]

[fo. iv. and fos. iir. and iiv. blank.]

[fo. 1r.]

At the Commee appointed to examine the States Estimates and Accots wch have been presented to the House and to report the Matter of Fact to the House.[2]

Mr Norris in the Chair.

Mercurij 15o die Dec. 1697.

[a] *In the clerk's own hand, the* 'e' *erased by wear. The two earliest folios are marked in pencil* 'i' *and* 'ii'. *Arabic folio numberings then begin.*

[b] *In small later hand.*

[c] *In large formal script.*

[d] *Also in small later hand. There is an ink erasure one inch long between* 'The' *and* 'Minute'.

(Since all references to the Commons Journal will be to vol. xii, the pages of the Journal referred to will be simply given in brackets.)

[1] 'particular' = 'select', i.e. a committee of limited membership as opposed to a committee of the whole House.

[2] Select Committee on Estimates and Accounts. This was appointed on 14 December (9) to consider accounts of the deficiencies in the previous year's revenue which had been presented the previous day (5, 6). The report of the select committee was read on 6 January, and set out in full in the Journal (30–2). Comparison of Courthope's minutes with the report shows that, apart from slight differences of drafting and one incorrect figure in the minutes, these are identical with the report as given in the Journal down to the end of the first account in the middle of p. 31 of the Journal. The rest of the committee's report, which was of some length, and dealt, first, with the causes of the deficiencies in the aids, including the evidence of two witnesses, and then with the arrears of pay and subsistence for the army, has no counterpart in these minutes, except for two lines at the end of the book (fo. 92v.) giving the total of arrears of pay from 1 April 1692 to 30 Sept. 1697, and of arrears of subsistence for the same time. The first of these figures is the same as that given in the Journal (31), though the period there stated is up to December 1697: the second figure has no exact counterpart in the Journal. It seems probable that after 16 December another clerk attended the committee.

The Comm^ee^ mett.

Ordered, That the Acco^ts^ be read according as they were delivered into the House, wch were read accordingly.

Adj^d^ till tomorrow morning 8 a clock.

(*A line here drawn across the page.*)

Jovis 16° die Dec. 1697.

The Comm^ee^ met and proceeded upon the Estimate of the deficiencyes of the last yeare's Aydes; and it does appear,

	£
That the 3^s^ in ye pound for the year 1697 was made a security for	1500000
That by a computacōn made the interest of the same, part at 6 and part at 8£ ℘ cent., will amo^t^ to	120000
Soe that the principall and interest to be made good out of the Ayd of 3^s^ in ye pound amo^ts^ to	1620000

(*A line here drawn across the page.*)

That by Mr Lounds [1] computacōn the Land Tax for 1697 will be near the same, in proporcōn, wth the 4^s^ Ayd for the year 1696 wch produced the sum̄e of 1706869. 10. 1, soe that computeing ¾^ths^ of that sum̄e to be the produce of the 3^s^ in the pound for the year 1697 but deducts 80000£ for soe much thereof as was paid in hammered money [2] but the Comm^ee^ thought that 67000£ was a nearer computation:

And then the neat produce of the 3^s^ in the pound will be about . 1213000

(*A line here drawn across the page.*)

Soe that by this computacōn there is a deficiency towards the dischargeing the principall and int. lent upon the 3^s^ in the pound amounting to the sum̄e of 407000

(*Here a double line drawn across the page at bottom of the folio.*)

[fo. 1v.]

The next was the Capitation Tax wch was made a security to discharge Bills of Creddit amounting in principall money to 1,500,000

That the interest at the rate of 5^d^ a day for every 100£ is by Act of Parl^t^ to attend the said Bills when they are not in ye Excheq, or in the hands of publick Receivers or Collecto^rs^; wch rate in the whole, from the time of makeing out those Bills till the time of cancelling the same, is computed at 100,000

[1] i.e. William Lowndes, M.P., Secretary to the Treasury.

[2] In the committee's report this passage reads as follows: 'But deducting 8d per ounce for so much as was paid in hammered money before the 1st of June 97, and 2d per ounce for what was paid in hammered money after that day: which deductions were computed at 80,000£; but the Committee thought that 67,000£ was sufficient for that allowance.'

Soe that the principall and interest to be made good out of the Capitac̄on Tax will amo^{t} to 1,600,000

The said Capitac̄on Tax will by computac̄on make abo^{t} 700,000$^{£}$ out of wch deducting 40,000$^{£}$ for the paym^{ts} in hammered money, and then the neat produce towards dischargeing the said Bills of Credit is estimated at 660,000

So by this computac̄on there will be a deficiency in the said Capitac̄on Tax amounting to the sume of 940,000

(*Here a double line ruled across the page.*)

The next was the Ayd of 1^{s} in the pound wch was given for . . 500,000

That the said Ayd of 1^{s} in y^{e} pound togeather with the new subsidy of Tunnage and Poundage were made a security to discharge Bills of Credit amounting to 1,200,000$^{£}$ principall money wth interest at the rate of 5^{d} a day for every 100$^{£}$, and the interest of so many of the said Bills as are to be cancelled on the said Ayd of 1^{s} in the pound singly is estimated at 33,000

So that the principall & interest to be made good out of the Ayd of 1^{s} in the pound will amo^{t} to 533,000

The neat produce of the 1^{s} in the pound, wch is estimated in proporc̄on with the 3^{s} in the pound, amo^{ts} to 404,000

And by this computation there will be a deficiency to be provided for towards dischargeing soe many of the said Bills of Creditt as are to be cancelled on the said Ayd of 1^{s} in the pound with the interest thereof amounting to the sum̄e of . . . . 90,000[1]

(*Here a single line ruled across the page.*)

By all wch computac̄ons ye totall of all ye princip^{ll} & int. moneys appointed by Parlt to be pd out of ye Fonds given ye last Sessions except ye subsidy of Tonnage & Poundage and Mault Duty wch Mr Lownds has not estimated amo^{ts} to ye sum̄e 3,753,000

(*Here a single line ruled across the page.*)

And ye sum̄e totall of all ye moneys wch will arise out of ye Ayd of 3^{s} in ye pound, ye Capitac̄on, and ye 1^{s} in ye pound, towards ye princip^{ll} & interest of ye sd loanes will amo^{t} to abo^{t} 2,277,000

(*Here a single line ruled across the page.*)

Soe y^{t} ye whole deficiency upon ye Ayd of 3^{s} in ye pound, the Capitac̄on & ye 1^{s} in ye pound given ye last Session is by this estimac̄on reckoned 1,476,000

(*Here a single line ruled across the page.*)

[fo. 2r. blank.]

[1] An error for 129,000£, correctly given in the Journal.

[fo. 2v.]

S[r] Hen. Colt in the Chair

Marriage Bill

Veneris [a] 7[o] die Jan. 1697.

At y[e] Comm[ee] to whom the ingrossed Bill from the Lords intituled An Act to prevent undue Marriages of Infants and for better secureing the Guardianship of them is committed.[1]

The Comm[ee] met and proceeded upon the Bill w[ch] was read once over and then paragraph by paragraph and went through y[e] same & made this amendment, viz.

Pr.[2] 1 L. ult. Leave out (six) and insert (twelve).

Ordered, That the Bill be reported wth this amendm[t] the first opportunity.

Knott's Bill.[b] Jovis 6[o] die Jan. 1697.

At y[e] Comm[ee] to whome the Bill to enable y[e] Trustees of W[m] Knott Gent. and his wife to sell a Lease of Houses in Breadstreet London for paym[t] of Debts and to settle another Estate of better value in lieu thereof is committed.[3]

The Comm[ee] mett and adj[d] to Saturday morning 9 a clock.

Sabti 8[o] die Jan. 1697.

Sir Jn[o] Bolls in y[e] Chair.

Knott's Bill.

The Comm[ee] mett and the Bill was read once over, and then the Preamble was again read and the Deeds therein recited were examined, and these parties following gave their Consents to the passing of the said Bill, viz:[c]

M[rs] Knott, widow.
M[rs] Eliz. Knott.
M[r] W[m] Knott
M[r] Sam[ll] Sterling.
M[r] Chase
M[rs] Wyburd &
M[rs] Jane Knott

And then the Comm[ee] adjourned till Monday morning 9 a clock.

Martis 11[o] Jan. 1697.[d]

[a] *Written over* Mercurij *erased.*
[b] At y[e] *imperfectly erased precede this title in margin.*
[c] *Followed by* and then the paragraph was agreed to be made part of y[e] Bill *erased.*
[d] *The minutes for this date are written in a different hand.*

---

[1] The Undue Marriages of Infants Bill was brought from the Lords and committed to a committee of 41 members on 30 December (19), and the committee was ordered to meet that afternoon in the Speaker's Chamber. The Bill was reported with one amendment on 7 April 1698 (33).

[2] *Sci.* press. The bill, having originated in the Lords, was ingrossed on parchment, each folio of which was called a press. The fees for ingrossment were so much per press.

[3] Knott's Estate Bill was presented on 20 December (13) and committed on 30 December (18) to a committee of 31 nominated members and the members for the counties of Yorks and Notts, to meet at 4 in the Speaker's Chamber. On 3 January (21) the petition of George Manwaring, a creditor, that he might not be prejudiced, was presented to the House and referred to the committee. It is curious that no allusion to this petition is made in the minutes or in the report of the bill which was made on 12 January (41). The amendments made were not recorded in the Journal.

The Comm^ee mett and proceeded upon ye Bill.

Fol. 5, L. 11 & 12. Fill ye 1st bla.[1] with (first), ye 2^d bla. with (March), & 3^d bla. w^th (ninety seaven).

5 & 6. Leave out (in) and insert (w^th), and before (convenient) insert (all), and leave out (time) and insert (speed) & leave out (with ye consent of the said Wm Knott).

Ordered, to report the same the first opportunity.

[fo. 3r.]
Bill ag^t Squibbs & Fireworks.
Sr H. Colt in ye Chair.

Lune 10° die Jan. 1697.

At ye Comm^ee to whome the Bill to prevent the Throwing and Fireing of Squibs Serpents and other Fireworks is committed.[2]

The Comm^ee mett and made these amendm^ts foll., viz.

Fol. 1st. L. 3. After (lost) add (their lives others).
Fol. 1. L. 8–9. Fill ye 1st blank w^th (25th), ye 2^d bla. w^th (March 1698), and leave out (now next comeing).
10. After (age) add (sex).
Fol. 2. L. 3. After (street) add (house, shopp, river).
5. Fill the blank w^th (a cōmon nusance).
6. After (age) add (sex).
7. Fill the first blank w^th (25th), ye 2^d bla. w^th (March).
8. Leave out (now next comeing) and after ye 2^d (shall) add (give).
15. Fill the bla. w^th (two).
Fol. 3. L. 1. Fill the bla. w^th (5^£).
2. Fill ye 1st bla. w^th (25th), ye 2^d bla. w^th (March), and leave out (now next comeing).
4. After (houses) add (shopps).
6. After (passage) add (or any other house or place whatsoever).
8. Fill the blank w^th (20^s).
12. Fill the blank w^th (halfe).
14. The same amendm^t.

[1] Private bills were not at this time printed before the committee stage, but were written in manuscript on folios of paper. Hence the place of amendments was determined by the number of the folio and the number of the line on that folio. The abbreviation 'bla.' means 'blank', i.e. a blank space in the manuscript bill (and at a later date in the printed bill) to be filled in during the committee stage. Blanks were usually left for the final insertion of proper names, dates, sums of money and so forth. In the nineteenth century words written in italics, which had formally to be moved for insertion, were substituted for blanks, both in public and in private bills.

[2] The Preventing Throwing Squibs &c. Bill was presented on 16 December (12) and after a division was committed on 22 December (15) to a committee of 44 nominated members with the members for London, Westminster and Southwark, to meet at 4 in the Speaker's Chamber. Sir H. Colt reported it with several amendments on 11 January (41), but the amendments were not recorded in the Journal.

17. After (age) add (sex).
Fol. 4. L. 1. Fill ye 1st bla. wth (25th),[a] ye 2d bla. wth (March), & leave out (now next comeing).
4. After (street) add (house, shopp, river) and after (passage) add (or any other place whatsoever).
6. Fill the bla. wth (20s).
Fol. 5. L. 1. Fill ye blank wth (one month).
Fol. 6. L. 11. Fill ye bla. wth (kebble).[b]
Ordered, to report the first opportunity.

[fol. 3v.]

Bread. Lune 10o die Jan. 1697.

At ye Commee to whome the Bill to Regulate and Ascertain the Assize of Bread is committed.[1]
The Commee met and adjd till tomorrow morning.

Martis 11o die Jan. 1697.

Bread. The Commee met and adjd till Fryday morning next.

Veneris 14o die Jan. 1697.

Bread. The Commee mett and adjd til tomorrow morning.

Sabti 15o die Jan. 1697.

Bread. The Commee met and adjd till Tuesday[c] morning next.

Martis 18o die Jan. 1697.

Bread. The Commee met and adjd till tomorrow morning.

Mercurij 19o die Jan. 1697.

Bread. The Commee met and proceeded upon ye Bill and made ye amendmts foll., viz.

[a] *Written above* March *erased.*
[b] *An illegible word erased precedes this word.*
[c] *Preceded by* tomorro *erased.*

[1] The Assize of Bread Bill was presented on 4 January (22) and committed on 10 January (38) to a committee of 36 nominated members with the members for London, Westminster, Surrey and Kent, ' all that come are to have voices ', which meant that the size of the committee was unlimited. This may account for the frequent adjournments of the committee here recorded. The committee first met on the day it was ordered to meet (10 January), but its first effective meeting was on 19 January when several amendments were made. Thereafter, on fos. 4r. and 5v. its meetings only to adjourn are intercalated with meetings of other committees, up to 2 February. There is no further entry referring to this committee until fo. 11v. with the dates 9 (or 10) March and 12 April. The committee minutes do not record the name of the chairman. It was Mr. Perry who, on 30 April (248), reported the bill with several amendments which, after several adjournments, were finally considered on 10 May (265). The amendments made are not recorded in the Journal.

Fol. 1. L. 19. Fill the first blank with (first), the 2d blank wth (May 1698).
Fol. 2. L. 1. Fill the blank wth (first).
5. Leave out (some) and insert (severall).
7. Fill the blank with (Five pounds).
11. After (fall) insert (sixpence).
16. Fill the blank wth (said first), the 2d blank wth (May).
20. After (that is to say) fill the blank wth these words (Halfpenny white loaves, penny white loaves, twopenny white loaves, halfpenny wheaten loaves, penny wheaten loaves, twopenny wheaten loaves, fourpenny wheaten loaves, sixpenny wheaten loaves, ninepenny wheaten loaves, 12 penny wheaten loaves, 18 penny wheaten loaves & two shilling wheaten loaves, penny household [a] loaves, 2 penny household loaves, 4 penny household loaves, 6 penny household loaves, 9 penny household loaves, 12 penny household loaves, 18 penny household loaves & two shilling household loaves made of wheate and loaves made of maslin according to ye weights and proporcons of wheaten bread and loaves made of rye according to ye weights and proporcons of household bread, and peck loaves & half peck loaves according to the table hereafter menconed).

And then the Commee adjd till Fryday morning next.

Veneris 21o die Jan. 1697.

Bread. The Commee mett and adjourned till tomorrow morning.

Fol. 3. L. 5. Fill the blank wth ye Table marked (A).[1]

[fo. 4r.]
At ye Comee to whome ye Bill intitul An Act to enable Rebecca Lassells wido to sell Coppyhold Lands & Houses in Ealeing in ye County of Middx.[2]

Veneris 21o die Jan. 1697.

Lassells. The Commee mett and adjd till Monday morning next.

Bread.[3] Sabti 22o die Jan. 1697.

The Commee met and adjd till Tuesday morning 8 a clock.

Lune 24o die Jan. 1697.

[a] *Written above* wheaten *erased*.

---

[1] The amendment recorded in the last line of this folio bears no certain date. It may belong to the proceedings of 19 January above. The committee clearly did no business on the 21st or 22nd (fo. 4r.).

[2] Lascells' Estate Bill came down from the Lords on 13 January (43), though Courthope did not enter that it was an ingrossed bill. It was committed on the 20th (56) to a committee of 32, to meet at 4 in the Speaker's Chamber. Mr. Whitaker reported it without amendments on the 27th (68).

[3] See fo. 5v. for the continuation of this committee.

Mr Whittaker in ye Chair.

Lassells' Bill. The Commee met [a] and proceeded upon the Bill and Mrs Lassells was present and consented to the same and produced the Admittance & ye Surrendᵉ of ye Copyhold premisses in the Bill menconed as also ye Will of the said Mr Lassells.

And the Commee passed the Bill without any amendmts.

[fo. 4v.]

Militia Comee.[1] Sr Richd Onslow in ye Chair. The Comee proceeded to take an Accompt of ye Militia of all ye Counties of England and Wales according to ye Returnes of ye Depty Lewtennts of ye sevll Countyes and is as foll., viz.

Counties	Troops	Comission Horse Officers	Number of Men	Compas	Comission Foot Officers	Number of Men	Regiments
Bedford	2	8	119	5	15	420	1
Berks	3	12	175	10	30	977	
Bucks	3	12	177	10	30	820	
Cambridge	3	12	151	5	15	677	
Chester	2	8	104	7	21	929	
City of Chester							
Cornwall	2	8	112	36	108	3001	4
Cumberld & Westmorld	1	4	70	7	21	537	
Derby	2	8	140	4	12	624	
Devon	3	12	226	41 [b]	13	4870	6
Exeter				8	24	480	1
Plymouth				5	15	467	
Dartmouth				1	3	60	
Dorsett	2	8	118	23	69	1790	2
Durham							
Essex	4	16	250	24	72	3070	3
Gloucester	6	24	243	36	108	2199	4
Bristoll				10	30	727	
Hereford							
Hertford	3	12	183	10	30	1025	1
Huntington	1	4	72	5	15	370	1

[a] *Preceded by* and *erased.*

[b] *An obvious error, should be* 13 compas 41 officers.

[1] The Militia Bill. On 17 December 1697 leave was given to bring in a bill to regulate the Militia and make them more useful. It was referred to a committee of 32 or any three of them to prepare and bring in the bill (12). On 8 January the House agreed to present a humble address for an account of the numbers of the Militia (37), and on 15 January (45, 46) this account was presented by Mr. Bridgman and referred to the committee: the contents of the account are not entered in the Journal. It seems likely that the detailed return of militia strengths by counties which appears on fos. 4v. and 5r. is the account then presented, thus filling an interesting gap in the Journal. There is no further record of the committee's proceedings in this minute book. Sir Richard Onslow presented the bill on 26 February (132).

Counties	Troops	Comission Horse Officers	Number of Men	Comp[as]	Comission Foot Officers	Number of Men	Regiments
Kent	4	16	226	36	108	3540	6
Cinq Ports . . .				20	60	1958	
Lancaster	3	12	150	22	66	1601	3
Leicester	3	12	175	6	18	609	1
Lincoln	4	16	333	15	45	1364	2
City of Lincoln . .				1	3	130	
Midlesex	2	8	131	26	78	3361	3
London				48	144	6770	6
Tower Hamlets . .				16	48	2000	2
Monmouth . . .	1	4	55	7	21	490	
Norfolk	6	24	335	28	84	3038	4
Lyn				2	6	250	
Great Yarmouth . .				4	12	536	
Norwich				6	18	621	
Northampton . . .							
Northumberland . .							
Nottingham . . .	2	8	120	6	18	400	
Oxford	1	6	130	8	24	732	
Rutland	1	4	53	1	3	93	
Salop	2	8	82	8	24	1050	1
Somerset	5	20	248	40	120	3434	5
Southampton . . .	2	8	120	34	102	2454	6
Portsm[o] & Gosper .				6	18	600	
Winchester . . .				1	3	150	
Southton City . .				1	3	200	
Isle of Wight . . .				17	51	1752	2
Stafford	2	8	120	5	15	500	
Suffolk	4	16	208	30	90	2190	4
Surrey	2	8	132	9	27	1209	1
Burr. of Southwark .				6	18	910	1
[fo. 5r.]							
Sussex	2	8	99	19	57	1543	2
Chichester				1	3	120	
Warwick	3	12	162	6	18	559	1
Coventry							
Wilts	16	4[a]	232	66[a]	22		
New Sarum . . .				3	9	128	
Worcester	2	8	120	7	21	786	1
York East Rideing .	2	8	128	8	24	671	
West Rideing .	3	12	213	18	54	1590	3
York City . .				7	21	520	1
North Rideing .	3	12	163	18	54	922	3
South Wales							
Glamorgan . . .	1	4	40	9	27	483	1
Carmarthen . .	1	4	40	6	18	341	1
Cardigan . . .	1	4	60	4	12	142	1

[a] *Two obvious transpositions in this line : should read* 4 troops 16 officers 232 men 22 comp[as] 66 officers.

Counties	Troops	Comission Horse Officers	Number of Men	Comp^as	Comission Foot Officers	Number of Men	Regiments
South Wales							
Pembroke . . .	1	4	36	7	21	456	1
Brecon & Radnor .	1	4	48	7	21	505	1
North Wales							
Mountgomery . .	1	4	56			364	1
Denbigh . . .	1	4	62			500	1
Flint	1	4	25			250	1
Merioneth and Carnarvan } . .	1	4	48			530	1
Anglesey	1	4	26			250	1

[fo. 5v.]
At ye Comm^ee to whom ye Peticõn of Tho. Oldershaw and John Williams of behalf of themselves and ye rest of ye Troopers who served in Coł. Langston's Regiment dureing the warrs of Ireland and since incorporated into ye sev^ll Regim^ts in Flanders is referred.[1]

Lune 24° die Jan. 1697.

Langston's Comm^ee. The Comm^ee met and adj^d till tomorrow morning.

Martis 25° die Jan. 1697.

Langston's Comm^ee. The Comm^ee met and adj^d till tomorrow morning.

Eodem die.

Bread Comm^ee.[2] The Comm^ee met and adj^d till tomorrow morning.

Mercurij 26° die Jan. 1697.

Troopers.[3] The Comm^ee met and adj^d till Fryday morning next.

Jovis 27° die Jan. 1697.

Bread. The Comm^ee mett and adj^d till Saturday morning next.

Veneris 28° die Jan. 1697.

Bread. The Comm^ee met and adjourned till till Tuesday morning.

Eodem die.

[1] This petition, one of several similar petitions from other regiments for arrears of pay, was presented on 17 January (47) and referred to a committee of 38, to meet at 5 in the Speaker's Chamber, and to have power to send for persons, papers and records. The marginal note to the Journal entries relating to these petitions was 'Irish Arrears'. Courthope uses the titles 'Langston's Committee' or 'Troopers'. The only effective meeting which he records is that of 3 February (fo. 6r.) when orders were made for the hearing of this and other petitions referred to the committee on various dates. See below, p. 11, n. 2.

[2] See p. 6, n. 1 above.

[3] See n. 1 above.

Troopers. The Commee met and adjourned till Tuesday morning.

Martis 1o die Feb. 1697/8.

At ye Commee to whome the Bill to oblige all Retailers of Salt to sell by weight is comitted.[1]

Fol. 2. L. 5. After (Retailer) add (Importer).
5, 6. Fill ye first bla. wth (25th), the 2d bla. wth (1698).
12. Fill the bla. wth (5th).
15. Fill the bla. wth (two).

Fol. 3. L. 10. Fill the bla. wth (two).
11. Fill the bla. wth (two).
16. Fill the bla. wth (six).
last. Leave out (off) and insert (for).
Att ye end of the Bill add Clause (A).
Adjd till Thursday next.

Veneris[a] 2o Feb. 1697.

Bread. The Commee met and adjd till Saturday morning next.

Jovis 3o die Feb. 1697.

Salt Bill. The Commee met and went through the Bill and ordered the same should be reported.

[fo. 6r.]

Mr Manly in ye Chair. Jovis 3o die Feb. 1697.

Troopers. The Commee met and proceeded upon the Peticons wch were read.
Ordered, That the Chairman doe from time to time issue out his summons for such persons to attend the said Commee as the Pets shall informe him to be necessary in this matter.
A Peticon of Tho. Oldershaw and John Williams &c. was read.
Ordered, That the said Peticon be taken into Consideration upon Saturday morning next.
Ordered, That Coll. Langston and Mr Roberts his late Agent doe then attend the said Commee.
A Peticon [2] of Archibald Lawrimer and Jacob Smith was read.

[a] *An error for* Mercurij.

[1] The Salt Bill was presented on 25 January by Mr. Foley (62), and committed on 29 January (75) to a committee of 38 to meet at 5 in the Speaker's Chamber. Mr. Foley, who is not mentioned as chairman in Courthope's minutes, reported the bill with several amendments (not recorded in the Journal) on 4 February (84).

[2] The petition of Lawrimer and Smith was presented on 3 January, and (see p. 12) that of the men of Arran's regiment and several other regiments of light horse on 20 January, on which day both were referred to the committee on Oldershaw's petition (21, 54). That of Jedbrough's dragoons was presented and referred to the committee on 27 January (69), and that of Lord Stainbock's regiment was presented and referred on 24 January (59, 60). This is the only effective meeting of this committee recorded in these minutes. On 4 May Mr. Manly, chairman of the committee, made a report relating to Lawrimer's petition (252–3): no report seems to have been made on the other petitions.

Ordered, That the said Peticõn be taken into Consideration upon Monday morning next.
The like Ord[e] for the Peticõn of the Troopers of ye Earl of Arran's Regim[t] [1] to be heard on Tuesday next.
The Ord[e] for ye Peticõn of the disbanded men in ye Lord Stainbock's Regim[t] [1] of Dutch Horse is to be heard on Wednsd. next.
The like Ord[e] for y[e] Peticõn of y[e] Soldiers discharged out of the Lord Jedbrough's Regim[t] [1] of Dragoons to be heard on this day seavenight.
And then the Comm[ee] adjourned till Saturday morning.

Sabati 5[o] Feb. 1697.

Langston. The Comm[ee] met and adj[d] till Monday morning next.

Lune 7[o] die Feb. 1697.

The Comm[ee] met and adj[d] till tomorrow morning.

[fo. 6v.]
S[r] Hen. Dutton Colt in y[e] Chair.
At y[e] Comm[ee] to whome the Peticõn of S[r] Henry Fitzharris Bar[t]. is referred.[2]

Sabti 5[o] die Feb. 1697.

The Comm[ee] met and adj[d] till tomorrow morning.

Lune 7[o] die Feb. 1697.

The Comm[ee] met and the Peticõn read wch sets forth, That the Pet[s] Grandfath[r] S[r] Edw[d] Fitzharris was seized of an estate of 2000£ ꝑ ann. in y[e] Countyes of Cork, Lymerick and Wexford in Ireland, and dureing the Rebellion resided peaceably in his own house. And the late K. Cha. y[e] 2[d] being informed thereof was pleased to make some provision for y[e] Pet[s] Grandfather soe as he and his heires should be incapable of the benefit intended him if any person could within six months time make appear to y[e] L[d] Lewtenn[t] & Counsell in Ireland that he had committed any massacre, murder or other heinous crimes as were then most falsely suggested ag[t] him by one Oliver who was then in possĩon of his estate by the Usurper. And notwithstanding he upon a full heareing before the said L[d] Lewtenn[t] and Counsell was acquitted of those false and scandalous imputacõns as appeares by a Report thereof

[1] See p. 11, n. 2.
[2] The petition of Sir Edward Fitzharris was presented on 28 January (72) and referred to a committee of 41 members to meet at 5 in the Speaker's Chamber: five more members were added to the committee on 3 February (81). Although the gist of the petition was entered in the Journal, it is only in these minutes that it is recorded *in toto*. The final entry on fo. 6v. shows the reason for the granting to this committee of power to send for persons, papers and records (88), and the proceedings of 8 February on the next folio show what order was made after this power had been granted. There is no further entry in this minute book relating to this committee: but the Journal records (*a*) that on 15 March the House resolved that, notwithstanding the order of the committee, persons summoned from Ireland should not be obliged to attend the committee (160), and (*b*) that on 21 April Sir Henry Colt reported the fact that in 1666 Fitzharris had been found innocent of the charges brought against him by Oliver.

dat^{d} 25 May 1666, yet he was not restored to his estate, and the said Oliver who still possesseth the same can neither mortgage, sell or make any settlement of all or any part thereof by reason of the reservacōn in the said Act for the [a] pet^{s} Grandfather and his heires.
That the said Oliver hath often solicited for a treaty wth the pet^{s} Grandfather [b] for y^{e} purchase of his title or to marry the pet^{s} sister.
That y^{e} said late King Cha. y^{e} 2^{d} being sensible of the great hardp̄s and want Sr Edwd was und^{r} in not being restored to his estate was pleased to allow him 150$^{£}$ ꝑ ann. for his maintenance till he should be restored to his estate soe unjustly kept from him.
The ye pet^{s} Father Edwd Fitzharris Esqr. being deceased had issue the pet^{r} and Judith his Sister who was comitted to the care of Sr Steph. Fox by K. Cha. y^{e} 2^{d} to be brought up in the protest^{t} Religion.
That Sr Edwd being a papist and seing his Grandchildren brought up in the protest^{t} Religion would not make any applicacōn to this Governm^{t} to be restored.
And their adversaryes there who are in poss̄ion of ye estate being rich and potent the pet^{r} is advised to apply himselfe to parliam^{t}.

He therefore prays he may have the liberty to bring in a Bill to restore him to his antient and paternall estate whereof he is soe wrongfully devested.
It was moved, That an Ord^{r} might be sent into Ireland to Oliver and such others as claymed right to ye estate to attend the Comm^{ee} to shew cause why a Bill should not be brought in Parliam^{t} to restore the Pet^{r} to his said estate. But ye Comm^{ee} finding they had noe such power by their Ord^{r}, *Ordered,* That the Chairman move the House that the Comm^{ee} may have power to send for persons, papers and records.

And then adj^{d} till tomorrow morning.

[fo. 7r.]

Martis 8° die Feb. 1697.

Fitzharris Comm^{ee}. The Comm^{ee} met and made this Ord^{r}.

Ordered, That Mr Oliver and all such other persons as claym any estate or interest to any part of the estate of the late Sr Edwd. Fitzharris Bar^{t}. deceased lying within the Kingdom of Ireland and now descended to his Grandson S^{r}. Henry Fitzharris Barr^{t}. doe attend the said Comm^{ee} on Tuesday the eighth day of March to shew cause why a Bill should not be brought in parliam^{t} to restore the said S^{r}. Henry Fitzharris to his antient and paternall estate according to the prayer of his peticōn, And that the said Mr Oliver and all other persons concerned doe at the same time produce and lay before the said Comm^{ee} all writeings, deeds and evidences by wch they claym their title to the said estate, and all other writeings relateing to the same.

And then the Comm^{ee} adjourned till Tuesday the 8th day of March next.

[a] *Written above* pet^{r} *erased.* [b] *Preceded by* Father *erased.*

At ye Commee to whome the Bill to make the Rivers Ayre and Calder Navigable at ye Charge of such persons as shall undertake ye same is committed.[1]

Veneris 11o die Feb. 1697.

The Commee met and adjd till tomorrow at 5 a clock in the afternoon.

Martis 15o die Feb. 1697.

The Commee met and adjd till tomorrow at 5 a clock in ye afternoon.

Jovis 17o die Feb. 1697.

Mr Gery in ye Chair.

The Commee met and the Bill was read and ye Peticõn of ye Mayor and Comonalty of the City of York was read.

Ordered, That Notice be given to ye Mayor and Comonalty of ye City of York that ye Comm doe intend to proceed upon ye said Bill on Monday ye 28th of Febr. next instant at wch time they may be heard by themselves or Counsell.

And then the Comm adjd till tomorrow 5 in ye afternoon.

[fo. 7v.] Sabti 19o die Feb. 1697/8.

Rivers Ayre & Calder.

The Commee met and severall Peticõns were read agt the Bill for makeing the Rivers Ayre and Calder navigable, viz.

1. The Peticõn of the Mayor and Comonalty of the City of York.
2. The Peticõn of ye Mayor, Aldermen, Burgesses, Gentł and other Inhabitants of the Town and Burrough of Pontefract.
3. The Peticõn of the Masters of Ships and Seamen belonging to the Antient City of York.
4. The Peticõn of ye Antient Burrough of Burroughbrigg in ye County of York.
5. The Peticõn of the Ship Carpenters of the Town of Cawood in ye County of York.
6. The Peticõn of the Burrough of Alborough in ye County of York.
7. The Peticõn of the Inhabitants of the Towne of Clifton in ye County of York.
8. The Peticõn of ye Inhabitants of ye Town of Wistow in ye County of York.

[1] Aire and Calder Navigation Bill. On the petition of Leeds Corporation to bring in a bill for this purpose, leave was given on 12 January (42), the bill was presented by Lord Fairfax on 1 February (76), and on 7 February it was committed to a committee of 56 members to meet at 5 in the Speaker's Chamber. It was ordered that all petitions should be referred to the committee, and that the committee should have power to receive clauses that the Newcastle and Sunderland coal trade should not be prejudiced. The petitions read on 19 February (fo. 7v.) were presented between 11 and 16 February, some in favour not being entered in the minutes (96, 98, 100–1, 104). The order made by the committee on that day that petitioners should be heard on 7 March was reinforced by an order of the House on 22 February (123) that all petitions were to be presented so that they might be heard on Monday, 7 March, and that no petitions should be admitted after that time. Several more petitions, some in favour, some against, and some praying to be heard were presented (124, 134, 145). Though Mr. Gery was chairman of the committee, it was Sir John Kay who reported the bill with several amendments on 8 April (198) when several new clauses were offered; but no entries in this minute book after 19 February relate to this bill, which passed the Commons but failed to pass the Lords. It was again introduced in the following session (fos. 55r.–57r.).

9. The Peticõn of ye Inhabitants of Gate Foulfold and Water Foulfold in Com̃. York.
10. The Peticõn of ye Inhabitants of Escrich in Com̃. York.
11. The Peticõn of ye Inhabitants of Northallerton in Com̃. York.
12. The Peticõn of the Inhabitants of the Antient Town of Easingwould in Com̃. York.
13. The Peticõn of Lords of Mannos upon ye River Ayre & Calder above Castleforth.
14. The Peticõn of ye Inhabitants of ye Town of Tadcaster in Com̃. York.
15. The Peticõn of Sr John Bland & ał.
16. The Peticõn of ye Inhabitants of ye Town of Heworth in Com̃. York.
17. The Peticõn of ye Inhabitants of ye Towns of Grimston & Heslington in Com̃. York.
18. The Peticõn of ye Inhabitants of Whaldrake in Com̃. York.

Ordered, That Notice be given to the severall Pets That the Commee will proceed upon the said Bill on Monday the 7th day of March next at wch time they may be heard by themselves or Counsell agt the said Bill if they think fit.

Lune 21o Feb. 1697.

London Derry Peticõn.[1]
At ye Commee to whome the Peticõn of the Mayor, Comonalty and Citizens of the City of London Derry in Ireland is referred.

The Commee met and ordered that the Pets should be heard to make good the Suggestions of their Peticõn on this day seavent.

[fo. 8r.]
At ye Commee. to whome ye Bill for Erecting of an Hospitall or Hospitalls, Workhouse or Workhouses, House or Houses of Correccõn within ye Townes and parish of Credinton in Devon for the better releife of the Poor there is committed.[2]

Sabti 26o die Feb. 1697

Crediton.
The Commee met and the Bill was read once over by the Clark. And then the Commee adjd till Monday 5 in ye afternoon.

Lune 28o die Feb. 1697

The Commee met and proceeded upon the Bill and made these amendmts following.

[1] See fo. 10r. and p. 19, n. 1.

[2] Crediton Workhouses Bill. Leave was given to bring in the bill on the petition of the inhabitants of Crediton on 26 January (63), and it was presented on 11 February (96) and committed to a committee of 42 nominated members with the members for Devon and Cornwall on 18 February (118) to meet at 5 in the Speaker's Chamber. The chairman, not named in the minutes, was probably Mr. Burrington, who reported the bill with several amendments on 11 March (153). The complete list of amendments made recorded in these folios is not otherwise recorded.

Fol. 1. L. 11, 12. Fill the 1st blank wth (first), the 2^{d} blank wth (June).

13. Fill ye bla. wth (8).[a]

15. Fill ye bla. wth (of the 12 Gov^{rs}. of ye Hereditam^{ts} and Goods of ye Church of Crediton als Kirton in ye said County of Devon for ye time being).

16. Fill the blank wth (10).

17. Fill the bla. wth (12 Govern^{s}).

19. The same amendm^{t}.

21. Fill ye bla. wth (10).

22. Fill ye bla. wth (12 Governo^{s} or ye greater Number of them).

24. Leave out (or) &[b] fill the blank wth (first).

25. Fill ye bla. wth (July).

26. Fill ye bla. wth (three).

27. Fill ye bla. wth (12 Governo^{s}).[c]

28. After (being) add (wch they are hereby impowered to doe).

29. Fill ye bla. wth (said Ten).

Fol. 2. L. 1. After (dye) add (or be removed).

2. Fill the bla. wth (12 Governo^{s}).

3. Fill ye bla. wth (3 months).

4. After (dyeing) add (or be removed), & fill ye bla. wth (10).

5.[d] Fill ye bla. wth (Assist^{t} to ye 12 Governo^{s} of ye Hereditam^{ts} & Goods of the Church of Crediton als Kyrton in ye County of Devon).

7. Fill ye bla. wth (12 Gov^{s}).

9. The same amendm^{t} & fill ye bla. wth (10).

[fo. 8v.]
Credington.

Fol. 2. L. 10. Fill ye 1st bla. wth (seaven), the 2^{d} bla. wth (12 Gov^{s}), ye 3^{d} bla. wth (one month).

11. Fill ye 1st bla. wth (three), ye 2^{d} bla. wth (10).

12, 13. Fill ye bla. wth (12 Gov^{rs}).

18. Fill ye 1st bla. wth (12 Governe^{s}), ye 2^{d} bla. wth (ten).

21. Fill ye bla. wth (12 Gov^{rs}., Assist^{ts} & Gardians for the better relief of the).

Fol. 3. L. 1. (Poor of the Townes and Parish of Crediton als Kyrton in the said County of Devon).[e]

5, 6. Fill the bla. wth (12 Gov^{s}).

6. Fill ye bla. wth (10), fill ye 2^{d} bla. wth (7), ye 3^{d} bla. wth (12 Gov^{rs}).

7, 8. Fill ye 1st bla. wth (first), the 2^{d} bla. wth (June).

10. Fill ye bla. wth (12 Gov^{rs}).

11. Fill ye bla. wth (7).

(12 Governo^{s}).

[a] *Preceded by* 1698 *erased.*

[b] *Preceded by* insert (or) *erased.*

[c] *Followed by* or ye greater Number of y^{m} *erased.*

[d] *The line above* 5. Fill the bla. wth (10) *erased.*

[e] *This is obviously the continuation of the words in the two preceding lines.*

12. Fill ye bla. wth (one).

14. (one) (12 Gov^{rs}.)

16. (seaven).

17. (12 Gov^{rs}.) (1st) (July 1698).

19. (one year), (12 Gov^{rs}. Assist^{ts}. & Guard:).

21. (seaven), (12 Gov^{rs}).

22. After (death) add (or removall).

Fol. 4. L. 5. (12)

6. (Gov^{rs}.), (12 Gov^{rs}.).

8. (12 Gov^{rs}.).

11. (12 Gov^{rs}.).

12, 13. Fill the bla. wth (2^{d} monday in every 2^{d} month in every year accompting Jan. for ye 1st month in the year).

14. Fill ye bla. wth (12), 2^{d} bla. (seaven).

15. Fill ye bla. wth (12 Gov^{rs}).

17. Fill ye bla. wth (nine).

[fo. 9r.]
Credington.

Fol. 4. L. 18. Fill ye bla. wth (eleaven), ye 2^{d} bla. wth (12 Gov^{rs}).

19. Fill ye bla. wth (11), ye 2^{d} bla. wth (one).

20. Fill the bla. wth (one).

21. Fill ye bla. wth (12 Gov^{rs}. Assist^{ts}. & Guardians).

22. Fill ye bla. wth (7).

23. Fill ye bla. wth (12 Gov^{rs}), ye 2^{d} bla. wth (two).

Fol. 5. L. 1. Fill ye bla. wth (12).

2. Fill ye bla. wth (7), ye 2^{d} bla. wth (12 Gov^{rs}).

6. Fill ye bla. wth (12).

8. Fill ye 1st bla. wth (7), ye 2^{d} bla. wth (12 Gov^{rs}.).

14. Fill the bla. wth (5 shilł.).

22. Fill ye bla. wth (2^{s} 6^{d}).

Fol. 6. L. 14. Fill ye bla. wth (sixteen).

20. Fill ye bla. wth (sixteen).

21. The same amendm^{t}.

23. Fill ye bla. wth (7).

Mercurij 2° die Martij 1697.

Fol. 7. L. 1. After (children) add (and also to such person & persons to whome such child or children shall be bound).

7, 8. Fill ye bla. wth (four five), ye 2^{d} bla. wth (12 Gov^{rs}. Assist^{ts} & Guardians).

8. Fill ye bla. wth (four), ye 2^{d} bla. wth (one).

9. After (power) add (and are herby impowered), and after (inflict) add (or cause to be inflicted).

15. Fill ye bla. wth (600£), 2d bla. wth (12 Govs).
20. After (same) add (at any one time).
Fol. 8. 14. Fill ye bla. wth (two).
22. Fill ye bla. wth (fifty).
Fol. 9. L. 1. Fill ye 1st bla. wth (13), ye 2d wth (seaven [a]), ye 3d wth (12).
2. Fill ye bla. wth (12 Govs).
5. Leave out (kind) and insert (sex).
12. Fill ye bla. wth (3).

[fo. 9v.]
Fol. 10. L. 8. Fill ye 1st bla. wth (seaven), the 2d bla. wth (12 Govs).
17. Leave out (the damages) and insert (dangers).
21. Fill ye bla. wth (12 Govs).
22. seaven: 12 Governors Assistants & Guardians.
Fol. 11. L. 3. Fill the bla. wth (two).
9. After (approve of) add (or give good security for ye same to be approved of as aforesaid).
9. After (Corporac̃on) add (or the major part of them), & after (shall) insert (direct and).
7. After (any) insert (money stock or other), and [b] after (things) add (whatsoever).
9. Fill ye bla. wth (double).
17. Fill ye bla. wth (5) [c]
22. Fill the bla. wth (two).
Fol. 12. L. 6. Fill ye bla. wth (2).
14. Fill ye bla. wth (2).
21. Fill ye bla. wth (treble).
Fol. 13. L. ult. Fill ye bla. wth (200).
Fol. 14. L. 1. Fill ye bla. wth (3).
9. Fill ye bla. wth (3).
9, 10. Fill ye bla. wth (2).
Fol. 15. L. 1. Fill ye bla. with (12 Govs).
Leave out the last Clause but one.[d]
Adjd till tomorrow in ye afternoon.

Jovis 3o die Martij 1697

After (Patents) insert (or any custome or usage relateing to the paymt of tythes within or between the said parish of Crediton als Kyrton and Hamlet of Sandford within the said parish but that all matts & things between the said parish and hamlet shall remain as they were before the makeing of this Act).

[a] *Written above* 12 Govs *erased.*
[b] *Preceded by* things *erased.*
[c] *Written above an illegible erasure.*
[d] *Followed by* & the last Clause *erased.*

[fo. 10r.]

At the Commee to whom the Peticõn of the Mayor, Comonalty and Citizens of the City of London Derry is referred.[1]

Veneris 18o die Feb. 1697.

The Com met and adjourned till Monday next.

Lune 21o die Feb. 1697.

The Commee met and adjd till Monday next.

Lune 28o die Feb. 1697.

The Commee met and adjd till Monday next.

London Derry.[a]

The Commee met & ye peticõn read and Mr Carnes was examined.

As to ye 1st head.

He was present when yt City was shutt upp, viz. 7 Dec. 1688, that they were apprehensive at that time that if they had not taken ye opportunity of shutting up ye City at yt time they should never have such another opportunity, for that there was a Regimt of Irish comeing into ye Town & just as they were entering in, he caused ye gates to be shutt up, and upon ye 9th of Dec. he had ye Comand.

That there was a consultacõn held in ye City & he was appointed to goe to Engł. to acqt. ye K. who went wth great hazard, by ye way of Scotland, wch he did and he returned back again wth ords from England wt to doe, he found many who

[a] *No date heads this entry ;* London Derry *is written in the margin.*

[1] Londonderry's petition was presented on 18 February (118) and was at once referred to a committee to examine the matter thereof, and report the same with their opinion to the House. The names of the members nominated were omitted from the Journal. Presumably Sir Robert Clayton who, as ordered by the committee, reported their resolutions on 9 April (199), was chairman of the committee. The entry for 21 February as recorded on this folio does not tally with that for the same date and same committee on fo. 7v. above. Probably Courthope had forgotten the latter entry when, before the final and effective meeting of the committee, he copied from his notes the record of its previous meetings. The script and the corrections show that Courthope was, on this last occasion, entering the committee's resolutions in his book as they went along: but the date of that meeting is uncertain. The committee is shown to have adjourned on 28 February till 7 March ; but that cannot have been the date of the final meeting at which the resolutions were passed, because on 24 March the committee were given leave to sit in a morning but not after 10 o'clock (176). The final meeting recorded here must have been subsequent to that date. The resolutions reported by Sir R. Clayton, as recorded in the Journal, are substantially the same as they appear in these minutes ; but no mention is made in the Journal of the interesting evidence by Mr. Carnes, the Governor of the city, of which Courthope took down the substance. On 9 April, after the report had been read, the House ordered the committee to draw up a humble address to the King on the matter, but there is no entry in Courthope's minutes of their meeting for this purpose. The address was reported on 2 May (249) and on 16 June (317) was recommitted to the committee after debate : on 23 June (328) the revised address was reported and ordered to be presented, and on 29 June (336) the King's favourable answer was announced. We should not know the exact reason for recommittal of the address but for the entry on fo. 42v. which gives it. The first draft had referred exclusively to the city, and made no mention of its defenders. A comparison of the first draft as given in the Journal with the address agreed to show what amendments in this sense were made. But Courthope does not record the meeting of the committee at which the revised address was agreed to.

were for quitting the Town but he encouraged them all he could, and it was resolved to defend ye Town.
The seige began ye 17th Apr. & ended in July.
2^d Head.
As to their losses in London Derry wch was laid out in defence of ye place.
An Acco^t was taken by Com^s of their losses and a Rep^t made to a Com^ee of ye parl^t of Ireland wch he produced in writeing, under ye hand of ye Chairman of ye Comm^ee appointed by that parl^t.
That there were sev^ll familiyes who were totally destroyed [a] wch were ruined, an acco^t of whose losses is not inserted.
That he has 20 houses lying in rubbish wch now lyes unbuilt.
That the computac̄on made by ye Com^ee of ye parl^t of Ireland is a very moderate computac̄on.

[fo. 10v.]
London Derry.
That ye H. of Commons in Ireland addresst ye Ld Capell Ld Lef^t of Ireland of their great losses of ye City of London Derry, wherein they pray that their case might be laid before the King.
They doe compute their losses to 29247: 16: 4.
agreed.[b]
Resolved, That it is the opinion of this Comm^ee That the Allegations contained in the Petic̄on are true.[c]
agreed.
Resolved, That it appeared to the Comm^ee upon examinac̄on of the Petic̄on That the publick losses, disbursem^ts and damages sustained by the Inhabitants of that City are in the said Petic̄on very moderately computed, and the losses besides to particular and private persons are very great.
agreed.
Resolved, That the Services and Sufferings of the said City on this late Revolution were very eminent and of great consequence to his Maj^ty's Service and the preservac̄on of these three Kingdomes.
agreed.
Resolved, That in regard thereof the said City [d] hath well deserved and ought to be refunded the money in the Petition menc̄oned, And to have some speciall Mark of His Maj^ty's Bounty for a lasting Monument to posterity.
agreed.
Resolved, That in order thereto, It is humbly proposed that something in particular which the Wisdom of this Honble House shall think meet be humbly Recommended to his Maj^ty to be done for the same.[e]

[a] *These two last words written above* destruct (?) *erased.*
[b] agreed *written in all cases in the margin against the resolutions.*
[c] *Here follows* Resolved, that the publick losses sustained by the said City wch appeared to be upon examinac̄on the sume of 29247: 16: 4 is a very moderate computac̄on *crossed out.*
[d] the said City *written above* it *erased.*
[e] *The last three resolutions are in another hand, but the final order is in Courthope's.*

Ordered, That Sr Robt Clayton Report the same the first opportunity.

[fo. 11r. blank.]

[fo. 11v.]

Bread. Jovis [a] 9° die Martij 1697/8.[1]

Fol. 3. L. 6. This Clause beginning in fol. 3 L. 6 is postponed to fol. 4 L. 5.
Fol. 4. L. 6. After (pointe) add (within the Kingdom of England & Dominion of Wales).
9. After (said) add (Churchwarden or).
10. After (said) add (City Towne or), and after (parish) add (under the penalty of 40[s] to be recovered [b] and disposed as hereafter is directed).
19. Fill the blank with (four).
20. After (hereafter) [c] add (in the daytime) & leave out (at seasonable houres).
Fol. 5. L. 4.[d] Leave out (scaled [e] wth the scale or marke of the baker of such bread & the price thereof thereon sett) & insert (as shall not be marked as by this Act is directed).
L. 6. After (Magistrate) add (Churchwarden or).
10. Leave out (or country).
13. Leave out (scale & price) & insert (marks).
16. After (be) add (cut insunder and).

Adj[d] to Fryday morning.

Martis 12° die Aprilis.

Fol. 6. L. 2. Fill y[e] bla. with (5[£]).
Fol. 6. L. 3. Fill the bla. w[th] (one).
11. Fill y[e] bla. w[th] (one month).
13. Fill y[e] bla. w[th] (one moiety thereof to y[e] poor of y[e] parish where y[e] offence shall be comitted & the other moiety thereof to y[e] Informer.[f]
15. After (think) add (him).
18. After (person) add (or persons).
After (his) leave out (or), and after (her) add (or their).
Fol. 7. L. 2. After (such) add (offender).
11. Fill y[e] 1st bla. w[th] (10[£]).
Fol. 7. L. 8.[g] After (incur) leave out (and to be lyable to etc.).

[a] *Should be either* Mercurij 9° *or* Jovis 10°.
[b] *Preceded by* disposed as *erased*.
[c] *Written above* Houres *erased*.
[d] *Preceded by a figure erased*.
[e] *Preceded by* as sh *erased*.
[f] *Followed by two or three illegible words erased*.
[g] *In a line above* After (lyable to) leave out *erased*.

---

[1] See p. 6, n. 1 above. The entry on fo. 12r., though it bears no heading, clearly refers to the committee on the Assize of Bread Bill.

[fo. 12r.]

Fol. 7. L. 18. Fill ye bla. w^th^ (treble).

L. 20. After (London) add (or the right of ether of ye two Universities of this Realm or of any other City or Town Coporate), and after (London) leave out (nor) & insert (or).

Line ult. After (respective) add (jurisdiccons), and after (frankpledge) add (according to the rules direccons and true intent and meaning of this Act).

19. After (shall) add (not).

Leave out the last Clause.

At ye end of ye Bill ad Clause A & B.

[fo. 12v.] Veneris 11o die Martij 1697.

Mr Bickerstaffe in ye Chair.

At ye Commee to whome the Bill [a] for ye better supplying the Town of Newcastle upon Tyne with fresh water is committed.[1]

The Bill was read over and the Articles betw. ye Town of Newcastle and Mr Yarrold dat. 11 Oct. last was compared wth ye Bill & agreed.

Mr Owen [2] appeared and desired a saveing for the right of the Lady Gerrard's water in her Mannor near the Town of Newcastle wch is saved by the amendmts following.

Fol. 2. L. ult. Fill the blank wth (twelve).

Fol. 3. L. 7. After (into) add (takeing away water or diverting any spring or springs stream or streams of water).

12. After (lands) add (and waters).

14. Fill the blank with (exchange).

16. After (lands) add (and waters).

17. Fill the blank with (eight).

27.[b] Fill the bla. wth (twelve).

Fol. 4. L. 6. After (into) add (take away water or divert any spring or springs stream or streams of water).

Fol. 5. L. 15. Fill the blank wth (five pounds).

Ordered, to report.

[fo. 13r.]

At ye Commee to whome the Bill for vesting the Mannos of Bastwick and Laviles in ye County of Norfolk part of the Estate of John Houghton Esqe. in Trustees

[a] *Preceded by* peticon *erased*. [b] *Preceded in margin by* Fol. 4. L. *erased*.

[1] Newcastle-upon-Tyne Waterworks Bill. Leave was given to bring in the bill on 14 February (100), it was presented on 24 February and committed on 5 March (126, 144) to a committee of 36. The bill was reported with amendments on 24 March (176) not by the chairman of the committee but by Sir William Blackett who had prepared and presented the bill.

[2] This appearance of counsel is very curious, since there is no record of any petition being presented by Lady Gerrard praying to be heard. It is difficult to conjecture how the committee conceived that they had power to hear counsel on her behalf without such petition and an order of the House consequent upon it.

to be sold for dischargeing Debts charged thereon and for settling another Estate in lieu thereof is committed.[1]

The Comm^ee mett and proceeded upon the Bill & made these amendm^ts.

Fol. 8. L. 6. Fill up the first blank w^th (Rich^d. Gipps), the 2^d blank w^th (Chyrurgeon).

Fol. 10. L. 1. Fill the blank w^th (Gipps).

Fol. 16. L. 15. Before (saveing) add Clause (A).

gave their [a] Consent to the passing of the Bill.

[fo. 13v.]

At ye Comm^ee to whome the Bill for supplying a defect in a Conveyance lately made by Sr Edwd Turner and Charles Turner Esq. his Son for ye more effectuall secureing the sume of 12000£ & interest upon their estate.[2]

Lune 21° die Martij 1697.

Sr Eliab Harvy in the Chair.

The Comm^ee met and the Bill was once read.

A Peticon of Francis Gee Gentl. and Sarah his wife one of the Daughters of Sr Edwd Turner Kn^t. was read.

Ordered, That notice be given to the Pet^s That the Comm^ee will proceed upon the said Bill on Wednesday next at 5 a clock in ye afternoon.

The like Notice to James Ward Esq. & Mr John Adams.

The like Notice to John Wilson Esq.

And then adj^d till Wednesday next at 5 in ye afternoone.

Mercurij 23° Martij 1697.

The Com^ee met and Mr Gee's Peticon was read, and he urged, That he desired Sr Edward Turner's marriage Settlem^t might be produced.

[a] *Blank space left at beginning of line for names not entered :* the Bill *erased under* gave their.

[1] Houghton's Estate Bill, presented on 22 February (124), was committed to a committee of 36 nominated members with all the members for Norfolk on 14 March (156–7), to meet that day at 5. No date is given for the entry in the minute book, nor is the chairman's name given. The meeting must have been after 14 March. Mr. Brotherton reported the bill with several amendments on 24 March (176), but the amendments are not set out in the Journal.

[2] Turner's Estate Bill, presented by Sir Eliab Harvey on 15 March (158), was committed on 21 March (167) to a committee of 41 nominated members and the members for Norfolk, Suffolk, Cambs. and Herts., to meet at 5 in the Speaker's Chamber. On the same day the petition of Francis Gee and his wife was presented and referred to the committee. Sir John Franklyn's petition was presented and referred on 25 March (178) and Mrs. Lee's petition on 29 March (181). All the petitioners prayed to be heard by counsel. Sir Eliab Harvey reported the bill with some amendments on 5 April, when a clause was added (193). There is no clue to the identity and right to appear of James Ward, John Adams and John Wilson. No petition in any of these names is recorded in the Journal or in the minutes of the committee, yet they seem to be parties, or creditors, bent on obtaining saving clauses to protect their rights. In the end, as will be seen, the committee rejected all their proposed clauses in favour of a general saving clause. The entries in Courthope's minute book have considerable interest, for they give the full course of a committee on an opposed estate bill at that date, including the gist of counsel's arguments.

Sr Edward produced the said deed & the Clause relateing to the porc̄ons for younger children was read.[a]

Adj^d to Fryday morning next.

Veneris 25° die Martij 1698.

The Comm^ee met and Mr Gee appeared and offered a Proviso.
Mr Wilson appeared and offered a proviso for a debt.
Mr Filmer objects ag^t ye Clause that ye settlem^t was made by Sr Edwd. If Mr Wilson has any objecc̄on the Agreem^t [b] betw. Sr Edwd & his Son does not affect Mr Wilson's Judgment, he can receive noe injury by the Bill. He has noe demand y^t can affect this estate. They hope ye Bill will not be cloged by this Clause for that there is a general Saveing.
Mr Addams whose debt is much greater than Mr Wilson is contented wth the General Saveing.
Mr Wilson desires a Clause for a particular Saveing or else the passing of the Bill will prejudice to ye Credito^s. He desires to be in ye same condic̄on as he was before ye passing of the Bill.[c]

Adj^d till ye afternoon.

[fo. 14r.] Veneris 25° Martij 1698.

Post Meridiem

Sr Edwd Turner's Bill.
The Comm^ee met and a Petic̄on of Sr John Franklyn and his wife was read.
Ordered, That Sr John Franklyn and his wife be heard by their Counsell on Wednesday morning next.

And then adjourned till Wednesday morning next.

Mercurij 30° die Martij 1698.

Sr John Franklin appeared and his petic̄on read.
A Petic̄on of Charity Lee widow was also read & she to be heard on Fryday morning next.
Mr Groundman for Sr John Franklin.
Sr John Franklin's Counsell not being here the Comm^ee thought fit to put it off till tomorrow at wch time Sr John Franklin is to be heard by his Counsell.

And then adj^d till tomorrow morning.

Jovis 31° die Martij 1697 [d]

The Com^ee met and Sr J. Franklin's Petic̄on.
Mr Northy of his Counsell that [e] Sr J. Fra. wife ex^s of Mr Clarke, Sr J. a judgm^t cred^e for 500^£.
They desire that ye Essex estate may be made a security for that judgm^t. They

[a] *The proceedings for this day are written in another hand.*
[b] *Written above* Settlem^t *erased.*
[c] *Above the line over the last four words* Deed of Settlem^t *not erased.*
[d] *Should be* 1698, *the new year (O.S.) began on 25 March.*
[e] *Preceded by* for *erased.*

desire a Clause may be inserted in the Bill wch they offered, That ye equity of redempcōn of the said estate mortgaled to Ja. Ward shall be a security for satisfyeing their debts.
The Clause was read.
Mr Wilson appeared and offered a another [a] Clause in lieu of that which he offered before.
And then the Commee adjd till tomorrow morning.

[fo. 14v.] Veneris 1o die Aprilis 1698.

Sir Edwd Turner's Commee.
The Commee proceeded upon the Bill and went thro' the same and made these amendmts following viz.

Fol. 5. L. 2. After (Turner) add (or the heires males of the body of the said Charles after the death of the said Charles).
12. After (them) the same amendmt.
13. Leave out (such) and insert (the).
Fol. 8. L. 18. After (son) add (or the heir male of the body of the said Charles after the death of the said Charles).
19. After (them) the same amendmt.
Fol. 10. L. 13. After (Chancellor) add (Lord Keeper or Comms of the Great Seal of England).

There being some Clauses for saveing the right of some judgmt & and other creds of Sr Edwd Turner, the Comee adjd till Monday morning next.

Lune 4o die Aprilis 1698.

The Commee met and proceeded upon the Clauses for [b] saveing the creds right.
Mr Wilson's Clause read & rejected.
Mr Gee's Clause read and rejected.
Sr John Franklin's Clause read & rejected.
Mrs Lee's Clause read & rejected.
A Generall Clause read & received.

[fo. 15r.]
At ye Commee to whome the Bill for setling ye estate of John Hall a Lunatiq subject to a debt charged thereon is committed.
Samll Ogle Esq in ye Chair.[1]

Mercurij 23o Martij 1697.

The Comee met & adjourned till tomorrow at 5 in afternoon.

[a] *Preceded by* Clause *erased.* [b] *Preceded by* agt *erased.*

[1] Hall's Estate Bill originated in the Lords. It came down on 15 March (158), and was read a second time and committed to a committee of 38 on 23 March (175), to meet at 5 in the Speaker's Chamber, which the minutes show that they did. On 25 March (177) seven members were added to the committee. Mr. Ogle reported the bill without amendments on 26 March (179).

Jovis 24° Martij 1697.

The Com^ee met and adj^d till tomorrow at 5 a clock in ye afternoon.

Veneris 25° die Martij 1697 [a]

The Comm^ee met and the Bill read and the mortgages produced.
The Bill agreed and ordered to be reported wth out amendm^ts.

Martis 19° die Aprilis 1698.

Malt.
At ye Comm^ee to whom the Bill [b] to repeale the Act made in ye 39th year of ye Reign of Queen Eliz. Entituled An Act to restrain the excessive makeing of Malt &c is committed.[1]

The Comm^ee met and passed the Bill wth out any amendm^ts & ordered the same to be reported.

[fo. 15v.] Martis 19° die Aprilis 1698.

At ye Comm^ee to whome the Bill to annex the Rectory of Whitbourne in Herefordshire to the Bishoprick of Hereford is comitted.[2]

The Comm^ee met and proceeded upon the Bill and went thro' the same without any amendm^ts.

Ordered, That the Rep^t be made the first opportunity.

Wooll and Fuller's Earth.

At ye Comm^ee to whome the Bill for ye Explanation and better Execuc̄on of former Acts made ag^t transportacon of Wooll and Fuller's Earth is committed.[3]

Martis 19° die Aprilis 1698.

[a] *Should be* 1698, *cf. note d on p. 24.* [b] *Preceded by* Act *erased.*

[1] On the petition of one Heathcote and others using the malt trade in Derbyshire, leave was given to bring in the Malt Bill on 3 February (81); Mr. Brotherton presented it on 21 February (122), and on 15 April (207) it was committed to a committee of 44 to meet at 5 in the Speaker's Chamber. Presumably Mr. Brotherton was chairman of the committee, though not here mentioned, for he reported the bill without amendment on 20 April (240).

[2] Whitbourne Rectory Bill was another Lords bill, which came down on 8 April (198), and was read a second time and committed on 18 April (236) to a committee of 34 nominated members with the members for Herefordshire, to meet at 5 in the Speaker's Chamber. Mr. Baldwin, presumably chairman of the committee though not here mentioned, reported the bill without amendment on 20 April (239).

[3] The Exporting Wool and Fuller's Earth Bill was, after leave had been given on 28 March (180), presented by Sir John Kay (184) on 31 March and committed on 15 April (207) to a committee of 45 nominated members and the members for the clothing counties, all that come to have voices, and to meet at 5 in the Speaker's Chamber. On 7 May (262) the committee was given power to send for persons, papers and records and to receive a clause to prevent exporting clay. On 28 May (289) Sir John Kay, who was presumably chairman of the committee, reported the bill with amendments, a clause relating to Winchelsea was added, and the bill ordered to be ingrossed. There is no record of any meeting of the committee on 20 April to which date it was adjourned on the 19th, and the continuation of the committee's proceedings only occurs, after a long gap, on fo. 32 (q.v.).

The Comm^{ee} met and adj^{d} till tomorrow at 4 in ye afternoon.[1]

[fos. 16, 17 and 18 entirely blank.]

[fo. 19r.]
Upon Challoner's Peticon.[2]

Martis 8° die Feb.[a] 1697.

The Comm^{ee} met and the Peticon read.

Ordered, That the Chairman doe issue out Ord^{s} for such Witnesses as shall be necessary to make good the Allegacons contained in the Peticon.

And also to issue out Ord^{s} for such persons as the Warden of the Mint shall give informacon.

And then the Comm^{ee} adj^{d} to Fryday morning 9 a clock.[b]

[fo. 19v.]
At ye Comm^{ee} to whome the Bill for ye better Improveing of the Woollen Manufacture is committed.[3]

Jovis 31° die Martij 1698.

The Com^{ee} met and the Bill read over and then adj^{d} till tomorrow at 5 in ye afternoon.

Sabti 2° die Aprilis 1698.

At ye Comm^{ee} to whome the Bill to Enable John Hawkes to sell lands in ye County of Salop for paym^{t} of debts is comitted.[4]

The Comm^{ee} met and adj^{d} till Monday next.

Mercurij 6° Apr. 1698.

[a] *An error for* Martij.

[b] *Followed by* Mercurij 9° die *in the middle of the page erased.*

---

[1] See p. 26, n. 3 above: no meeting on 20 April is recorded.

[2] It is curious that the meeting of a committee on 8 February should be entered on so late a folio. It looks as though the entry was an afterthought of Courthope's, all the more since the date must be wrong. The petition of William Challoner, praying for redress since he had been falsely imprisoned by some persons in the Mint for having in the previous session discovered some abuses in the Mint, was not presented until 18 February (119), when it was referred to a committee of 44 to meet at 5 in the Speaker's Chamber, with power to send for persons, papers and records. Other members were added on 2 and 28 March (138, 180), and on 7 March (146) the committee were given leave to sit the following morning. No report on this petition appears in the Journal, and no further reference to it in this minute book. See R. Ruding, *Annals of the Coinage of Britain* (3rd ed.), ii. 53, n. 4, for Challoner's case.

[3] The Improving Woollen Manufacture Bill was read a second time on 29 March (182) and committed to a committee of 29 nominated members and the members for Somerset, Wilts, Gloucestershire and Yorks, to meet at 5 in the Speaker's Chamber. There is no further reference to the bill in the Journal or in Courthope's minutes.

[4] Hawkes' Estate Bill, after leave given on 21 March (168), was presented by Mr. Edward Harley on 28 March (180) and on 2 April committed to a committee of 32 nominated members and those for Herefordshire, Worcestershire and Staffordshire (189), to meet at 5 in the Speaker's Chamber. Mr. Harley reported the bill with some amendments on 8 April (197). The amendments here entered are not recorded elsewhere.

M^r Ed. Harley in the Chair.

The Comm^ee met and the Bill once read.

The marriage Settlement examined dat. 5 Feb. 4 Jac. 2^d.

The Will of John Hawkes examined.

Mr Hawkes examined who said, That he was a prisoner a year & a halfe a prisoner for ye paym^t of ye Legacyes his father left to ye Children wch his mother imbezzled.

Mr Hawkes & his wife consented to ye passing of the Bill.

Fol. 6. L. 11, 12. Fill the blank w^th (W^m. Dawes of ye parish of S^t. Clem^t. Danes in ye County of Midłe D^r of phisick).

Fol. 7. L. 2. Fill ye bla. w^th (Wm Dawes).

[fo. 20r.]

At ye Comm^ee to whome the Peticõn of ye Proprieto^s of Million Lottery Tickets is referred.[1]

Mercurij 30° die Martij 1698.

Mr Lowndes in the Chair.

The Comm^ee mett and adjourned till tomorrow morning.

Jovis 31° die Martij 1698.

The Comm^ee met and adjourned till tomorrow morning.

Veneris 1° die Aprilis 1698.

The Comm^ee met and adj^d till tomorrow morning.[a]

Sabati 2° die Apr. 1698.

The Comm^ee met and the Peticõn read and Mr Taylor was examined as 20000^£. for ye 120000^£ wch become due at Michas

20000^£ in benefits N. from one to 2500

[a] *Preceded by* Morrow *erased.*

[1] Claims on Lottery Tickets. The petition of the proprietors of Lottery tickets for provision to be made for payments was presented on 29 March (179) and referred to a committee of 43, to meet at 5 in the Speaker's Chamber. On 30 March they were given leave to sit in a morning not after 10 o'clock, and on 31 March the petition of persons who had advanced money on the credit of an Act of 1695 granting certain rates on marriages, births and burials for payment of interest due was also referred to them (184). Two members were added on 15 April (207) and two others besides the members for Cornwall and Yorks were added on 16 April (208). Mr. Lowndes reported the matter and the committee's resolutions on 16 April (208), and he was ordered to prepare and bring in a bill pursuant to the resolutions. The bill was presented on 28 April (246) and committed on 3 May (252) to a committee of 31 to meet at 5 in the Speaker's Chamber. For the proceedings of the committee on that bill, see fo. 30r.

The resolutions put forward, as here recorded, on 2 April and agreed to on 6 April, and the account presented by Mr. Taylor on the latter date are reproduced in the report as entered in the Journal. It is to be noted that the committee did not receive power to send for persons, etc., yet they ordered Mr. Taylor, presumably of the Lottery Office, to deliver an account. As regards the petition relating to rates on marriages, births and burials, see p. 30, n. 1.

There is due at Lady[a] day upon 2500 beneft. tickets	20000£
At Michas upon 97500 blanks	97500
At Michas upon 2500 benefits	20000
102500	137500£

It is proposed that ye tickets shall be paid in course after this method. The lowest numbers to be paid 1st one year and the highest numbers to be paid first the next year, and one year shall be cleared[b] before the other begins.

Mr Herne opposed it, and said that the middle tickets will be always best.

These Questions following were proposed and the Commee took time till Tuesday morning next to consider of the same.

Res., That ye growing weekly paymts comeing into ye Excheq, from the Addic̄onall Excise for paymt of the Lottery tickets be first applyed to the paymt. of the tickets of those half yeares wch are already incurred and growne due, except the tickets of Michas 1696 and Lady day 1697 wch are appointed to be satisfyed out of the Land Tax.

That for the future the growing weekly paymts comeing into ye Excheq, from the Addic̄onall Excise for paymt of the Lottery tickets be applyed to [fo. 20v.] paymt of the tickets of every halfe year wch shall first incurr or become due soe that the tickets of every preceding halfe yeare shall be cleared or money reserved for them before any paymts be made upon any tickets of a subsequent halfe year.

3. That for the more orderly paymt of the Lottery ticketts those for twenty shillings a peece commonly called Blank Tickets shall be paid in arithmeticall progression beginning first with Number one and proceeding to the Number 97500, and those called benefit or prize tickets shall in the next place be paid in course from No. 1 to No. 2500 and afterwards[c] the blank tickets shall be paid from N. 97500 to No. 1 and the benefit tickets from No. 2500 to N. 1, and soe forwards alternately.

4. That ye ninepence p. barrell Excise be appropriated dureing the whole term of sixteen yeares to the paymt. of the said tickets untill they be fully satisfyed.

Adjd till Tuesday morning next.

Martis 5o die Aprilis 1698.

Ordered, That Mr Taylor doe lay before the Commee an Accot of what sumes of money are due upon ye Million Lottery tickets upon Lady day 1696, Michas 1697 and Lady day 1698 or any other former halfe year except the year provided for by parliamt. and what cash remaines in his hands towards paymt thereof.

And then adjourned till tomorrow morning 8[d] a clock.

[fo. 21r.] Mercurij 6o die Aprilis 1698.

Lottery Tickets.

Mr Tayler according to ordr. delivered in to ye Commee an accot. of what is due upon ye Mill. Lottery tickets and[e] what remaines in his hands viz.

	£	s	d
Remanes yet unpaid of ye Million Lottery tickets due at Lady day 1696	18342.	10.	0

[a] *Preceded by* Michas *erased.*
[b] *Preceded by* paid *erased.*
[c] *Preceded by* the benefit and *only imperfectly erased.*
[d] *Preceded by* 9 *erased.*
[e] *Preceded by* viz. *erased.*

There is also unpaid of 120000£ due at Michas 1697 the sume of	43000. 00. 00	
Towards wch there is in ye Excheq	3000. 00. 00	
Soe remaines to be provided for		40000. 00. 00
There is also due at Lady day 1698		20000. 00. 00
		78342. 10. 00
Received upon 14 Tallies of Pro struck for paymts of ye tickets of the year 1695	7912£	
Out of wch deducting for ye tickets of yt year yt remained unpaid	6363	
There will remain to lessen the above deficiency		1549. 0. 0
		76793. 10. –

Then the Resolucōns were read and sevll proprietos present approved of the same and the said Resolucōns were agreed to.

Mr Taylor informed the Commee that he spoke wth Mr Herne and that Mr Hern said he was willing that the tickets should be paid in such course as desired by ye peticōn provided the parlt. would provide for the deficiency upon ye Lottery tickets.

Mr Hern appeared & said the deficiency arises by ye parlt's. takeing away ye fund, viz. the Salt Duty, soe that there is a deficiency of 200098£ wch he hopes the parlt. will make good.

There is above 50000£ misapplyed of ye money come in since Mich. last.

The Clause of the Act read relateing to ye commencemt of ye Dutye whereby it appear that it commences from Lady day 1694.

Mr Hern. noe tickets is to be paid till La. day 1695 & there ought [a] to be a yeare's paymt in cash before any are paid.

There is due at Lady day 1698 78342£. 10s wch is to be reported.

Mr Taylor. there is abot. 2000£ a week comes in upon ye Excise.

Ordered, That Mr Lownds doe report the matter to the House.

[fo. 21v.]
Births & Burials.[1]

Mercurij 6o Aprilis 1698.

The peticōn read.
The Agents of ye Excheqr. appeared. Mr Dewy, That there have been Supervisors appointed by the late Act, that the [b] Supervisors have made great improvemts made upon ye duty upon houses and they are now entring upon the births &

[a] *Preceded by one illegible word erased.* [b] *Preceded by* these have *erased.*

[1] The committee on the claims on Lottery tickets, having agreed to their report, turned immediately to the consideration of the second petition referred to them (see p. 28 n. 1), as here recorded. The evidence of, and the committee's discussions with, the Agents of the Exchequer as noted by Courthope is a highly interesting addition to our knowledge: for further comment, see p. 34, n. 1 below.

burials wch he hopes will make a great improvem^{t}, but ye duty is very much evaded[a] & ye Supervisors discouraged by the Justices of ye peace.
Sr Tho. Lane, one reason of the deficiency of the Act is because of persons dyeing in one place and buryed in another, and liveing in one parish & marryeing in another. They offered severall Clauses to be inserted.
It is proposed that ye duty upon marriages to be paid upon his takeing out a lycence.
Mr Dewy, There is direccons sent to ye Justices of the peace to hear ye compl^{ts}. of y^{e}[b] supervisors, who give little incouragem^{t}.
Sr T. Lane, merch^{ts} & foreig^{s} come into sev^{ll} great cityes & townes. &
Ordered, That the Agents doe attend on Saturday morning.
And then ye Comm^{ee} adj^{d} till Saturday merid.

Sabti 9° die Aprilis 1698.

The Comm^{ee} met and the Peticon read, and the Agents of the Excheq, appeared.
Sr Tho. Lane appeared and offered some Clauses to make the Act relateing to births and marriages more effectuall.
Mr Squires proposed that the person wch is to pay the duty[c] shall pay the same wthin such a time under[d] a certain penalty.
A Clause was read.

[fo. 22r.]
Sr Tho. Lane that where ever any person shall be christened[e] maryed[e] & buryed the duty shall be paid in ye very place where[f] they are christened maryed or buryed to ye Collector of that place or parish, and a more effectuall reg^{s}. kept & there shall be certificates given[g] of the duty being paid before they are marryed, buryed & christened.[h]
It was objected as to christenings that children might be like to dye and perhaps before a certificate could be gott the child might dye unchristened.
Sr Tho. Lane proposes that where it should happen that certificates could not be got, then the Ecclcall person shall receive the duty & be accomptable himselfe.
Sr S. Dashwood as to marriages, That the reg^{s}. are defective, that in Holborn above 100 have been marryed & not above 5 wch paid the duty.
He proposes that the parson shall be lyable to a fine[i] wch marryes any one wthout[j] produces a certificate that he has paid the duty.
It was objected that there may be counterfeited certificates.
The Collector of the parish where they are married shall give the certificate that[k] the duty has been paid.
A Clause to enjoyne the Justices of the peace to meet once in 3[l] months upon this Act.[m]

[a] *The* e *written above* J *erased.* [b] *Followed by* Ju *erased.*
[c] *Written above* money *not erased.* [d] *Preceded by two short words erased.*
[e] *Preceded by* buryed *erased.* [f] *Preceded by* before *erased.*
[g] *Preceded by* be *erased.*
[h] *Followed by* It was objected as to children being *on a fresh line erased.*
[i] *Followed by* ul unless *erased.* [j] *Preceded by* that *erased.*
[k] *Preceded by* where they are mar *erased.*
[l] *Written above* two *erased.* [m] *Followed by* Sr S. Dashwood *on a fresh line erased.*

An allowance to ye parson of every parish to keep an exact register and deliver the same to the petty Session.
Mr Dewy, That Supervisors are appointed for every county in Engld. upon ye duties upon houses, births, marriages & burialls.
That great improvemts have been made upon ye houses & they are now entred upon the births & do not doubt but [a] to improve that revenue.
That the Justices of peace doe not meet upon the matter as they ought to doe.
That they have sent direccons to the Supervisors how to improve this duty.
Adj to Fryday next [b] Saturday morning.[1]

[fos. 22v. and 23r. blank.]

[fo. 23v.] Mercurij 30o die Martij 1698.

Coll. Perry in ye Chair.
At ye Commee to whome ye Engrossed Bill for ye better enabling Sr R. Hare Bart. to make a joynture & settle his estate and raise porcons & maintenance for his younger children is comitted.[2]
The Commee met and proceeded upon the Bill and went through the same. And My Ld Hare and Sr R. Hare & Sr Robt Dashwood consented to ye passing of the Bill.
The Report to be made the first opportunity.

Mercurij 6o die Aprilis 1698.

At ye Commee to whome the Bill to enable John Jenkins Mercht to sell some part of his [c] estate for ye paymt of his debts is committed.[3]
The Bill read & the Deed exaed,
A cop: of the Mortgage produced.
Mr Horsmandine consented to ye passing of the Bill.
Ms. Jenkins also consented to the passing of the Bill.
Adjd to Tuesday next next.[4]

[fo. 24r.] Sabti 12o die Martij 1697.

At ye Commee to whom the Peticon of Fra. Strutt, Hen. Eeles, Edmd Woodward,

[a] *Followed by* that *erased.* [b] Fry *very imperfectly erased.*
[c] *Written above* the *erased.*

[1] The adjournment was obviously till Saturday, 16 April, as shown by the continuation of this committee's proceedings on fo. 25r.
[2] Hare's Estate Bill originated in the Lords: it came down on 21 March (168), and was read a second time and committed on 30 April (182) to a committee of 42 nominated members and those for Norfolk, to meet at 5 in the Speaker's Chamber. Col. Perry reported the bill with one amendment (which does not appear in these minutes) on 2 April (189).
[3] Jenkin's Estate Bill, after leave given on 29 March (182), was presented on 1 April (188), and on 6 April (193) committed to a committee of 30 nominated members with those for Kent and Sussex. Mr. Brewer, not mentioned here as chairman, reported the bill with some amendments on 23 May (283).
[4] The continuation of this committee is on fo. 31v. with date 18 May. There are no entries relating to it between 6 April and that date.

Edwd White, Tho. Marlow, Edwd Goldgay and Jno Eeles on behalf of themselves and severall other Serv^ts of his late Ma^ty. K. Cha. ye 2^d is referred.[1]
Sr J. Bolls in ye Chair.
The Comm^ee met and
Ordered, the Clarks belonging to his Ma^ts Wardrobe, the Dep^ty or Clark belonging to the Treasurer of his Ma^ts Chambers, the Dep^ty or Clark to his Ma^ts Coferer, and the Dep^ty or Chiefe Clerk to ye Auditor of the Excheq, doe lay before this Com^ee on Tuesday next such papers and books of acco^t as relate to ye acco^ts and paym^ts of 60000^£ wch by a late Act was appointed to be paid and distributed equally and proporconably to & among the serv^ts of the late King Cha. the 2^d who were serv^ts at ye time of his death and to shew how when and to whome the paym^ts & distribucons have been made.

Adj^d to Tuesday next.

Lune 28° die Martij 1698.

Ordered, That the Clarks of the Treasury or some of them doe on Thursday morning next at 8 a clock lay before the Comm^ee on acco^t. of how much of the 6000^£ hath been paid to the serv^ts of the late K. Charles in pursuance of the late Act of parliam^t made in the 1st year of the reign of his present Ma^ty and the late Queen Entituled An Act for appropriating certain dutyes for paying the States Generall of the United Provinces their charges for his Ma^ts expedicon into this Kingdom and for other uses; and to what Offices the same hath been paid into.

Jovis 31° Martij 1698.

The Comm^ee met but the Clarks of the Treasury not[a] attending according to the former Ord^r the same Ord^r was made for them to attend on Saturday morning next.

And then adj^d till Saturday morning next.

[fo. 24v.] Sabti 2° die Aprilis 1698.

King's Serv^ts Pet.
The Comm^ee met and Mr Powis and Mr Tilson attended and (according to Order) delivered in to the Comm^ee an acct. how and to what Offices the sume of 60000^£ appropriated to the paym^t of wages due to such of the serv^ts of the late King Charles the 2^d as were actually his serv^ts at the time of his decease was paid.
W^ch acco^t. was read.
Ordered, That the Clerks of the Excheq, or some of them doe on Wednesday morning next lay before the said Comm^ee an acco^t of how much of the 31164. 3^s. 4 (w^ch

[a] *Preceded by* not (?) *erased*.

---

[1] The petition of the Servants of King Charles II. On 3 March (139) the petition of several servants of Charles II who were in his service at his death was presented and read, but there is a blank in the Journal where the contents should have been set forth. There is also a blank for the surname of Francis Strutt, which is thus filled by Courthope. The names of the committee to whom the petition was referred are also omitted from the Journal, though 6 named members were added on 5 March (143) and 10 more on 25 March. No report of this committee appears in the Journal, so that Courthope's minutes fill a gap by showing the nature of the claim and the steps taken by the committee in their inquiry, so far as it is recorded.

was paid into the Excheq, for the use of such of the servts of the late King Charles the second as were payable there) was actually paid & to whome the same was paid and how much to each person.
The like Ords to the Clerks of belonging to the Treasurer of the Chamber.
The like Ords to the Clerks of the Great Wardrobe.
The like Ords to ye paymaster of the Band of penconers.
And then adjd till Wednesday morning next.

Mercurij 6o die Aprilis 1698.

Ks. servts pet.
The Commee met and adjd till Monday morning next 8 a clock.

[fo. 25r.] Sabti 16o Aprilis 1698.[1]
The Commee met, and the Pets were called in.
Mr Squire, that the persons to pay the duty may have an oath given them.
S Tho. Lane.
Mr Serjt Ryly. The causes of the deficiency of the Act are the want of Justices of the peace in remote places.
The Comms of ye Act of 3s in ye pound may be impowered to put the Act in execucōn.
Clandestine marriages at Knightsbridge and severall other places whereby the duty is defrauded.
It is proposed that persons marrying out of the parish where they resided shall produce Cert. that ye duty hath been paid under a certain penalty, That ye duty shall be paid before ye offices shall be performed.
Batchellos [a] of & widowers to enter their names [b] where ever they remove undr a penalty.
Great defects in the regs that are kept. He proposes that every person shall enter his place of abode.
A Clause of retrospeccōn one part to ye informer & the other to ye King.
The Comms may have power levy all penaltyes.
The Comms may be authorized to examine the Colls upon oaths touching the dutyes.
S Tho. Lane, That all persons are to pay the duty wthin such a time.[c]

[a] *Preceded by* The Duty of *erased.* [b] *Preceded by* Ab *erased.*
[c] *Followed on fresh line by* That the Assessos *erased.*

[1] See p. 30, n. 1 above. Although no heading except the date is given at the top of this folio, the contents make it clear that this is the continuation, from fo. 22r., of the committee on births, marriages and burials. The proceedings of the committee continue without interruption to the end of fo. 27r. The sitting recorded on fo. 25v. bearing the same date as that on fo. 25r., must presumably have occurred in the afternoon. The proceedings of 16 and 20 April as here entered by Courthope cover most of the report as it was made by Mr. Lowndes on 28 April (245–6), save that the 10th resolution entered in the minutes was not reported, another resolution being substituted, that the poundage to the collectors should be increased. On consideration of the report, the 2nd resolution (bachelors and widowers) was negatived on division, and the 9th (the King may farm) negatived. Mr. Lowndes was ordered to prepare and present a bill, which he did on 28 May (289). This was committed to a committee of the whole House on 31 May (293) and eventually passed.

A Clause that every person shall pay the dutyes wthin such a time therein to be limited.
A Clause that ye Collecto^{s} shall make their paym^{ts} and give [a] their acco^{ts} upon oath.
That there may be liberty to farm it.

[fo. 25v.]

Births and Marriages Sabti 16° die Aprilis 1698.

The Comm^{ee} met and sev^{ll} of the Pet^{s} appeared.
The Agents of the Excheqꝫ also appeared and delivered in to the Comm^{ee} severall proposals for the better ascertaining and collecting the rates and duties upon marriages, births & buralls and upon batchellors and Widowers, wch are as followes, viz.

1st That to supply the defect of Justices of the Peace in severall places the same Comm^{s} that were authorized the first year of granting the said dutyes or the Comm^{s} for the present Ayd of 3^{s} in ye pound may be generally authorized to put this Act in execuc̃on.

2dly That to prevent for the future the loss sustained by persons marryeing in parishes or places wherein they are not resident, it may be enacted that the duties for such marriages be paid before such office ꝑformed and that it may be made penall for any parson, viccar &c. to marry such person untill they shall have produced a certificate under the hands of the Collecto^{s} of the same parish where they reside of ye paym^{t} of the duty accordingly, and the forgeing of any such certificate to be penall as in other cases of forgery, and that the like provision may be made for the duties upon births and burialls of persons either christened or buryed in other places than where they resided or that the said dutyes be paid in   dayes or else the party to pay double or greater or other penalty.

3dly That batchello^{s} and widowers lyable to the payment of the said dutyes may be obliged on or before the 24th day June next to enter their names, sur-names, qualityes and places of abode with the parochiall Collecto^{s} respectively under a penalty, and soe from time to time upon removeall of such persons.

4^{thly} That the registers to be kept pursuant to the Act 7° & 8° of his Ma^{ts} Reign may containe the names, qualityes and places of aboade of all persons marryed, buryed and born or christened according to the best and most particular informac̃on under the penalty as in the said Act.

5^{thly} That in the case of removeall of any person without payment of the duty the Comm^{s} or any two of them to certify.

[fo. 26r. blank.]

[fo. 26v.] Mercurij 20 die Aprilis 1698.

Marriages.
The Comm^{ee} met and Mr Squire offered some other proposalls for advanceing ye duty on births & marriages.

[a] *Written above an illegible word erased.*

1st That no administracon̄ be granted nor probat of wills allowed unless ye duty be first paid.

2 Clause of retrospeccon̄.

That ye King have leave to farm it.

The Comee came to sevll Resolucon̄s, viz.

1st That [a] in many places there being few Justices of the peace to act for these casuall duties and the Justices of peace having new trusts and dutyes comitted to ym by severall [b] Acts of parlt., It is ye opinion of this Commee that for ye year 1698 the persons nominated Coms for this year's [c] Land Tax be [e] also authorized [f] for executing the Acts for the said dutyes upon marriages, births & burialls, batchellos & widowers.

ts. article agreed agreed.[d]

The 2d Article postponed.

3 Art. agreed. That batchellos and widowers lyable to the paymt of the said dutyes shall be obliged on or before the 24th day of June next to give an accot in writeing of their names, surnames, qualityes and places of aboad with the parochiall Collector where they reside respectively under a penalty and soe from time to time upon removeall of such persons they shall be obliged to give the like notice to the Collector of the place to wch they remove within 3 months after their comeing to such new place or residence.

4th Art. agreed. That the regs be kept pursuant to ye Act 6o & 7o of his Mats Reign shall[g] contain the names, qualityes and places of abode of all persons marryed buryed, born and christened according to ye best and most particular informacon̄, and that the persons who ought to pay the sd. duty shall give or cause to be given to the Minister the said addicon̄s truely [h] under a penalty to be inflicted in default thereof.

5 Article. agreed. That in the case of removeall of any person without payment of the duty the Comms or any two of them to certify such default under their hands & seals and such certificate

to be

[fo. 27r.]

to be sufficient ground for the like number of Comms in any county or place where such person shall reside to levy the duty by distress in case of non-paymt.

6th agreed That all penaltyes be levyed by warrt of the Comms or any two of them except the penalty of 100£ for not keeping the regs and that to be levyed in manner the Acts.

7th agreed That the Collectos for the said dutyes doe render their accots upon oath to be administered by two or more Coms.

8th agreed That every person for the time to come shall pay or tender the said dutyes to the Collectos within a certain time under a penalty.

[a] *Preceded by* Resolved *erased.*
[b] *Preceded by* the *erased.*
[c] *Written above* the *erased.*
[d] *The first* agreed *written hastily.*
[e] *Preceded by* of the same year *erased.*
[f] *Followed by* to act wth the Justices of the peace *erased.*
[g] *Preceded by* may *erased.*
[h] *Preceded by a small illegible word erased.*

9 agreed — That the King shall have power (if his Ma^ty think it will be most for the improvem^t of the said dutyes) to farm the same.

10th agreed — That the Assessm^ts be brought to the Comm^s every three months and allowed and duplicates thereof returned.

Adj^d till tomorrow morning 8 a clock.

[fo. 27v.] Jovis 28o Aprilis 1698.

At ye Comm^ee to whome the Peticõn of Andrew Perrot, Sam^ll Dawson and other Inhabitants of the City of York is referred.[1]

The [a] Comm^ee met and the Peticõn read.[b]

Ordered, That the Warden of the Mint,[2] Mr Hall, Mr Ambrose, Mr Brattle,[3] Mr Briant and Mr Foquier [4] doe attend the said Comm^ee on Saturday morning next. Mr Neale be [5] desired to bring an acco^t of what money is due to the publick and private importers in the severall Mints and what due to the severall Officers and workmen and [c] what new money remaines in the Mint.

Ordered, that Mr Barton and Mr Tuly doe attend the said Comm^ee on Saturday morning next.

And then adj^d till Saturday morning.

Sabti 30o die Aprilis 1698.

The Comm^ee met and Mr Neal produced an acco^t of w^t is due to the Mints in generall.

[a] *Preceded by* Ordered That *erased.*

[b] *Followed on a fresh line by* M^r (*illegible*). A deficiency of all ye Mints except Bristoll. A loss by the badness of ye coyn and also in ye sweepings. Abo^t 20000£ or 30000£ loss to the importers and till that be made good there will be continuall complaints. *crossed out.*

[c] *Written above* in *erased.*

---

[1] 'Hammered Money' is the marginal note of the Journal references to this matter. Courthope does not give the substance of the petition, which was that the petitioners had delivered £3,000 of hammered money to the Master worker of the Mint at York, but had had no payment. It was an incident in the long and rather expensive effort of this reign to restore the coinage. On the whole subject, see Ruding, *Annals of the Coinage of Britain* (ed. 1840), ii. 29–60, though the author makes no specific reference to this committee. These minutes would have furnished him with some interesting details. See also Sir John Craig, *The Mint* (1953), pp. 194–6.

The petition was presented on 20 April (240) and immediately referred to a committee of 28 nominated members with the members for Yorkshire and other counties where there were Mints, to meet at 5 in the Speaker's Chamber, and to have power to consider of the deficiency at all the Mints. On 5 May (254) a petition of divers traders of the City of London complaining that they could not get new money for parcels of silver carried to the Tower Mint was referred to the same committee, who were ordered to sit *de die in diem,* which they did not do, as Courthope's minutes show. On 2 June (297–8) Sir Marmaduke Wyvell, who was one of the Commissioners of the Treasury and presumably chairman of the committee, though not mentioned as such in the minutes, reported the matter at length with the committee's resolutions, which were amended and agreed to. Courthope's minutes of this committee occupy, with two interruptions, 6½ folios.

[2] The Warden of the Mint at this date was Isaac Newton: he is the Mr. Newton whose name appears more than once in these minutes.

[3] Mr. Brattle was Assay Master, and Mr. Bryant was Provo of the Moneyers.

[4] Fauquiere is the correct spelling. He was Master's Assayer.

[5] Mr. Neale was Master of the Mint till succeeded by Newton in 1699.

Mr Newton. The Officers delivered into y^{e} L^{ds} of y^{e} Treasury an acco^{t} of w^{t} due to y^{e} Mints [a] wch he produced to y^{e} Committee by wch it appeared y^{t} at there was due in y^{e} whole.
Mr Foquier. If y^{e} coynage be made good the private importes will be paid.
Mr Barton said that he owes not above 1200$^{£}$ to the King. He made up his acco^{ts} at York wth the Mint, but they cannot agree abo^{t} their acco^{ts}.
[fo. 28r.]
Ordered, That Mr Barton doe lay before the Comm^{ee} on Thursday [b] next his [c] acco^{t} [d] wth the Mint at York and w^{t} is due to the importers and what due to him.
Ordered, That Mr Neal doe at the same time lay before the Com^{ee} an acco^{t} of what is due to every particular Mint and what due to the severall Officers and workmen and what new money remaines in the Mints.

And then adj^{d} till Thursday morning next.

Jovis 5° die Maij 1698.

Mr Barton [e] delivered in to the Comm^{ee} an acco^{t} whereby he makes himself debtor to the King 27.
Mr Tuly objected ag^{t} Mr Barton's acco^{t} and said that Mr Barton was debtor to the King at 3756. 4. 10.
Mr Tuly said that their money comes out of the Mint at York worse than in other Mints.
Mr Foquier that the Master Worker is to receive 18^{d} p. pound, and when that is made good the Mints will be paid.
Ordered, That an acco^{t} be laid before the [f] Com^{ee} of what has been come in upon the Act for [g] wine and brandy.
Ordered, That the Lords of the Treasury be desired to ord^{r} an acco^{t} be laid before the Comm^{ee} what money has been issued [h] for the supply of the severall Mints in the Country.
The Warden, Mr Foquier, Mr Haines, Mr Briant to attend tomorrow morning.

And then adj^{d} till tomorrow morning.[1]

[fo. 28v.] Lune 9° die Maij 1698.[2]

M Tilson [i]

[fo. 29r.] Lune 2° die Maij 1698.

[a] *The words following down to* whole *are written in a very hasty scribble.*
[b] *Written above* Wednesday *erased.*
[c] *Preceded by* how *erased.*
[d] *Followed by* stands *erased.*
[e] *Written above* Thompson *erased.*
[f] *Followed by* Ho *erased.*
[g] *Preceded by* for y *erased.*
[h] *Followed by* to the sever *erased.*
[i] *The remainder of fo. 28v. is blank.*

[1] There is no entry of any meeting on 6 May: see next n. and p. 39, n. 2.
[2] This abortive entry clearly belongs to the committee on hammered money. Mr. Tilson was an official of the Exchequer: see p. 39, n. 2.

At ye Commee to whome the Peticõn of Andrew and Jeronimy Clifford is referred.[1]
The Commee mett and Mr Jero. Clifford produced the Articles of Peace betw. ye English and Dutch relateing to Surinam, whereby it was agreed that the English might have liberty to transport themselves and familyes & effects.[a]
That he was fined 4000£ abt a negro & kept a prisoner 4 yeares in Surinam and at last was discharged by his Mats intercession wth the States Generall.
And produced an Ord£ of the States Generall to ye Governo£ of Surinam to release the pet£. Jeronomy Clifford and to suffer him to depart from Surinam wth his goods & effects.
To prove ẏt they fined him and seized his effects to ye damage of 20000£ & upwards.
That he demanded satisfaccõn of ye Dutch West India Compa. and likewise of the States Generall.

Martis 3o die Maij 1698.[2]

Mr Tilson delivered in to ye Comee an accot of the issues made at the Excheq, for ye supply of the sevll Mints wch was read.
A peticõn of the Traders of ye City of London was read.
Mr [b] Neal's accot of the debt of ye severall Mints was read.
Mr Lownds moved, That a more particular accot be brought in by the Master of the Mint.
The Warden of the Mint said they cannot make a more particular accot in soe short a time.
Mr Barton's accot recd whereby Mr Barton owned himselfe indebted to ye King 2749. 17. 8 and when he is paid what due to him he will pay that sum̄e.
Mr Barton desires 6 weeks time to make up the sweep, and when he has settled his accot with Mr Neal there will not be above 1500£ for him to pay of ye 2749. 17. 8 & when the sweep is made up it will pay that.

[fo. 29v.]

~~2749. 17. 8~~
~~1096. 19. 6~~
~~1652. 18. 2~~ [3]

[a] *Followed by* to Jamaica (?) *erased*. [b] *Preceded by two small erasures.*

[1] The petition of Andrew and Jeronomy Clifford, lately inhabitants of Surinam, was presented and read on 18 April (235) and was immediately referred to a committee of 24 to meet at 5 in the Speaker's Chamber. Ten more members were added on 30 April (247), and there is no further reference to it in the Journal. Moreover, there is a blank in the Journal where the substance of the petition should have been set forth, so that Courthope's minutes, though incomplete, fill a gap in our knowledge.

[2] This date is obviously wrong. It will be seen at the top of fo. 29v. that the committee adjourned till 'tomorrow', and met again on 10 May. The abortive entry on fo. 28v. which begins 'Mr Tilson' under the date 9 May must furnish the correct date for this entry, which begins with the same words. It should be 'Lune 9o die Maij'. The minutes continue from the end of fo. 29v. to fo. 34r.

[3] These erased figures refer to the reduction likely to be made in Mr. Barton's total by settling his account with Mr. Neal (see end of fo. 29r.).

Mr Barton did offer in 3 weeks time to cleer half ye money what is due to the sweep.

Adjd till tomorrow.

Martis 10o Maij 1698.

Mr Neal delivered in to ye Commee (according to ordr) a particular accot of what is due to ye Mint at ye Tower.
That the Mint is chargable to ye Comrs of Excise as standards.
That out of yt money they take out ye charge of coynage.
Mr Lo.[1] That there has been imprest to ye Mar of ye Mint great sumes of money.
That in ye accot ye Mar reckons 2s p. pd. wt. whereas ye Act of parlt allowes but 16d½.
Mr Lounds said, Itt is necessary ye Mar of ye Mint should give an accot of wt money has been imprested to him, there being above 100000£ imprest to him within this two yeares.
There remains in ye Mint in ye Tower saved out of ye 2d wch was stopt out of ye publick money the sume of 7343. 1s. 5¼d 7 or 8000£ p.[a] ann. appropriated towards[b] the charge of ye Mint.
Mr Neale. There is 20711. 3. 11 due to ye Mint, but if they had 10000£ of that debt will be sufficient to keep[c] up the creddit of ye Mint.
Ordered, That Mr Hall bring an accot of wt money hath been imprest to him and how he hath disposed of the same.
Mr Foquier. Hall has returned 2000£ to ye Mint this day.

[fo. 30r.] Jovis 5o die Maij 1698.

Lottery Ticket Bill.

At ye Commee to whom the Bill for the better and more orderly paymt of the Lottery Tickets now payable out of certain addiconall Dutyes of Excise was[d] comitted.[2]

Mr Lowndes in ye Chair.

The Commee met and proceeded upon the Bill.

Fol. 2. L. 8. Fill ye 1st bla. wth (fifteenth), the 2d bla. wth (May 1698).

[a] *Preceded by* app *erased.*
[b] *Preceded by an erasure of one illegible word.*
[c] *Preceded by* ma *erased.*
[d] *Followed by* read ye 2d time *erased.*

---

[1] I.e. Lowndes.

[2] This bill was the outcome of the select committee's report on the claims on Lottery tickets (see fos. 20r.–21r. and p. 28, n. 1 above). On the day when the bill was committed (252) the committee were ordered to take into consideration a petition lodged on the previous day (249) from certain annuitants who had lent money upon the credit of the tonnage duties for payment of arrears. It will be observed that, after ordering the bill to be reported, the committee ordered the petitioners above-mentioned to attend on the following Monday, i.e. 9 May: but the Journal (263) shows that Mr. Lowndes reported the bill with amendments on 7 May. There is no entry here of any sitting of the committee on 9 May. Nevertheless, when the bill was passed (269), the title shows that it included payment of the annuities. The Act is 9 & 10 William III, c. 34.

Fol. 3. L. 11. Fill ye bla. wth (his office).
12. Fill ye bla. wth (100£).
line ult.[a] Fill ye bla. wth (treble costs).
Fill ye bla. wth (2500£).
Ordered, that the Bill be reported to the House ye 1st opportunity
Ordered, That the pets upon ye Annuityes doe attend the Commee on Monday next.[1]

[fo. 30v.] Jovis 5o die Maij 1698.

Hull Workhouse.
At ye Commee to whome the Bill for erecting Workhouses and Houses of Correccōn in ye Town of Kingston upon Hull for ye imployment and maintenance of ye poor there is comitted.[2]

The Commee met and adjd till tomorrow morning.

Veneris 6o die Maij 1698.

The[b] Commee met and proceeded upon the Bill and made severall amendmts thereto wch was ordered to be reported.

Veneris 20o die Maij 1698.

At ye Commee to whom ye Bill for vesting a Coperas Work part of ye estate of Robt Mascall Esq, decēd in Trustees to be sold for paymt of debts & other charges thereupon is comitted.[3]

The Commee met and the Bill was read.
And then the Comee adjd till tomorrow morning.

Sab̄ti[c] 21o Maij 1698.

Fol. 3. L. 15. Leave out (lawfully) & insert (fully).
After (ended) insert (wthout impeachmt of or for any manner of wast).
Fol. 5. L. 4. After (another) leave[d] out (as they & every of them should have been in) & insert (according to their).
Fol. 5. L. 10. Leave out (they had happened) and insert (any[e] such had been).
Fol. 6. L. 6. Before[f] (such) insert (the body of).

[a] *Preceded on line above by* 13 f *erased*.
[b] *Preceded by* At ye Commee to whom the Bill *erased*.
[c] *Preceded by* Veneris *erased*.
[d] *Written above* add *erased*.
[e] *Preceded by* if *erased*.
[f] *Written above* After *erased*.

[1] See p. 40, n. 2.

[2] Kingston-upon-Hull Workhouse Bill, after leave being given on 27 April (244), was presented on 29 April (247) and on 3 May was read a second time and committed to a committee of 29 to meet at 5 in the Speaker's Chamber (251). Mr. Lowther, presumably the chairman, reported the bill on 10 May (265). Courthope was negligent in not setting out the amendments.

[3] Mascall's Debts Bill, after leave being given on 5 May (254), was presented on 11 May (266) and on 16 May (271) committed to a committee of 45 nominated members with those for Kent and Surrey. Sir Henry Colt, presumably chairman, reported the bill with amendments on 26 May (286).

Fol. 7. L. 2. Leave out (but).
Fol. 8. L. 17. After[a] (seniority) add (of age).

Ordered, That Mr Hackshaw doe attend ye Comm^{ee} on Monday morning next.

Ordered, That M Scrimpshire[b] and Mrs Eliz. Scrimpshire do also then attend.

[fo. 31r.]
Mascall's Comm^{ee}.

Lune 23° Maij 1698.

The Comm^{ee} met and made a further progress in the Bill and then adj^{d} till tomorrow morning.[1]

[fo. 31v.] Veneris 6° die Maij 1698.

Sr J. Churchill Bill
At the Com^{ee} to whome the Bill to confirm the Sale of part of the estate of Sr John Chrchill Kn^{t} lattely deced pursuant to his last Will and two Decrees in Chancery for performance thereof is committed.[2]
Mr Yates in ye Chair.
The Comm^{ee} proceeded upon the Bill
F. 1. L. 1. Leave out (the said) and after (Churchill) add (late of Churchill in ye County of Somerset Kn^{t}.).

Adj^{d} till Monday 4 in ye afternoon.

Jovis 12° Maij 1698.

The Com^{ee} met and proceeded upon ye Bill: Sr John Churchill Will produced.
The probate of the will produced.
The Ld Chanc^{s} Decree for sale of ye estate sold.
Press 3. L. 20. Leave out (seaventh) and insert (ninth).
Pr. 4. L. 21. After[c]

Martis[d] 18° Maij 1698.

At ye Com^{ee} to whom ye Bill to enable John Jenkens[3]
The Comm^{ee} met and proceeded upon the Bill paragraph by paragraph.
Fo. 10. L. 11. Fill ye 1st blank wth (24th), the 2^{d} bla. wth (June 1698).[e]

[a] *Preceded by* sen *erased.* [b] *Between* Scrimp *and* shire *is* haw *erased.*
[c] *Followed by* (Chancery) add (soe farr as the same relate to or concern the sale of the said Mannor & Lands only) *erased.*
[d] *Should be* Mercurij. [e] *Above is written* in ye year of o *not erased.*

---

[1] There are no further minutes of this committee.
[2] Churchill's Estate Bill came down from the Lords on 15 April (208), and was read a second time and committed on 27 April (244) to a committee of 44 nominated members and all those for Somerset, to meet at 5 in the Speaker's Chamber. On 12 May all the members for Devon and Dorset were added (267). Mr. Yates reported the bill with one amendment on 14 May (269).
[3] Continued from fo. 23v., see p. 32, n. 4 above.

Fill ye bla. wth (John Cason, Cha. Bargrave Esq, [a] & John Bates [b]) mercht.

f. Fill y bla. wth

After (heires) add (Exs Adms & Assignes).

Fo. 11. L. ult. After (mortgage) add (wth such int as shall become due for ye sume).

[fo. 32r.]

At ye Commee to whome the the Bill for the better Explanacon of former Acts made agt Exportacon of Wooll is comitted.[1]

Martis 10o die Maij.

The Commee met and went thro' the Bill and made severall amendmts to the same.
A Clause was offered to be added to the Bill to prevent the exportacon of Teasles [c]: and upon debate of the said Clause it was moved, That Witnesses might be examined relateing thereto.[2]

Edwd Woodcote of Axbridge informed the Commee that abt 20 yeares since this Nacon was supplyed with teasles from France.

That he had advice from Holland by an eminent mercht that there are 1200 pecks of teasles bought up at Roan in France and some of them arrived at Rotterdam.

That the French teasles are better then the English and will yeild from 64 to 68 guilders a peck, and the mercht sayes they are alwayes esteemed 50£ p. cent better then the English.

A peck of teasles will dress abt 28 peices of cloth.

That 30 or 40 parishes abot Exbridge wch sowe nothing but teasles and many thousands of poor are thereby maintained.

John Hayes, Clothworker, saith that he has bought many pecks of French teasles and they are generally better then English teasles wch growes abot Somersetshire, but there are some wch grow near Newberry and Reading wch exceed some French.

That the French teasles were 3£ p. peck and he has known 7£ given, but since the great improvemt ye English have made of them they are brought down to a low ebb.

That ye French supplyes Holland wth vast quantityes.

That since our English teasles were exported they are cheaper then before.

Mr Woodcote saith that he has advice from France that they are able to supply all Europe with teasles.

[a] *Written above* gent. *erased.*
[b] *Followed by* gent *erased;* mercht *follows the closure of the bracket.*
[c] *Preceded by* Wooll *erased.*

---

[1] See fo. 15v. and p. 26, n. 3 above. None of the evidence taken and recorded on this folio and the next was reported to the House. For similar evidence about the illicit exportation of wool in the following session, see fos. 46v., 51r.–53r., etc.

[2] The committee had been granted power to send for persons, papers and records, see p. 26, n. 3.

[fo. 32v.]

Edward Anderson, being examined relateing to the exportacon of wooll to France said that great quantityes of wooll are dayly transported to France out of Sussex and in and near the Isle of Thannet in Kent wch might be prevented were there a sufficient number of Officers placed in those parts.

In Augt last being in compa with a seaman at St Margts wth a seaman at St Margts near Dover he told him he was lately come from Calais being a prisoner there abot two months dureing wch time there was brought into Calais near eight hundred packs of wooll.

Abt six weekes since being in compa wth Mr Hen. Allen, a messenger being in France tending upon the Ld Portland, the said Allen told him that he saw great quantityes of wooll brought into Calais, and that he was told there was near 100 packs of wooll brought thither every week.

About three weekes since being in compa in London with Capt. John Ellisdon, a Rideing Surveyor for Romney Marsh, he told me the week before he came to town he and his man took in the night time near Dungeness on the coast of Romney Marsh 17 packs of wooll just at the sea side goeing to be put on board a French boat.

Abot three weekes since Capt. Marsh who has comand of a Custome House smack he and his man took severall packs of wooll goeing to be put on board near the Isle of Oxney.

A letter was produced to the Comee directed to Capt. Goodwin from one Mr Pollard the substance whereof was,

that severall ships had gone from Ireland to France with wooll and from Scotland to France, and that some ships have taken in their wooll in Ireland designed for England according to their dockets and have come from Ireland into some part of England and have received a certificate that the said wooll was landed in England, soe their bonds in Ireland are cleared of course.

[fo. 33 r. and v. blank.]

[fo. 34r.] Jovis 12o die Maij 1698.

Mint Comee.[1]

The Comee met and Mr Hall produced (according to Ordr) an accot of silver ingots imprested to him at ye Excheq, for ye use of the Country Mints.

Mr Hall to give an accot of ye house money wch he has received to pay the 6d.

He also delivered an accot of the silver ingots & also ye 6d.[a]

3000£ more towards paying the importers in Mr Hall's hands.

2000£ in ye Excheq, &

2000£ more in Mr Foquier's hands.

Mr Hall is ordered to give an accot of wt he paid to every particular Mint, wch he did accordingly.

Mr Foquier delivered in to ye Comm an accot of what has been imprested to him.

[a] *On next line* 4000£ towards paying the importers *erased*.

---

[1] Continued from fo. 29v.

There [a] is 7000£ in ye hands of the Mint to be abated out of ye 2d wch was allowed for coynage 1000£ of wch is for ye private importers.
Money in ye hands of the Melter and in ye Moneyers' & Refiners' hands.
That by accots. produced by the Officers of the Mint there appeares to be due to private importers.

Veneris 13o die Maij 1698.

The Comee met and Mr Lo. moved that the officers might [b] give an accot of wt is due to ye Melters to ye Refiners & Moneyers.
Mr Neal accordingly gave in ye accot as foll. viz.

				£	s.	d.
Publick Money	5396726oz.	19dwt.	13gr.	6346.	0.	6
Private Money	847896			997.	0.	10
	6244622.	19.	13	7343.	1.	5

[fo. 34v.]
Mr Russell saith that out of ye 18000£ there is due to ye Moneyers 10000£.
The Moneyers have engaged to pay in ye Mas of ye Mint's hands the sum̃e of 7684. 17. 0 (being the ballance of what due to ye importers) in 3 dayes time.
The Refiners' ballance wch he is to make good is [1]

[fo. 35 r. and v. blank.]

[fo. 36r.]

Sword Hilts.[2]

Fol. 2. L. 6. Fill ye 1st bla, wth (24th), ye 2d bla, wth (June 1698).
L. 10. Fill ye bla, wth (the Coms of his Maty Customes for the time being or any five of them) and leave out (or such other persons as his Maty shall appoint for yt purpose).

At the end of the Bill add Clause (A).

At ye Commee appointed to draw up reasons to be offered to the Lords for disagreeing to the amendmt made by their Lordships to the engrossed Bill intituled An Act for the more Effectuall suppressing of Blasphemy and Profaneness.[3]

The Lords Amendmt to ye Bill was in ye 1st skinn Line the 13th & 14. Leave out (haveing been educated in or at any time haveing made profession of the Christian Religion).

[a] *Preceded by* M Foquier There *erased.* [b] *Preceded by* given (?) *erased.*

[1] Continued on fo. 36v.

[2] The single entry referring to this committee bears no date. On 22 January (58) leave was given to bring in a bill to explain an Act of 7 & 8 W. III to encourage bringing of plate to Mints, to remedy the ill state of the coinage and to give leave for exporting watches, sword-hilts and other manufactures of silver. On 2 May (250) the bill was read a second time and committed to a committee of 29 to meet at 5 in the Speaker's Chamber. Sir Thomas Mompesson reported the Exporting Watches Bill with amendments on 19 May (277). It became 9 & 10 W. III, c. 28.

[3] The Lords amendments to the Suppressing Profaneness, etc., Bill were considered on 18 May (276) after a division, and the first amendment was disagreed to. A committee of 23 was appointed to draw up reasons, to meet at 5 in the Speaker's Chamber. Courthope's minutes bear no date, but since eleven members were added to the committee on 19 May (276) and Sir John Philips reported the reasons as entered in the minutes on 21 May (280), the date of meeting was probably 20 or 21 May.

The Commee met and the reasons for disagreeing to the said amendmt were read and are as followeth, viz.
The Commons doe conceive that the 1st amendmt 1st skin L. 14, 15 [a] made by yoe Lordps will subject the Jews who live amongst us to all the paines and penaltyes contained in the Bill wch must therefore of necessity ruin them or drive them out of the Kingdom and cannot be thought was the intencon of yoe Lordps since here they have the meanes and opportunityes to be informed of and rightly instructed in the principles of the true Xtian Religion, for wch Reasons the Commons disagree wth yoe Lordps in the said amendmt.
Ordered, That Sr John Phillips doe report these Reasons to the House.

[fo. 36v.] Martis 18o [b] Maij 1698.

Chester Mint.[1]
Mr Hawley delivered in to ye Commee an accot of Chester Mint.

Debtr [c]	6564.	19.	1
Cr.	4722,	7.	4
Ballance	1842.	1.	9 [d]

Q. whether any part of ye 2500£ upon ye accot of utensils allowed for ye London Mints for [e] ye Moneyers be any part of ye Article of [f] 350 for Incident Charges.
In their former accot nothing was charged for tooles.
There is 1842£. 1s. 9d due to clear Chester Mint.
Exeter Mint.[g]
Mr Hayes delivered in an accot of Exeter Mint, whereby it appeared that there is due to clear Exeter Mint ye sume of 5000£.
The charge of coynage is reckoned as well to ye publick as private importers.
Mr Lo. The whole charge of coynage ought [h] to be deducted.
Mr Hayes, more money of private importers then King's money. 85000li.wt. coyned of private importers.
The Receivers were alowed 5s an ounce.
That there is abot 440£ [i] wch must be paid according to the severall appropriacons & must be [j] added to ye demands to Exeter Mint.
There will [k] remain to clear ye Mint at Exeter abt 5000£.
Q, why ye ingots are not brought to accot wch Mr Hall sent down to pay y 6d.
Mr Hayes. That wt was brought to ye Mint was paid out wt, for wt. & why ye 2700£ wch was imprest towards ye charge at Exeter Mint was not put into this accot.

[a] *Written above* 13, 14 *erased.*
[b] *Should be Mercurij 18 or Martis 17.*
[c] *Preceded by* Credr. *erased.*
[d] *Beneath this figure and the line drawn under it is written* 350, *and in the blank space higher up to the right* & 2 : *presumably notes for the ensuing para.*
[e] *Preceded by* claymed by *erased.*
[f] *Preceded by* in *erased.*
[g] *Followed by* D *erased.*
[h] *Written above* out *erased.*
[i] *Written above two erasures of other figures.*
[j] *Preceded by* ad *erased.*
[k] *Preceded by* is *erased.*

[1] Continued from fo. 34v.

[fo. 37r.] Jovis 26° Maij 1698.

The Com^{ee} met and Mr Hayes delivered in an acco^{t} of w^{t} is due to y^{e} Mint at Exeter wch is the sume of 5462$^{£}$. 18. 7^{d} due to make good the Mint at Exeter.
Resolved, That the sume of 3000$^{£}$ [a] is necessary to be first [b] provided to pay off the debt due to the private importers.
That there is a sume of 5462. 18. 7 due to make good the Mint at Exeter.
Mr Newton the Warden of the Mint delivered in to y^{e} Com^{ee} an acco^{t} of w^{t} is due to y^{e} Mint at Bristoll.
There is [c] 3000$^{£}$ due to y^{e} importers at Bristoll.
There is wanting to clear y^{e} whole Mint at Bristoll the sume of 2200 of wch 1500$^{£}$ is to be paid to private importers.
Mr Hall delivered in to y^{e} Com^{ee} an acco^{t} of Norwich Mint.
Nothing due to private importers at Norwich.
To clear y^{e} Mint at Norwich there is wanting 2737, 13^{s}. 0.
He also delivered in an acco^{t} of York Mint whereof

The totall D^{r} is . . . . . . 7850. 15. 0.
The totall Cred^{s} . . . . . . 7850. 15. 0.

1947$^{£}$ to pay y^{e} private & publick importers.
Ordered, That Mr Barton attend y^{e} Com^{ee} tomorrow night.
2500$^{£}$ to be provided to pay off y^{e} workmen in y^{e} sev^{ll} Mints.

Adj^{d} till tomorrow at 5 a clock in y^{e} [1]

[fo. 38 r and v. blank.]

[fo. 39r.]
Phamphlett.

Lune 23° die Maij 1698.

Att y^{e} Comm^{ee} appointed to examine into a printed pamphlet intituled The Case of Ireland being bound by the Acts of parl^{t} in England stated, and to report such passages as they doe find denying the authority of the parl^{t} of England.[2]

[a] *Written above* 4000$^{£}$ *erased.* [b] *Followed by* suppl *erased.*
[c] *Followed by* due *erased.*

[1] This is the last entry relating to the committee on hammered money.
[2] Privilege: Unconstitutional Pamphlet. On 21 May (281) complaint was made of passages denying the authority of the English Parliament in a printed pamphlet bearing the title given at the head of the minutes. A committee was appointed to examine the said pamphlet, and to inquire into the author thereof, and report such passages as they find denying the authority of the Parliament of England, and also what proceedings have been had in Ireland that might occasion the said pamphlet. There is a blank in the Journal where the names of the members nominated should have been entered. The House also resolved to present a humble address to the King desiring him to direct that an inquiry should be made into the author, so that he might be punished. The name of the author was Molyneux. Three members were added to the committee on 3 June (299), and on 22 June Mr. Boscawen's report was read and entered in full in the Journal (324–7). On 27 June (331) the House resolved that the book was of dangerous consequence to the Crown and people of England, and the same committee was ordered to draw up a humble address representing these matters to his Majesty. The address as amended was agreed to on 30 June (337). Courthope's minutes, covering sittings during the end of May and the first half of June, do not contain the committee's report.

Mr Buscawen in ye Chair.

The Commee met and part of the Book was read, viz. to ye 20th fol., and then the Commee adjd till tomorr. morning 8 a clock.

Lune 30o die Maij 1698.

Ordered, That the Clerk of the Crown doe lay before the said Commee on Wednesday morning next all Bills transmitted under the great Seal of Ireland since the late K. James' Reign wch have been considered at ye Counsell board in England and rejected or approved there.

Adjd till Wednesday morning next.

Mercurij 1o die Maij [a] 1698.

The Clerk of the Crown (according to Ords) attended & delivered to the Commee the Bills transmitted under the great Seal of Ireland into England since the late K. Jam: reign togeather wth a list thereof wch were ordered to be left in ye hands of the Clark attending ye Commee till the Comee had perused the same.

Jovis 2o die Maij [a] 1698.

The Commee being informed yt Mr Yard one of ye Cheif Clerks in ye Secretarye's Office hath in his custody or power the printed Votes of the parlt of Ireland of the last Session, and the Commee conceiveing the same may be of some service to them in this matter, it is therefore *Ordered*, That the said Mr Yard do tomorrow morning at 8 of the clock in ye Speaker's Chamber cause the said Votes of the last Session of the parliamt of Ireland to be laid before the said Commee in order to their perusal of the same.

Adjd till tomorrow morning.[1]

[fo. 39v.]

At ye Commee to whome the Peticon of severall workmen belonging to ye Victualling Office is referred.[2]

Mr Berty in ye Chair.

The Comms of ye Victualling Office to attend a Monday in ye afternoon.

Martis 31o die Maij 1698.

The Comee met and ye Peticon read.

The Pets to prove that there is 15 months wages due to them.

[a] *Error for* Junij.

---

[1] Continued on fo. 42r.

[2] Victualling Office Arrears. On 27 May (287) a petition of working coopers, brewers' servants, bakers' servants and labourers belonging to the Victualling Office in London was presented and read. It set forth that they had fifteen months' pay due to them, and that the Commissioners offered to pay them only three months' pay in salt tallies, by which they would lose four shillings in the pound, taking no account of their arrears for twelve months. It was at once referred to a committee of 42, with power to send for persons, papers and records, to meet at 5 in the Speaker's Chamber. There is no further entry in the Journal relating to this matter. Courthope's minutes therefore fill a gap, incomplete as they are, since they show that the committee got to work and heard the complaints of several petitioners. The date of the first meeting is not given. It may well have been 27 May.

The Com^{s} of ye Victualling Office deny that there is soe much due to them.

M Ja. Hoar, That there is 2 months due to him, wch is 4. 09. 00 wch was due in Jan. & Feb. last.

Mr Papillion,[1] That ye Com^{s} never meddle wth any money.

That by and ord^{r} from ye Lords of ye Treasury they are [a] to pay ye wages due before [b] ye 1st of May in Salt Tallyes.

That they moved that they might receive ye int. upon ye Salt Tallyes in their hands for ye paym^{t} of of the labourers because of their poverty.

John Wise, saith there is 13 months due to him, viz. Aug^{t}., Sept. to Jan., Feb., March, Ap., May.

The Com^{s} say there is but 11 months due to him.

Tho. Tindall That there is 13 months due to him.

Hen. Howman, That there is not above 8 months due to him wch ye Com^{s} owne.

Cha. Griffin, That there is 12 [c] months wages due to him wch ye Com^{s} admit.

Cha. Hoar, That there is 15 months due to him wch ye Com^{s} do not admitt. The Com^{s} say that he was [d] offered 2 months pay viz. July [e] & Augt., he refused, Aprill and May he received.

W^{m}. Beers, That there is 14 months due to him to ye last of Apr.[f] wch ye Com^{s} admitt.

M York, Clark to ye Cooperige, saith that he had 3 months wages in his hands wch Beers knew.

Mr Beers said that he did not know that Mr York had any in his hands.

Tho. Wishaw, That there is 8 months due to him wch ye Com^{s} doe admitt. That Mr Papillion told him that Mr York must sell their tallyes & they must allow the disco^{t}.

Mr Mayn, That they were comanded that they should pay in Salt Tallyes all the [g] debts contracted before ye 1st of May 1697.

[fo. 40r.]

Robt Gent, That there is abo^{t} 8 months due to him wch ye Com^{s} doe admit.

Dan^{ll} Gibb, That [h] there is 15 months due to him.

Mr Moor saith that he was offered 3 months in Tallyes & 2 in Excheq Bills.

[fo. 40v.]

At ye Comm^{ee} to whom ye Engrossed Bill for vesting in Tho. Rogers Gent. an absolute Estate of Inheritance in fee simple in ye Manno^{r} of West Court & other Lands in Kent.[2]

Mr Brewer in ye Chair.

[a] *Preceded by* have *erased*.
[b] *Written above* to *erased*.
[c] *Written above* month *erased*.
[d] he was *written above* they were *erased*.
[e] June *is written above the line*.
[f] *Written above* May *erased*.
[g] *Preceded by* that *erased*.
[h] *Preceded by* That he *erased*.

---

[1] Thomas Papillon, who became the chief commissioner in 1689; see *The Sergison Papers* (Navy Record Soc. 1950), p. 235.

[2] Rogers' Estate Bill came down from the Lords on 25 May (285), and was read a second time and committed on 30 May (291) to a committee of 41 nominated members with those for Kent, to meet at 5 in the Speaker's Chamber. Mr. Brewer reported the bill without amendment on 1 June (294).

Mercurij 1° die Junij 1698.

The Comm^{ee} met and the Bill read.
M^{s} Higons and her four daughters consented to ye Bill.
Sev^{ll} Deeds were examined & agreed wth the Recitall of the Bill.
Ordered, That Mr Brewer doe report the same to the House the first opportunity.

[fo. 41r.] Veneris [a] 3° die Junij 1698.

Ordered, That the Chairman doe write to Mr Southwell [b] to desire him to send to the Comm^{ee}.[1]

[fo. 41v.]
At y^{e} Comm^{ee} to whom the Bill for enabling Humphrey Trafford Esq. to raise 4000$^{£}$ upon his Estate for paym^{t} of his debts is comitted.[2]
Mr Brotherton in y^{e} Chair.

Jovis 9° die Junij 1698.

The Comm^{ee} met and proceeded upon the Bill.
Fol. 1. L. 2. Leave out (tenth) and insert (4th).
3. Leave out (said).
Mr Tho. Goodin proved y^{t} Edm^{d} & Cecill Trafford are dead wthout issue & y^{t} Humph. Trafford is ab^{t} 16 years of age.
Fol. 8. L. 13. Leave out (Descendants).
14. After the first (Trafford) add (deceased or either of them).

[fo. 42r.]
Pamphlett.[3]

Sabti 11° Junij 1698.

The Comm^{ee} met and the passages wch were taken out of Mr Molyneux' book were read and ordered to be reported to the House.
The Votes of the Parliam^{t} of Ireland in 1697 were delivered in to ye Comm^{ee} and left with the Clerk to be perused by the Members.
And then adj^{d} to Wednesday morning 8 a clock.

Mercurij 15° die Junij 1698.

The Comm^{ee} met, and Irish Votes of ye parl^{t} of 1697 were produced and some Ord^{s} read whereby it appeared that ye parl^{t} of Ireland doe prepare Bills and heads of Bills and order them to be read the 1st & 2^{d} time & then comit the same and

[a] *Preceded by* Jo *erased.* [b] *Written above an illegible word erased.*

---

[1] This fragmentary entry may refer to the committee on Molyneux' pamphlet, which adjourned on 2 June till the morrow (see fo. 39r.).
[2] Trafford's Estate Bill, after leave being given on 26 May (286), was presented by Mr. Brotherton on 30 May (291), and read a second time and committed on 6 June (301) to a committee of 41 nominated members with those for Lancs and Yorks, to meet at 5 in the Speaker's Chamber. On 11 June (309) Mr. Brotherton reported the bill with some amendments.
[3] Continued from fo. 39r., or possibly fo. 41r. (see n. 1 above).

report them with their amendmts [a] and use the same method and goe the same steps as the Parlt of England doe in prepareing their Bills.
Ordered, That some of ye passages in the Irish Votes be transcribed and reported to the House.
Ordered, That the Irish [b] Act for preservacõn of the King's person be laid before the Commee tomorrow morning.

And then adjd till tomorrow morning 8 a clock.

Jovis 16o die Junij 1698.

The Comee met and the passages wch were taken out of ye Irish Votes were read, and that part wherein Mr Molsworth was named was ordered to be struck out. The Irish Act for the preservacõn of the King's person was read, wch [c] was re-enacting part of the Articles [d] wch have been made in [e] Engld and for altering some other part of it.
That Bills have been transmitted from Ireland into England to re-enact Laws made in England to bind Ireland and to make alteracons in the same.

Adj till tomorrow morning.[1]

[fo. 42v.]
London Derry Address.[2]

Jovis 15o [f] die Junij 1698.

The Commee met and the Order read.
The Address ought to be made generall not only for the City of London Derry only but for [g] officers and other persons that had come into ye Town and ventured their lives in defence of the same.[h]

Adjd till Saturday morning 8 a clock.

[fo. 43r.]
Pamphlet.

Veneris 17o Junij 1698.

The Commee met and proceeded to take an accot of some part of [i] Irish Acts wch have been transmitted into England [j] [3]
[fos. 43v., 44 r. and v., and 45 r. and v. blank.]

[a] same . . . amendmts *written above the line, one illegible word being erased after* the.
[b] *Preceded by* A *erased.*
[c] *Preceded by* That *erased.*
[d] part . . . Articles *written above* Laws *erased.*
[e] *Followed by an illegible word erased.*
[f] *Should be* 16o.
[g] *Preceded by* th *erased, and followed by* those *erased with* the Governos *erased above* those, officers & other *written above* that had.
[h] *Preceded by* said City *erased.*
[i] *Followed by* of the *erased.*
[j] *Followed by* and are Re w *erased except for the isolated* w.

---

[1] Continued on fo. 43r.
[2] See p. 19, n. 1.
[3] This is the last entry in Courthope's minutes for the session, which ended on 5 July.

[fo. 46r.] Mercurij 21o die Decembris 1698.

At ye Commee to whome the Bill for continueing a Former Act for ye cleering, preserving, maintaining and repairing the Haven and Peer of Great Yarmouth in ye County of Norfolk, is comitted.[1]
Yarmouth Peer.
The Commee met and adjd till tomorrow 5 a clock post meridiem

Jovis 22o die Dec. 1698.

Fol. 2. L. 9. Leave out (for) and fill the blank wth (from & after the 24th day of July wch shall be in the year of our Lord 1699).
10. Leave out (from and after) and fill the blank wth (for 21 [a] yeares and to the end of the then next Session of parliamt).
Fol. 3. L. 5. Fill the blank wth (twelve pence).
12. Fill the blank wth (21 yeares and to ye end of the then next Session of parliamt).
Fol. 4. L. 9.[b] Fill the blank wth (twelve).[c]
12. Fill the blank wth (three).[d]
14. Fill the bla. wth (three).[d]
Fill the bla, wth (twelve).[c]
Fill ye bla, wth (three).[d]
Fill the bla, wth (twelve).[c]
Fill the bla, wth (three).[d]
Fill ye bla, wth (five).
Fill ye bla, wth (five).
Fill ye bla, wth (five).
Fill ye bla. wth (one).
Fill the bla. wth (two pence).
Fol. 7. L. 3. After (Haven) add (or Road).
7. Fill ye first bla, wth (one), ye 2d bla, wth (one).
12. Fill ye bla. wth (ten).[2]

[fo. 46v.] Lune 9o die Jan. 1698.

[a] *Written above* 14 (?) *erased.* [b] *Written above* 9 & *erased.*
[c] *Written above* eight *erased.* [d] *Written above* two *erased.*

---

[1] Yarmouth Harbour Bill, after leave given on 17 December 1698 (358), was presented on 19 December (359) and on 21 December (360) committed to a committee of 37 nominated members and the members for (here a blank in the Journal). No order as to meeting occurs in the Journal, but since the committee met on the day the bill was committed, the usual order was presumably made. On 25 January Mr. England, who had presented the bill and was presumably chairman of the committee, reported the bill with several amendments (449), whereupon the bill was recommitted to the committee, who were to meet at 5 in the Speaker's Chamber. On 7 February Mr. England reported the re-committed bill with several amendments. It was eventually passed and became 10 & 11 W. III, c. 5 (see p. 53, n. 3 below).
[2] Continued on fo. 46v., see p. 53, n. 3.

At ye Comm^{ee} to whom the peticōn of ye Inhabitants of ye Town of Taunton and parts adjacent relateing to the Exportacōn of Wooll, is referred.[1]

The Comm^{ee} met and made choice of Sr Robert Davers for their Chairman.

And then adj^{d} till tomorrow 3 in ye afternoon.[2]

Lune 6° die Feb. 1698.[3]

Fol. 2. L. 5. After (preserved) add (and ye channell of y^{t} part of ye river leading from Great Yarmouth aforesd to ye City of Norwich called Brayden depthned & made more navigable for boats & keels usually passing the same).

Fol. 3. L. 6. After (Comonalty) insert (of ye said Borough).

Fol. 4. L. 3. After (the) insert (said).

8. After (piers) insert (and depthning the chanell aforesaid).

Fol. 4. L. 9. Leave out (from time to time).

Fol. 5. 1 & 2. Leave out (Aldrēn & Comons) and insert (Sheriffs Citizens & Comonalty).

7. Fill ye blank wth (number of y^{m} 5 being of ye Countyes of Norfolk, Suffolk & City of Norwich), & leave out (or more of y^{m}).

12. The same amendm^{t}.

14. The same amendm^{t}.

Fol. 6. L. 10. Fill ye bla. wth (sixpence).

[fo. 47r.]

Fol. 7. L. 12. Leave out (wthin) & insert (for).

[1] Exporting Wool. For a committee on much the same subject, see fo. 32r. and p. 26, n. 3 above: also on the illicit export of wool and the endeavours of the clothiers to prevent it, see E. Lipson, *Economic History of England* (2nd ed., 1934), iii. 23–34. The petition from Taunton, the substance of which is left blank in the Journal, was presented and read on 17 December 1698 (358). A committee was at once appointed 'to consider of ways for the better preventing the exportation of wool from England and Ireland into foreign parts, and to consider of the most proper methods to encourage the woolen manufactures of this Kingdom'. The committee was nominated of 34 members with all those for Devon, Somerset, Wilts, Southampton, Worcestershire, Gloucestershire and Yorks to meet at 5 in the Speaker's Chamber and to have power to send for persons, papers and records. They were also instructed to inquire what proceedings had been had in the Parliament of Ireland, since the last session, in relation to woollen and linen manufactures. The Taunton petition was referred to the committee. A further instruction was given to the committee on 20 December (360), to examine and inquire into the nature of the licences for exporting wool from Ireland, and the bonds given in relation thereto, and how they had been prosecuted, and how they might be more effectually prosecuted. Between 5 January and 27 February several more petitions from towns in the clothing counties were presented and referred to the committee (387, 423, 513, 516, 518, 530). The meeting of the committee on 9 January—more than three weeks after they had been ordered to meet—was obviously the first, since the choice of chairman is recorded. Sir Robert Davers reported the heads of a bill on 28 February (532), most of which were agreed; the bill was brought in and eventually became the Act 10 & 11 W. III, c. 10.

[2] Continued on fo. 51r. under date 18 January. There is no entry of any meeting on 10 January.

[3] No heading is given, except the date, to these proceedings, the contents of which show that they relate to the Yarmouth Harbour Bill. Moreover, they must be proceedings of the committee on re-committal of the bill, since the report on recommittal was made the following day, see p. 52, n. 1 above.

At ye end of ye Bill add Clauses A. B & C.[1]

[fo. 47 v.]
At ye Comm^ee^ to whom the Bill for makeing the River Tone navigable from Bridgwater to Taunton in the County of Somerset, is committed.[2]
Mr Clark in ye Chair.

Lune 16° die Jan. 1698.

The Bill was read over.[a]
Deed dat^d^ 4th March 1697.
A Deed was produced and read being a Conveyance of the Earl of Sandwich & his Countess & others unto John Freind in consideracõn of [b] 330^£^ by him pd to them of the Letters pattents formerly granted to John Mallet.

Then was produced and read over Articles of Agreem^t^ made ye 11th Nov. 1698 betw. John Freind of ye one part, Tho. Baker & others of ye other part, whereby the said John Freind doth declare That ye aforesaid purchase of ye Lett^s^ patents & right of navigacõn [c] & his name was used in trust only for all ye partyes menconed in ye said Articles of Agreem^t^.

Then the preamble was read over and agreed to stand [d] part of the Bill.[3]

And then ye Com^ee^ adj^d^ till Wednesday next 4 in ye afternoon.[4]

Veneris 20 die Jan. 1698.

The Com^ee^ met.
Fol. 2. L. 22. Leave out (any) and fill ye bla, w^th^ (the major part).
Fol. 3. L. 21. The same amendm^t^.
Fol 4. L. 1. The same amendm^t^.
6. Fill the bla. w^th^ (it shall and may be lawfull to and for the Sheriffe

[a] *Followed by* and the preamble agreed to *erased*.
[b] *Followed by some figures erased.*
[c] *Followed by* was *erased*. [d] *Written above* be made *erased*.

---

[1] This entry clearly completes the proceedings on the re-committed Yarmouth Harbour Bill.

[2] Tone Navigation Bill. On 16 December 1698 a petition was read from the inhabitants of Taunton praying for leave to bring in a bill for making the river Tone navigable from Bridgwater to Taunton, for the carriage of sea-coal and other heavy goods (355). Leave was given, and Mr. Clark presented the bill on 5 January (386). On 10 January (391) a motion to commit the bill to a committee of the whole House was negatived and it was committed to a committee of 34 nominated members with those for Devon, Somerset and Dorset, to meet at 5 in the Speaker's Chamber. A motion that all who come have voices was negatived. Petitions in favour of the bill were presented on 17 and 19 January (423, 441). Mr. Clark reported the bill with amendments on 25 January (449), and it eventually passed both Houses.

[3] These minutes give very few instances of any decisions of a committee regarding the preamble of a private bill. By modern standards it would be incorrect for a committee to agree to the preamble, which contains the allegations on which the bill is based, or to resolve that it stand part of the bill: they must by standing order report whether or no the allegations of the preamble have been proved.

[4] There is no entry of any meeting on this day (18 January). The proceedings of this committee continue from 20 January on this folio without interruption till they are completed at the top of fo. 49v.

for ye time being of ye sd County, and the said Sheriffe is hereby authorized & required either in person or by his Under Sheriffe wthin 30 dayes after request by ye sd Conservators or ye major part of ym to him for yt purpose made in writeing & at ye cost & charges of ye said Conservators by a Jury of 24 Indifferent men of ye neighbourhood neither interested in ye said Undertaking nor in any of ye sd lands thro' wch ye said river now is or shall be made navigable and by examining witnesses upon oath in ye presence of ye sd Jury wch ye sd sheriff or Under Sheriff is hereby empowered to administer, and upon hearing ye partyes interested or any of them or on default of their appearance at such enquiry without hearing them).[a]

10. Fill the bla, wth (twenty).
17. Fill ye bla. wth (Jury or the major part of them).
Fol. 5. L. 1.[b] Fill ye bla. wth (the [c] major part [d]),
Fol. 5. L. 2. Fill ye bla. wth (Jury [e] or ye major part of them).
3. Fill ye bla. wth (four).

[fo. 48r.]
Fol. 5. L. 7.[f] After (persons) add (or at his her or their dwelling house or usuall place of abode).
9. Fill [g] ye bla. wth (ye major part).
15. Fill ye bla. wth (Jury or ye major part of them).
17. The same amendmt.
24 & 25.[h] Leave out (and [i] a reasonable time allowed them therein for their appearance).
ult. Fill ye bla. wth (Jury or the major part of them),
Fol. 6. L. 3. Fill ye bla. wth (the major part).
15. Fill ye bla. wth (six).
16. After (p. cent) add (p, ann).
20. Fill ye bla. wth (the major part).
22. Fill ye bla. wth (four pence).

Adjd. to Monday 4 in ye afternoon.

Lune 23° die Jan. 1698.

Fol. 6. L. 23. Fill ye bla. wth (48 bushells by heap of ye measure now used at Bridgwater wch is equall in quantity to two chalders or 72 bushells Winchester measure by heap and also in like manner).
24. Fill ye bla. wth (two pence).[j]

[a] *Followed by two lines erased, viz.* 7. Leave out (w), 8. Leave out (are hereby empowered).
[b] *Preceded by* L *erased.*
[c] *Preceded by* or *erased.*
[d] *Followed by* of them *erased.*
[e] *Preceded by* the said *erased.*
[f] *Above this line is written* Fol. 5. L. 9 Fill ye bla. wth *erased.*
[g] *Preceded by* Leave out (any) *erased.*
[h] *Preceded in margin by* ult. *above* 24 *both erased.*
[i] *Written above* in *partially erased.*
[j] *The line above:* 24. Fill ye bla. wth *erased.*

Fol. 7. L. 1. Fill ye bla. w^th (at a certain place [a] on ye said river comonly call or know by ye name of Knap: Bride or Bridges).[b]

3. Fill ye bla. w^th (or either).

4. Fill ye bla. w^th (stop arrest or detain such boat, barge or vessel wth all its apparrell & tackle and all ye coales, goods, wares & merchandizes laden in or on ye same).

. Fill ye bla. w^th (four pence).

6. Fill ye bla. w^th (two pence).

Fol. 7. L. 10. Fill ye bla. w^th (the first or lowermost lock that shall be built or made on ye said river above a certain house or place near the said Ham Mill comonly called or known by the name of Coal Harbour).

[fo. 48 v.]

River Tone.[c]

Fol. 7. L. 11. Fill ye bla. w^th (four shillings).

12. After (vessell) add (wch shall be from time to time set & appointed by ye sđ Conservators or the major part of them).

13. And in ye same line after (also) add (in like manner).

13. Fill ye bla. w^th (2^s).

15. Fill ye bla. w^th (lock soe to be built or made).

18. Fill ye bla. w^th (stopp arrest or detaine such boat barg or vessell wth all its apparrell & tackle & all ye coals goods wares & merchandize laden in or on ye same).

19. Fill ye bla. w^th (4^s).

20. Fill ye bla. w^th (2^s).

Fol. 8. L. 4. Fill ye bla. w^th (the major part).

5. Fill ye bla. w^th (one shilling).

8. Fill ye bla. w^th (first or uppermost lock y^t shall be built or made on ye sđ river next ye said Town of Taunton).[d]

10. Fill ye bla. w^th (or either).

11. Fill ye bla. w^th (stop [e] arrest or [f] detain such boat barge or vessell with all its apparrell & tackle & all ye coals goods wares & merchandize laden in or on ye same).

13. Fill ye bla. w^th (one shilling).

22. Fill ye bla. w^th (one penny).

23. The same amendm^t.

Fol. 9. L. 2. Fill ye bla. w^th (Knap [g] Bridge or Bridges).

3. Fill ye bla. w^th (one shilling).

[a] *Followed by* comonl *erased.*

[b] *Followed by* 3. Leave out (any) & fill ye bla. w^th *on fresh line erased.*

[c] *Following these words are* At ye Comm^ee to whom ye Peticon̄ of Tho. Chute Esqr. Clerk of the Crown is referred setting forth that all Writts *erased, and underneath them in the margin* Com^ee on Mr Chute's Peticon̄ *erased.*

[d] *Followed by* & leave out (*illegible word*) *erased.*

[e] *Preceded by* to *erased.* [f] *Preceded by small illegible erasure.*

[g] *Preceded by* at *erased.*

4\. Fill ye bla. wth (six pence).
7\. Fill ye bla. wth (the first or lowermost lock yt shall be built or made on ye said river above the said place comonly [a] called or know by the name of Coal Harbour aforesaid).

[fo. 49r.]
Fol. 10. L. 9. After (hale up) insert (boats barges & other vessells).
Fol. 10. L. 21. Fill ye bla. wth (The Rt Reverend the Lord Bp̄p̄ of Bath & Wells [b] for ye time being and the Justices of ye peace for [c] ye said County for ye time being).
23\. Fill ye bla. wth (seaven).
24\. Fill ye 1st bla. wth (ten), ye 2d bla. wth (three).
26\. Fill ye bla. wth (Lord Bp̄p̄ & Justices).
Fol. 11. L. 1. Fill ye bla. wth (seaven).
13\. Fill ye 1st bla. wth (twenty fourth), ye 2d bla. wth (June).
14\. Fill ye bla. wth (Ld Bp̄p̄ & Justices).
15\. Fill ye 1st bla. wth (seaven), ye 2d bla. wth (one month).
16\. Fill ye bla. wth (Ld Bp̄p̄ & Justices), ye 2d bla. wth (seaven).
23\. Fill ye 1st bla. wth (Ld Bp̄p̄ & Justices), ye 2d bla. wth (seaven).
24\. Fill ye bla. wth (Ld Bp̄p̄ & Justices).
25\. Fill ye bla. wth (seaven).
Fol. 12. L. 12. Fill ye bla. wth (the major part).
14\. Fill ye bla. wth (twenty).
16\. Fill ye bla. wth (six), and after (notice) add (in [d] writeing to be affixed on [e] ye Market Cross in ye sd̄ Town of Taunton [f] whereof proclamac̄on shall be then made in open market).
16\. Fill ye bla. wth (the major part).[g]
17\. Fill ye bla. wth (other).
19\. Fill ye bla. wth -thirty).
25\. Fill ye bla. wth (major), yr 2d bla. wεh (five).
26\. Fill ye bla. wth (major).
Fol. 13. L. 11. Fill ye bla. wth (major).
25\. Fill ye 1st bla. wth (Ld Bp̄p̄ & Justices), ye 2d bla. wth (seaven).
Fol. 14. L. 3. Fill ye bla. wth (ten [h] dayes).
10\. Fill ye bla. wth (major).
11\. Fill ye bla. wth (ye major part of ye whole number then liveing).

[fo. 49v.]
River Tone.
Fol. 14. L. 25. Fill ye bla. wth (double).

(*Here a line drawn across the page.*)

[a] *The last five words written above* near ye said Town of Taunton *erased.*
[b] *Followed by* & the Justices *erased.*
[c] *Written above* of *erased.*
[d] *Preceded by* as *erased.*
[e] *Written above* at *erased.*
[f] *Followed by* and *erased.*
[g] *Followed by two lines erased, viz.* 17. Fill ye bla. wth (one), & after (person) add (or persons). 19. Fill ye bla. wth (thirty).
[h] *Preceded by* T *erased.*

At ye Commee to whome the Peticõn of Tho. Chute Esqr., Clerk of ye Crown, is referred.[1]

The Commee met and the Peticõn read.

Mr Chute said, That ye Course has been to have the [a] returnes made to ye Clerk of ye Crown at ye day mencõned in ye Writt & wthin 2 or 3 dayes after, but this parlt some [b] returnes have been brought to him 2 or 3 months after & brought by boys and porters.

That he has a small fee of 2s. for a Burgess and 4s. for a Knt of ye Shire for ye fyleing the return.

That there is but 3 days time now allowed for ye Cinq; Ports for delivering the [c] precepts.

That ye returnes should be made by ye Sherriffe himself or some other creditable person.

That in K. Ja. 1st time ye fees of all officers were setled.

That by ye late Act of parlt ye fee of 4s. for a Knt of ye Shire & 2s. for a Burgess is taken away.

That ye time for delivering ye precepts to ye Warden of ye Cinq; Ports ought to be 6 days whereas now 3 dayes are allowed.

Mr Lo: That ye Sheriffe shall be obliged to returne ye Writt by ye day of ye return or within 10 days under a penalty.

Mr Chute says that this parlt sevll returns have come to him open.[d]

To report ye matter wth their opinions.

Adjd till Saturday morning.[e]

[fo. 50r.]

Upon Mr Chute's Peticõn.

[a] *Followed by* Writts *erased.*
[b] *Preceded by* they have not *erased.*
[c] *Preceded by* Writts *erased.*
[d] *Preceded by* oppen *erased.*
[e] *In the margin* Mr Turner for ye Cinq; Ports *erased.*

[1] The date of this entry is not given: but since the committee adjourned till Saturday, 4 February, it must have been one day in the week beginning Monday, 30 January. The petition of Thomas Chute, Clerk of the Crown, was presented and read on 10 January (390). It is set out at length in the Journal, and it complained of irregularities in the delivery of returns of elections to the petitioner, and to the loss of his fees. The petition was referred to a committee of 39 to examine the matters and report their opinion, to meet at 5 in the Speaker's Chamber, and to have power to send for persons, papers and records. They were also instructed to consider of enlarging the time allowed for delivering the precepts in the Cinque Ports for the election of members. On 21 January all the members for the Cinque Ports were added. Mr. Clark, whose chairmanship of the committee is just recorded by Courthope, made a report to the House on 6 February (484). This report, as entered in the Journal, contains much more than the three resolutions entered in the minutes, namely, the findings of fact upon which they were based. It is strange that Courthope made no allusion to that part of the report, which must have been formally agreed to by the committee. On the report being agreed to by the House, a bill was ordered to be brought in upon the resolutions, and to provide that the officers of cities, boroughs and Cinque Ports made their returns to the sheriffs, and the sheriffs their returns to the Clerk of the Crown, in a reasonable time. Mr. Clark who, with two other members, had been ordered to prepare the bill presented it on 18 February. This was the Elections, Preventing Irregularities Bill, and on 21 February (521) it was committed to a committee of 36, to meet on the following day at 8 a.m. in the Speaker's Chamber. Mr. Clark reported the bill with some amendments on 6 March (522), and it became the Act 10 & 11 W. III, c. 7. See pp. 59, 70.

Sabti 4o die Feb. 1698.

The Commee met and the Report was read paragraph by paragraph, and ye Comee came to this Resolucõn upon ye 1st head.

Resolved, That the only way to prevent these mischeifs is to [a] enforce the antient course of returnes [b] of members to serve in Parl by the Sheriffes [c] or other proper Officers of their Deputyes who are obliged to make such returnes. ('agreed' *in margin.*)

The 2d head.

Resolved &c, That the time for issueing and delivery of precepts in the Cinq, Ports be inlarged [d] to six dayes.

To ye 3d head.

Resolved, That the antient fee paid to the Clerk of the Crowne be paid as formerly and that the Sheriffs and other Officers obliged to make such returnes be allowed the same upon their account [e] in ye Excheq, and elsewhere.

[fo. 50v.]

At ye Comee to whom the Bill for pŕeventing Irregular proceedings of Sheriffes and other Officers in makeing ye Returnes of Members chosen to serve in Parliamt is comitted.

Mr Clark in the Chair.[1]

Mercurij 22o die Feb. 1698.

The Commee met and adjd to Fryday.[2]

[fo. 51r.]

Wooll.

Mercurij 18o die Jan. 1698.

At ye Commee appointed to consider of wayes for ye better preventing the Exportacõn of Wooll from England & Ireland into foreign parts and to consider of ye most proper methods to encourage ye woollen manufactures of this Kingdom.[3]

[a] *Followed by* to L *erased.*

[b] of returnes *is written above the line, and* course *is followed by* by obliging the Sheriffe or his Deputy to (*followed by* Re *erased*) make the returnes to the Clerk of the Crown *erased.*

[c] *Followed by* or his Deputy *erased.*

[d] *Followed by* by allowing three dayes *erased.*

[e] *Followed by* ing *erased, with* ts *erased above the line.*

---

[1] See preceding note. The committee met on the day ordered.

[2] Continued on fo. 59v. under date 24 February. It is typical of Courthope's haphazard methods that he should have allowed so many folios to intervene between two consecutive meetings of a committee.

[3] Continued from fo. 46v., see p. 53, n. 1. From this point for nine folios, with a long interruption after the fifth, we get the heads of the extensive evidence heard before the committee on the exportation of wool with regard to the smuggling of wool out of the country and the measures recommended to stop it (cf. the evidence given in the previous session by Mr. Anderson on fo. 32v.). None of this evidence was reported to the House, so that its details supply new information. Professor Lipson (*op. cit.* on p. 53, n. 1) mentions Mr. Carter as an inveterate foe of the 'owling' trade which he pursued in several pamphlets exposing their practices. The petitions mentioned at the beginning of the proceedings on 20 January were read and referred to the committee on 17 January (423).

Mr. Cary proposes [a] to have all wooll brought to be registred & to set up work-houses to settle a generall Credit & the wooll to be brought into publick storehouses. *Ordered,* That Mr Cary doe attend ye Commee on Fryday morning and bring his proposalls in writeing for ye better preventing ye exportacōn of wooll.

Veneris 20o Jan. 1698.

The Commee met and the Peticōn from Cirencester & anoth from ye Clothiers of Gloucshire were [b] read.
Mr Cary delivered his proposalls wch were read.
Mr Carter appeared and delivered [c] some heads for a Bill.
Mr Devereux appeared and said the great incouragemt is given to ye Officers on ye coast for to connive at ye exportacōn of wooll so that they let vast quantityes be run.
That it is easy to send 10000 packs of wooll in despite of all ye Officers.
That ye Officers imployed there are very remiss and negligent.
That if vessells were constantly sent out upon the coast, it would prevent the exportacōn of wooll. Small vessells are more convenient in this place.
That within this six weeks there has been 4 times wooll carryed into France.
Ordered, That Mr Devereux bring what he has to say in writeing.
Mr Benry appeared, That he had returned out of ye West of England & observed some abuses in relacōn to ye wooll.
That fisherboats carry away great quantityes wool ready combed near Topsham & other parts in ye West.
At Tinmouth & sevll other parts where wool is carryed off

[fo. 51v.]
That no boat should goe out not above but to bring a certificate how [d] they have disposed of their fish, for under pretence of fishing [e] they carry vast quantityes of wooll.
Mr Blanch saith that in Flanders they are now under consideracōn of discourageing our woollen manufactures, upon consideracōn that their lynnens are discouraged here in England.
Mr Doyly appeared & proposed that if people were obliged to be marryed in woollen as they are when they are buryed, it would make a great consumpcōn of ye woollen manufactures.
Another proposall wch was delivered in by [f] Mr Jervoise a Member of ye House wch was sent him from Romsey.

6. agreed.[g] That ye Clause in ye Act of ye last parliamt relateing to buying wooll in Kent and Sussex within 15 miles of the sea may be made generall to all persons within 15 miles of the sea & of ye borders of Scotland in all Countyes.
7. agreed.[g] That if any wooll, fullers' clay or scouring [h] clay be found on board any vessell, the Master of the ship shall be adjudged to be the exporter, and the

[a] *Preceded by* Mr Cary *erased.*
[b] *Preceded by* wch *erased.*
[c] *Preceded by* acq *erased.*
[d] *Written above* what *erased.*
[e] *Preceded by* carrying *erased.*
[f] *Written above* to *erased.*
[g] *In the margin.*
[h] *Written above* &c. *erased.*

ship forfeited, unless he shall in a time to be lymitted make known ye person that shipped or ordered ye same to be shipped.

disagreed.[a] That whereas great quantityes of wooll in many places within 20 miles of the sea is washed & combed fitt for spinning and is sold and disposed without being converted into cloth by the persons by or for whom the same is so washed and combed, That some expedient may be found that such persons may be obliged to make entryes of such quantityes as they comb and not to sell or dispose of it without a certificate as in case of fleece wooll in ye foremenconed Act.

Mercurij 25° die Jan 1698.

The Commee mett and Mr Haynes[b]

Mr Jobson, That ye delay of armeing ye sloops wch was delayed near a 12 month was a great prejudice to ye preventing wooll.

That Mr Edwards imployed by them has been much discouraged by some Officers of ye Customes.

[fo. 52r.]

Mr Jobson, That abot Malden in Essex great quantityes of wooll is exported.
Necessary to have some officers to be imployed to look after ye exportac̄on of wooll.
To have ye offenders transported.
That they have sent[c] out a sloop comanded by one Edwards wch has cost them abot 1000£ in fitting out.
That vast quantityes of wooll are exported from Whitehaven to Scotland & from thence to Rotterdam.
That ye persons to be employed by ye merchts will undertake to prevent ye exportac̄on of wooll for half ye charge that ye King is now at for ye same.

Mr Busfield, That it is necessary to have a fund settled for ye imploying officers to prevent ye exportac̄on of wooll.

Ordered, That ye Secretary of[d] ye Admiralty do give an accot of what Men of War and other vessells have been imployed to prevent ye exportac̄on of wooll & what the charge hath been for that same.

The like to ye Coms of ye Customes.

Adjd to Fryday morning next.

Veneris 27° die Jan. 1698.

Mr Burket (according to Ords.) delivered in to ye Comee from ye Admiralty Office an accot of what ships and vessells are employed in cruizing pursuant to a late Act of parliament for preventing ye exportac̄on of wooll, wth ye yearly charge of each of the said shipps and vessells for wages, victualls, wear and tear, exclusive of ye charge of ye Office of Ordnance, wch was read.

Capt. Baker appeared and according to Ords delivered in to ye Comee an accot of wt seizures have been made by vertue of his comission to prevent ye exportac̄on of wooll.

[a] *In the margin.*
[b] *Preceded by* An *erased.*
[c] *Preceded by* be *erased.*
[d] *Preceded by* doe g *erased.*

That he has been employed in this service near 2 yeares. That within this 2 years there has been seized in Kent & Sussex 450 packs. That he will undertake to break ye neck of that trade upon ye coast of Kent & Sussex.
That he has given ords to prosecute sevll persons for exporting of wooll & smugling of silks & lace.

[fo. 52v.]
Wooll.
That he has 30 persons in execucōn: and above 200 unds prosecucōn, and a verdict agt 80.
That ye Gaol at Dover Castle is not in a condicōn to hold offends.
Mr Sanson (according to Ords) delivered in to ye Comee an Accot of the Sloops established on ye coast of Kent, as also an Accot of all Wooll imported from Ireland pursuant to ye late Act of parlt, as also,
a Warrant from ye Treasury for ye stacōns on ye coast [a] and ye Comands, as also a Copy of Instruccōns from ye Coms of ye Customes to ye Comander.
Capt. Baker, called in again, said, that there has been verdicts obtained to ye amot of 12000£ some whereof is paid in.
That 30 are now unds execucōn.
Since wch there has been seizures to ye amot of 5000£.
There are above 200 persons now under process.
There are 80 persons that are ready to be brought to tryall.
That he desires that a Clause may be enacted to this effect, viz.

> That whoever shall transgress agt ye Act of 12o Car. 2d for prohibiting ye exportacōn of wooll or of any subseqt Act relateing to ye exportacōn of wooll shall be prosecuted in any suit or informacōn & a Capias shall issue out ye first process specifyeing ye penalty sued for & ye offender shall give bayl by English men to ye Officer executeing ye process to answer such suit, and shall at ye time of such appearance give good security in ye sd Court to answer & pay the forfeiture incurred for such offence in case he shall be convict.

That he has gone thro' ye coast of Kent & Sussex and he has observed that ye Officers of ye Customes in those parts doe drive the smugling & owling trade themselves.
That he has some people wch gives him an accot, that a great many English boats wth English men [b] carry wooll there, that ye Gravesend boat carry wooll there.
8.[c]
He proposes yt a [d] Clause may be made, That any Englishman carrying English or Irish wooll into France or other foreign parts in any English vessells

[fo. 53r.] of 30 tunns or unds shall forfeit [e] , & ye person in France that informes of this practice shall be sufficient evidence.

Adjd to Tuesday morning 8 a clock.

[a] *Followed by* of Kent *erased.*
[b] *Followed by* Bring in Woo *erased.*
[c] *Written in margin preceding* He *in next line.*
[d] *Preceded by* any Eng *erased.*
[e] *Followed by a blank space.*

Martis 31° die Jan. 1698.

Mr Carter appeared and acquainted y^{e} Com^{ee}, That he had something to propose. That y^{e} duty laid on wooll in Ireland be taken off 1$^{s.}$ 3$^{d.}$ a stone laid for y^{e} K. 4^{d} a stone for y^{e} Service of y^{e} Governo^{r} for his lycence.
Mr Davis [a] delivered in his proposalls for encourageing y^{e} woollen manufactures.
Mr Anderson delivered his proposalls in writeing wch were read.

Adj^{d} Fryday 5 in y^{e} afternoon.[1]

Martis 7° Feb. 1698.

The Comm^{ee} met and Mr Devereux delivered in his proposall wch was read.
Mr Busfield desired that a fund might be setled for defraying the charge to prevent ye exportac̃on of wooll; he produced lett^{s} from Deal giveing an acco^{t} of a hoy being seized.
Mr Lomb delivered a proposall in writeing.
Ordered, That Capt. Baker do give an acco^{t} to ye Com^{ee} what quantityes of wooll have been seized in Kent and Sussex since he has been imployed, by whom seized, and where and what prosecuc̃ons have been thereon, what money he has received out of ye Treasury for that service, and what money has been paid into the Excheq, recovered upon those prosecuc̃ons.

Adj^{d} to Fryday 4 in ye afternoon.[2]

[fo. 53v.] Jovis 2° die Feb. 1698/9.

Sr John Manwareing in ye Chair.
At ye Comm^{ee} appointed to draw up an Address to be presented to his Ma^{ty} to give him thanks for his most gracious Speech to both Houses.[3]

The Comm^{ee} met and ordered that ye Chairman should prepare an Address and present ye same to ye Com^{ee} tomorrow morning.

And then adjourned till tomorrow morning 9 a clock.

Veneris 3° die Feb. 1698/9.

The Comm^{ee} met, the Address was read twice over & agreed to wth some amendm^{ts}.

Ordered, That ye same be reported to ye House.

[fo. 54r.]
Tho. Foley Esqr in ye Chair.

[a] *Preceded on line above by* Mr Harg *erased.*

---

[1] There is no entry of any meeting on this day.

[2] There is no entry of a meeting on Friday, 10 February. The proceedings continue on fo. 57v. under date Thursday, 16 February.

[3] On 1 February (468) the House agreed that a humble address of thanks for the King's speech should be presented, and the drafting was referred to the Chancellor of the Exchequer and 35 members, to meet on the morrow at 9 a.m. in the Speaker's Chamber. Sir John Manwaring reported the address on 3 February (481) and it was agreed to with amendments. Courthope's laxity in recording neither the draft address nor the amendments made to it in the committee is to be noted.

At ye Comm^ee appointed to bring in a Bill upon ye debate of ye House to make the Militia more usefull.[1]

Veneris [a] 10° Feb. 1698.

The Comm^ee met and sev^ll Acts of parl^t relateing to ye Militia was read.

Sabti 11° Feb. 1698.

The Comm^ee met and adj^d till Monday.

Lune 13° Feb. 1698.

The Comm^ee met and adj^d till tomorrow.

[fo. 54v.]

At ye Com^ee to whome is committed the Bill to Enable Edwd Price Esqr to transfer a charge of one thousand pounds for ye use of his younger children from an estate in ye County of Mountgomery to an estate in the Countyes of Hereford & Radnor of a better value.[2]

Martis 21 die Feb. 1698.

The Comm^ee met and the Bill read.
The Deeds were read over, viz.
The Settlem^t upon the marriage of Mr Edw. Price dat 30 June 1666.
Mr Adam Price's Settlem^t dat 16 Nov. 1695.
The Deed to declare ye uses dat 28 Mar. 1691.
The Supplementall Deed dat 1° Oct. 1691.
The Fine & Recovery.

Fol. 4. L. 13. After (purchasor) add (towards the paym^t of the debts of the said Edward Price), and leave out from (purchasor) to (and) in ye 16th line.

Fol. 5. L. 2. Fill ye bla. w^th (five hundred).

[fo. 55r.]

[a] *Preceded by* Jovis *erased*.

[1] On 6 February (484) the House proceeded to take into consideration the King's speech of 1 February in which he reproached the House for insisting on disbanding his army, and warned them that it was incumbent on them to provide sufficient strength for the safety of the kingdom. After debate, it was ordered that a bill should be brought in to make the Militia more useful, and the preparation of the bill was referred to a committee of 21 nominated members or any 5 of them, to meet on the morrow at 9 a.m. in the Speaker's Chamber and to sit *de die in diem*. On 8 February (491) 17 members were added. On 2 March (540) Mr. Foley presented the bill, which did not reach the committee stage. Courthope's minutes, which end on this folio, do not record an effective meeting.

[2] Price's Estate Bill, after leave given on 25 January (449), was presented by Mr. Price on 8 February (493), and on 15 February (512) was committed to a committee of 24 nominated members with those for Wales and Herefordshire. Mr. Price reported the bill with amendments on 27 February (529).

Air & Calder Bill.[1] Mercurij [a] 8° die Feb. 1698.

The Comm^{ee} met and adj^{d} till Saturday morning.

Sabt 11° die Feb.

S^{r} Jo. Bland in ye Chair.
The Comm^{ee} met and the Bill read.
A Peticõn from ye City of York was read.
Ordered, That [b] the Pet^{s} be heard by their Counsell on Wednsday fortnight [c] next.
A Peticõn of Fra. Nevill Esqr. read.
Ordered, That he be heard by his Counsell, at ye same time.
Ordered, That ye Master and Wardens of Trinity House doe attend [d] at ye same time & produce the Report in relacõn to ye makeing ye said rivers navigable, and y^{t} they have a Copy of the Bill in ye mean time.
Adj^{d} to this day seaven^{t}.

Sabbti 18° die Feb. 1698.

The Comm^{ee} met and adjourned to Wednsday the first day of March next.

Martis [e] 1° die Martij 1698/9.[f]

The Counsell was called in, viz.
Mr Serj^{t} Wright for ye City of York: Mr Northy for ye Bill.
The Report from Trinity House read.
M Serj^{t} Wright, That ye Report is partiall. It will be ye ruin of ye City of York. When it flowes at ye mouth of ye river Ayr it ebbs at ye Humber. It must draw of ye water from ye City of York.
The City of York drive a great trade from cheese, butter &c. and also for cloth.

[a] *At top of folio* Ven *erased.* [b] *Followed by* N *erased.*
[c] *Written above* seaven *erased.* [d] *Followed by* on Wed *erased.*
[e] *Should be* Mercurij. [f] *Preceded by* 1689 *of which the first three figures erased.*

---

[1] For the Aire and Calder Navigation Bill of the previous session, see fos. 7r and 7v. On 11 January 1698/9 (395) a petition from Leeds for leave to bring in the bill was presented and read. Leave was given Lord Fairfax and Mr. Brotherton to prepare and bring in the bill. Lord Fairfax presented it on 18 January (425), and on 7 February (486) it was read a second time. After a motion (negatived) that it be referred to a committee of the whole House it was committed to a committee of 40 nominated members with those for Yorks, Durham, Lancs, Northumberland and Cumberland, to meet at 5 in the Speaker's Chamber, and to have power to send for persons, papers and records. On the same day a petition from the City of York against the bill, and another from Francis Nevill praying to be heard were presented, and the House ordered that both should be heard by counsel before the committee. On 27 February (530) 8 members were added; on 8 March (554) it was ordered that the report should be made on Monday morning next (13 March); and on that day Sir John Bland reported the bill with several amendments. One clause was negatived by the House, but the bill passed both Houses this session and became the Act 10 & 11 W. III, c. 19. The proceedings of the committee on 1 March, when counsel on both sides presented their cases and called their witnesses, are extremely interesting as an example (remarkably modern in form) of the hearing of an opposed local bill in committee, instead of at the bar of the House, as became more usual in the eighteenth century.

[fo. 55v.]
Witnesses for ye Pets.
John Moor, known ye river, that ye water is lost a foot in his time since Gold Sluice was down.
That ye trade of ye City is very great.
If Knottingly Mill Dam be kept up as it is now, will not prejudice the river Ouze.
Mr Hadley for ye Bill.
There will be no cutt to divert ye current of ye water.
John Buttery for ye Pets.
The tide does not flow so [a] much by a foot at York since Gold Sluce was down.
If the river Ouze be not cut, it will not hurt them.
The sludging of ye river Ouze is [b] a prejudice to [c] ye flowing of ye river.
John Bacon.
When Gold Sluce was up, it flowed above a foot higher then now in ye river Ayr.
Simon Richardson.
The tide does not flow so strong above Gold Sluce as it did abot 20 yeares agoe.
That there is near 100 vessells belong to York [d] City.
That he does not conceive it will be any prejudice.
Tho. Ward.
Mr Northy for the Bill, It will be no prejudice to the City of York.
It will be very advantagious to ye whole country, and ye charge of carriage of goods 2 thirds cheaper.
Mr Serjt Write desires there may be a Clause to oblige the Undertakers to keep up the locks to be erected.
Mr Hadley.
There must be locks. It will be noe prejudice to ye river Ouze. The first lock will be set up about Hadlesey.[e]

Adjd till tomorrow morning.

[fo. 56r.] Jovis 2o Marcij 1698.

The Commee met and proceeded upon the Bill.
Fol. 1. L. 1. After (makeing) add (and keeping).
Fol. 1. L. 2. Fill ye bla. wth (from a place called Weeland situate upon the river Ayr).
L. 10. Fill ye bla. wth (Mr Caleb Askwth present Mayor of Leeds, Wm Rook, Josuah Ibbetson, Tho. Kitchmann, Hen. Jocson, John Dodgson, Wm Milner, John Rontree, Tho. Laisenby Gent., Aldren of ye Corporation of Leeds, Sr Lyon Pilkington Bart., John Goodrich Esqr., Robt Benson Esqr., Richd Wilton Esqr., Theoph. Shelton, Joseph Watkinson, John Smith, Abra. Beavers & Richd Ellis Gent. in and nigh the Town of Wakefield).

[a] *Preceded by* by *erased and followed by* as *erased.*
[b] *Followed by* ye occasion of *erased.*
[c] *Followed by* to *erased.*
[d] *Preceded by* Co *erased.*
[e] *Preceded by an illegible name erased.*

Fol. 2. L. 2. Fill y^{e} bla. wth (nine).
6. Fill y^{e} bla. wth (Weeland).
Fol. 5. L. 2. Fill y^{e} bla. wth
4. Fill y^{e} bla. wth (seaven).
Fol. 6. L. 8. Fill y^{e} bla. wth (seaven).
10. The same.
14. Fill y^{e} bla. wth (5$^{£}$).
ult. Fill y^{e} bla. wth (20$^{s.}$).
Fol. 7. L. 5. Fill y^{e} bla. wth (seaven).
12.[a] The same.
Fol. 8. L. 6. The same.
8. Fill y^{e} bla. wth (twenty).

[fo. 56v.]
Ayr & Calder.
Fol. 9. L. 4. Fill y^{e} bla. wth (seaven).
Fol. 11. L. 1. Fill y^{e} bla. wth (eleaven).
5. Fill y^{e} bla. wth (200$^{£}$).
6. Fill y^{e} bla. wth (4000$^{£}$).
Fol. 12. L. 8. Fill y^{e} bla. wth (Weeland aforesaid).
10. Fill y^{e} 1st bla. wth (Weeland), y^{e} 2^{d} bla. wth (first).
11. Fill y^{e} bla. wth (May).
12. Fill y^{e} 1st bla. wth (10$^{s.}$), y^{e} 2^{d} bla. wth (first).
13. Fill y^{e} 1st bla. wth (Oct.), y^{e} 2^{d} bla. wth (first).
15. Fill y^{e} bla. wth (16$^{s.}$).
Fol. 14. L. 12. Fill y^{e} bla. wth (damages).
13. Fill y^{e} bla. wth (full costs).
Fol. 15. L. 11. Leave out (by) and insert (ag^{t}).
Fol. 16. L. 3. Fill y^{e} bla. wth (full).
10. Fill y^{e} bla. wth (seaven).
Fol. 17. L. 9.[b] Leave out (and) and insert (or), & after (their) add (own proper).
11. Fill ye bla. (7).
13. Fill ye bla. wth (20).
Fol. 18. L. 3.[b] After (royaltyes) add (rights).
8. After (royaltyes) add (rights tolls).

Adj^{d} till Saturday morning next.

Sabti 4° die Martis 1698.

Clause [c] (A) read twice.

Adj^{d} till Monday morning 8 a clock.

[fo. 57r.]
Ayr & Calder.

Lune 6° die Martij 1698/9.

The Comm^{ee} meet and two Clauses were offered to the Bill and agreed to.
Ordered, That the Bill wth the amendm^{ts} be reported.

[a] *Followed by* 11 *erased.* [b] *Incorrect figures erased.* [c] *Preceded by* A *erased.*

[fo. 57v.] Jovis 16° die Feb. 1698.[1]

Wooll.
The Com^{ee} met and Capt. Baker attended and delivered into y^{e} Com^{ee} an acco^{t} of what seizures has been made & w^{t} returned into y^{e} Excheq^{r}. to y^{e} amo^{t} of 3000$^{£}$ or thereabouts.
That [a] abo^{t} 30 persons are now under execuc͠on.
That 200 are now under prosecuc͠on.
That he has obtained verdicts ag^{t} sev^{ll} ꝑsons to y^{e} amo^{t} of near 12000$^{£}$.
Mr Baker,[b] being asked what money he has paid for prosecuc͠ons upon y^{e} acco^{t} of exporting wooll & to whome he hath paid y^{e} same and what other sumes he hath expended relateing to the service, said cannot give an acc^{t} of ꝑticular sumes but will do as well as he can if time given.
Ordered, That he have till this day sevenn^{t} at 8 in the morning.
M Jobson đđ a proposall which was read & said that W^{t} Haven is a port unfitt to have leave to export wooll which comes there from Scotland & convey it to Holland & Ireland.
Adj. till Saturđ. next at 9 in the morñ.

Sab͞ti 18° die Feb. 1698.

Wooll.
M Edwards, Capt. of ye Blackwell Hall sloop, said he has a deputac͠on to seize wooll.
That he seized a parcell of wooll at Ramsgate in ye store-houses there, but ye Custome House Officer said he had an ord^{r}. from ye Com^{s} of ye Customes to shipp the same for that it was Spanish wooll.
That he seized another ship laden wth wooll in Dover [c] peer come from Rotterdam wch lay 21 dayes betw. the two brigantines y^{t} are ordered to cruize there.

[fo. 58r.]
That at [d] Ramsgate the officer John Mockford told him he would break his head if he offered to meddle wth it, for that the said Mockford told him he had an ord^{r} from ye Com^{s} of Cust^{s}. to ship the same, it being Spanish wooll.
That in Augt last ye packet boat carryed great quantityes of wooll.
That Cha. Cawsey exports great quantityes of wooll into France in his sloope wch sayles wth French colours.
That in Dec. last a vessell com. from France came into Dover peer, that he seized brandy & alamods therein, that he found 2 peices of silks, that the Collector at Dover refused to send the said goods to ye Custome House in London, that he seized sev^{ll} parcell of brandy afterwards.

[a] *On line above* That *not erased, rest of line blank.* [b] *Followed by* saith *erased.*
[c] *Preceded by a semi-erasure of an abbreviation, probably by writing* y *over it.*
[d] *Preceded by* y *erased.*

[1] Continued from fo. 53r., see p. 63, n. 2.

That ye Captns of ye brigantines threatened him, viz.
Capt. Coward
Capt. Windson } threatened to sink him.
Capt. Layton
Capt. Clifton
That abot 10 dayes agoo he took 3 packs of comb'd wooll out of 3 [a] Dutch hoys in ye Downes, wch came directly from Holland.
That ye wooll was stored at ye bottom of ye hoy und^ε other goods.
Mr Haines,

That ye officers sent down to prevent ye exportacon of wooll have be sevll times attacked by Scotch [b] Dragoons, who carred sevll packs into Scotland.
Mr Moor,

That he was knocked down by some of ye Scotch Dragoons & they carryed off 2 packs of wooll into Scotland.
That they have seized sevll packs of wooll in Northumberland goeing into Scotland.
That ye owners of ye wooll carry ye same into Scotland.
Fenwick Downes at Hexham arrested Mr Ussell for seizing wooll goeing into Scotland.

Adjd to Wednsday.

[fo. 58v.] Mercurij 22o die Feb. 1698.

Wooll.
Capt. Edwards said, That he was kept a close prisoner from Thursday to Fryday & he desired to go to drink a pint of wine & the goaler made him pay 5s. for ye same.
That he offered sufficient bayle, but the gayler refused to take bayle at first.[c]
Mr Goodw

Jovis 23o die Feb. 1698.

Wooll.
The Comee [d] met and Capt. Baker pursuant to ye Ord^ε of ye Comee delivered an accot to ye Comee [e] a particular accot of all moneys disburst and paid by him relating to prosecucons and other services relating to ye transportacon of wooll, wch was read.

Adjd to Monday morning.[1]

[fo. 59r.] Jovis 23o die Feb. 1698.

At ye Commee to whome the Bill for Sale of some part of ye Estate late Sr Tho. Darcy deceased for paymt of his debs is comitted.[2]

[a] *Written over* a.
[b] *Preceded by* ye *erased.*
[c] *Followed on next line by* Ordered That *erased.*
[d] *Followed by* ad *erased.*
[e] *Followed by* of *erased.*

[1] Continued on fo. 60r.
[2] Darcy's Estate Bill, after leave given on 10 February (495), was presented by Mr. Hammond on 15 February (512) and on 23 February (523) was read a second time and committed to a committee of 27 nominated members and those for Essex, to meet at 5 in the Speaker's Chamber. On 27 February Mr. Hammond (530) reported the bill without amendment.

Mr Hammond in ye Chair.

The Commee met and adjourned till tomorrow morning.

Veneris 24o die Feb. 1698.

Darcy.
The Comee mett and the Bill read; and the Commee took the consents of the three daughters of Sr Tho. Darcy deceased, viz.
Frances now ye wife of Sr Wm Dawes Bart.
Mary Darcy }
Eliz. Darcy } unde 21 yeares of age.

And then ye Commee adjourned till tomorrow morning.

Sabti 25o die Feb. 1698.

The Commee proceeded upon the Bill and went thro' the same.
The Will was produced & examined.

[fo. 59v.] Veneris 24o die Febr. 1698 ante meridiem.

At ye Commee to whom ye Bill for preventing irregular proceedings of Sheriffs and other Officers in makeing the Returnes to ye Clerk of ye Crown of Members chosen to sit in Parliamt is comitted.[1]
Mr Clerk in ye Chair.

The Commee met and adjd till ye afternoon.

The Commee met and ye Bill read & preamble postponed.

Adjd to Monday 4 in ye afternoon. [a] [2]

Veneris 3o Martij 1698.

Fol. 1. L. 8, 9. Fill ye 1st bla. wth (the day that any such [b] parliamt shall be appointed to meet).
The 2d bla. wth (fourteen).

Fol. 2. L. ult. At ye end of the Bill add (for every such offence the sume of 500£ one moiety [c] thereof shall be to his Maty and ye other moiety [d] to him or them that shall sue for the same, to be recovered by accon of debt, bill, plaint or informacon in any of his Mats Courts of Record at Westme wherein no essoign, proteccon, priviledge or wager of law shall be allowed nor any more than one imparlance).[3]

[fo. 60r.]
Wooll.[4]

[a] *On the same line in margin* Fol. 1. L. 8 & 9 *erased.*
[b] *Written above* future *erased.*
[c] *Written above* half part *erased.*
[d] *Preceded by* half *erased.*

---

[1] Continued from fo. 50v.
[2] There is no entry of a meeting on this day.
[3] Continued on fo. 60v.
[4] Continued from fo. 58v.

Lune 27o die Feb. 1698.

Mr Spicer at Southampton seized a parcell of wooll in ye Isabella Man of War, Capt. Warner Comander, 230 pd of combed wooll. The pilate's name was De Croy who carried it on board in ye night wthout ye Captns knowledge.
That [a] it was ship't by pidgeon.
That he stopt 5 baggs of wooll wch came from Barnaby Street designed for Jersey.
That the Master had 23 lb. in his cabbin wch he bought of pigeon upon his own accot.
Mr Hoar produced a letter from one in France giveing an accot that great quantitys of wooll are exported from Ireland into France made up in barrlls & entred at ye Custom House for beefe &c.[b]

[fo. 60v.]
Writs of Error.
At ye Comee to whom ye Bill for limiting certain times [c] wthin wch Writts of Error shall be brought for Reversing Fines, Comon Recoveries & Ancient Judgmts is committed.[1]

Martis 7o die Martij 1698.

Mr Lowther in ye Chair.
The Commee met and proceeded upon ye Bill and made these amendmts.
Fol. L. 11. Fill ye 1st bla. wth (first), ye 2d bla. wth (May 1699).
13. Fill ye bla. wth (twenty).
19. The same amendmt.
Fol. 2. L. 1. Fill ye bla. wth (five).
Ordered, That ye Bill wth ye amendmts be reported to ye House.

At ye Comee to whom ye Bill for setling Augmentations on some small Viccariges for ever is comitted.[2]

Martis 7o die Martij 1698/9.

The Commee met and adjourned till tomorrow morning.

Mercurij 8o die Martij 1698/9.

Foot Onslow Esq. in ye Chair.
The Bill was read and sevll amendmts made.

[a] *Preceded by* That ye *erased.*
[b] *Followed by* from ye Isle *erased.*
[c] *Followed by* for Reversing *erased.*

[1] The Writs of Error Bill, after leave given on 5 January (387), was presented by Mr. Thursby on 14 January (406), and on 18 January (425) was read a second time and committed to a committee of 31 nominated members and all the gentlemen of the long robe, to meet at 5 in the Speaker's Chamber. Mr. Lowther reported the bill with several amendments on 7 March (553), and it became the Act 10 & 11 W. III, c. 14.

[2] The Augmenting Vicarages Bill, after leave given on 18 February (517), was presented by Mr. Pelham on 23 February (523) and on 1 March was read a second time and committed to a committee of 32 nominated members and those for Surrey and Sussex, to meet at 5 in the Speaker's Chamber. Mr. Onslow reported the bill with amendments on 9 March (557), but it did not reach the Statute book.

Fol. 3. L. 19. Fill y^{e} bla. wth (thirty pounds).
Fol. 4. L. 6. Fill y^{e} bla. wth (twelve).
9. Fill y^{e} bla. wth (40$^{s.}$).

Adj^{d} till tomorrow.

Jovis 9° die Martij 1698.

Viccaridges.
The Com^{ee} [a] met and went thro' the Bill and at the end of the Bill a [b] Clause was offered & agreed to.
Ordered, to report the same.

[fo. 61r.]
At y^{e} Comm^{ee} to whom y^{e} Bill for makeing the River Trent in y^{e} Countyes of Leic^{s}., Derb̄. & Stafford Navigable is committed.[1]

Veneris 10° die Martij 1698.

The Hon [c] Henry Paget in ye Chair.
The Comm^{ee} met and adj^{d} till tomorrow morning.

Sab̄t̄i 11° die Martij.

The Comm^{ee} met and proceeded upon the Bill & made these fo

Fol. 3. L. 2. Fill ye bla [d] wth (five).
Fol. 4. L. 11. Fill ye bla. wth (five).
L. ult. Fill ye blank wth.
Fol. 5. L. 4. Fill ye bla. wth (five).
ult. The same amendm^{t}.
Fol. 6. L. 7. Fill y^{e} bla. wth (ten).
11. Fill y^{e} bla. wth (5).
ult. The [d] same amendm^{t}.
Fol. 7. L. 3. The same amendm^{t}.
9. The same amendm^{t}.
13. The same amendm^{t}.
15. The same.
Fol. 8. L. 2. The same.
12. The same.
Fol. 9. L. 5. Fill y^{e} bla. wth (10$^{£}$).
15. Fill y^{e} bla. wth (5).

[a] *Preceded by* Cla *erased.*
[b] *Unintentionally erased by a blot.*
[c] *Preceded by* Right *erased* (*in margin*).
[d] *Preceded by* f *erased.*

[1] Trent Navigation Bill, after leave given on 16 February (514), was presented by Mr. Paget on 3 March (542), and on 9 March (557) was committed to a committee of 39 nominated members and those for Leicestershire, Derbyshire, Staffordshire and Warwickshire, to meet on the morrow at 8 a.m. in the Speaker's Chamber. On 11 March (583) 4 members were added. On 17 March Mr. Paget reported the bill (592) with several amendments, and it became the Act 10 & 11 W. III, c. 20.

Fol. 10.[a] L. 2. Fill ye bla. wth (seaven).[b]
6. Fill ye bla. wth (nine).
10. Fill ye bla. wth (twenty).

[fo. 61v.]
Mr Paget in ye Chair. Lune 13o die Martij 1698.

River Trent.
The Commee proceeded upon the Bill & made these amendmts, viz.
Fol. 11. L. 7. Fill ye bla. wth (three pence).
15. Fill ye bla. wth (five).
Fol. 12. L. 11. Fill ye bla. wth (five).
Fol. 13. L. 5. Fill ye bla. wth (five).
L. 13. Fill ye bla. wth (six).[c]
Fol. 14. L. 13. Fill ye bla. wth (five).
Fol. 15. L. 6. Fill ye bla. wth (five).
Fol. 16. L. 6. Fill ye bla. wth (five).
L. 13. The same.
Fol. 17. L. 1. Fill ye bla. wth (600£).
L. 7. Fill ye bla. wth (five).
L. 10. Fill ye bla. wth (10£).
Fol. 18. L. 3. Fill ye bla. wth (five).
7. Fill ye bla. wth (Burton upon Trent or some other [d] convenient place upon the said river wth in seaven miles of the said Town [e]).
L. 8. Fill ye bla. wth (five).
Ordered, to report the Bill wth the amendmts.

[fo. 62r.] Jovis 16o die Martij 1698/9.

At ye Commee to whome the Bill for Vesting part of the Estate of Tho. Methold Esq. in Trustees for raising the sume of one thousand two hundred pounds expended in the improvemt of the said Estate is committed.[1]

The Bill read and severall Deeds exmd, viz. ye Deed of Settlemt dat 2 June 1676.

Mr Methold and his wife consented to the Bill.

Mr Hoar in ye Chair.

The Preamble agreed to.

Fol. 10. L. Fill ye blank wth (Stephen Harvey of ye Middle Temple London Esq., Wm Wigan of Kensington in ye County of Midlx, Clerk, Samll Diggle of Gray's Inn in ye County of Midlx Gentl.
Ordered to report ye first opportunity.

[a] *Written above another figure erased.* [b] *Preceded by* (six) (?) *erased.*
[c] *Preceded by* three *erased.*
[d] *Followed by* con *erased.* [e] *Written above* same *erased.*

[1] Methwold's Estate Bill. On 11 February the petition of Thomas Methwold (or Methold) and his wife for leave to bring in the bill was read (497) and leave was given. On 27 February (529) Mr. Harvey presented the bill, which on 10 March (558) was read a second time and committed to a committee of 35, to meet at 5 in the Speaker's Chamber. On 16 March (591) two members were added. On 21 March Mr. Hoar reported the bill (605) with some amendments.

[fo. 62v.]
At ye Commee to whome the Bill to Enable Robt Aldworth & Ann his wife to sell their Estate in or near Wantage in ye County of Berks for ye Raising of 300£ for paymt of his debts & for applying ye Residue of ye moneys ariseing by ye Sale for ye purchaseing some other Estate for ye sole benefit of his wife & children, is comitted.[1]

Lune 27o die Martij 1699.

Fol. 4. L. 5. Fill the blank wth (Hen. Izard, Fellow of New College in Oxford, Seymour Wood of London, Oyleman, & Robt. Greeway of Thavye's Inne in St Andrew's Holbon London, Gent.)
6. The same amendmt.
11. The same amendmt.
18. The same amendmt.
23. The same amendmt.
The same amendmt.
Fol. 5. L. 24. The same amendmt.
Fol. 6. L. 3. The same amendmt.
21. The same amendmt.
Fol. 7. L. 8. Leave out (his) and insert (The King's most Excellt).
Mr Aldworth and his wife and Mr Wood & Mr Greeway, two of the Trustees, consented to ye passing the Bill.
The Deed of Settlemt upon Mr Aldworth's marriage read.
Ordered, to report the Bill wth the amendmts.

[fo. 63r.]
At ye Commee to whom the Bill for ye Sale of ye Estate of Zenobia Hough for ye paymt of the debts of her husband & other uses is committed.[2]
Mr Brotherton in ye Chair.

Lune 27o die Martij 1699.

The Bill read.
The Deed produced and read.
The Fine & Recovery read.
Fol. 1. L. 10. Leave out (lands) and insert (lanes).

[1] On 11 March (561) the petition of Robert Aldworth and his wife for leave to bring in the bill was read, and leave given. On 18 March (599) Mr. Rowny presented the bill, which on 25 March (613) was read a second time and committed to a committee of 28, to meet at 5 in the Speaker's Chamber. On 28 March (619) Mr. Rowny reported the bill with some amendments.

[2] On 10 March (558) the petition of Zenobia Hough for leave to bring in the bill was read, and leave given. On 15 March Mr. Brotherton presented the bill, which on 24 March (612) was read a second time and committed to a committee of 34 nominated members and those for Yorks and Lancs, to meet at 5 in the Speaker's Chamber. On 28 March (619) Mr. Brotherton reported the bill with some amendments.

Fol. 6. L. 2, 3. Fill ye blank w^th^ (the said John Tanner & W^m^. Etterick of the Middle Temple London, Esq.)

Mr Tanner
M^r^ [a] Zenobia Hough
Mr Benoni Hough
M^s^ Abigail Hough
Mr Minshall
M^r^ Ra. Hough
} consented to ye passing of the Bill.

Ordered, to report.

[fo. 63v.]
At ye Comm^ee^ to whom the Bill for Encourageing the Trade to Newfoundland is comitted.[1]

Lune 27° Martij 1699.

The Comm^ee^ mett and adj^d^ till tomorr morning.
Newfoundland Bill.

Martis 28° die Martij 1699.

The Comm^ee^ met and made choice of Mr Gwyn for Chairman, and then adj^d^ till Thursday morning next.[2]

At ye Comm^ee^ to whom the Bill for Vesting the Reall Estate late of Thomas Lassells Esqr. deced in Trustees to be sold for ye paym^t^ of his debts is committed.[3]

The Bill read and the Com^ee^ went thro' the same w^th^out any amendm^ts^.

Mr Metcalf appeared and gave his consent to the Bill.

M^r^ W^m^. Wilson not being present a writeing und^r^ his hand & seale was produced signifying his consent.

[a] *Obvious error for* M^s^.

---

[1] Newfoundland Trade Bill. On 20 February (519) leave was given to bring in a bill for encouraging trade to Newfoundland, Sir Edward Seymour, Mr. Gwyn and Mr. Scobell to prepare the bill, which was presented by the first-named on 25 March (613). On 27 March (615) it was read a second time and committed to a committee of 24 nominated members with those for Cornwall, Devon, Dorset and the seaports, and all that were merchants, to meet at 5 in the Speaker's Chamber. Courthope records that the committee met that day. On 15 April a petition was read from the Greenland Company against the additional duty on tonnage and poundage imposed by two recent acts (644): it was ordered that the committee, to whom this petition was also referred, on the Newfoundland Bill have power to receive a clause to explain the said acts. On 24 April (661) the bill was ordered to be reported on the following day, and on 25 April (664) Mr. Gwyn reported that the committee had considered the bill and the Greenland petition and had made several amendments. On 1 May (674), after several postponements, the motion for taking the report into consideration was carried on a division, and the amendments were agreed to. It became the Act 10 & 11 W. III, c. 25.

[2] Here is another instance of the choice of chairman being entered in the minutes. The proceedings are continued on fo. 64r.

[3] Lascells' Estate Bill came down from the Lords on 25 March (615), and on 1 April (627) it was read a second time and committed to a committee of 32 nominated members and those for Yorks. On 4 April Sir William Hustler, who was presumably chairman of the committee, reported the bill without amendment (631). No date is given by Courthope for this entry, but it was probably Monday 3 April or the following day.

[fo. 64r.] Jovis 30° die Martij 1698.[a]

Mr Gwyn in ye Chair.
At ye Commee to whome the Bill for Encourageing the Trade to Newfoundland is committed.[1]
Newfoundland Bill.
The Bill read over, and severall merchts appeared and made their objeccons to the Bill, viz.
Mr Nisbet.

That ye restrayning this trade would be a great detrimt to Engld.

That if ye planters shall be removed 6 miles from ye sea coasts it will be a great prejudice to ye merchts.
Mr Manston.

By Boats takes up the ye ships' fishing ground & become planters, and great numbers goe & settle in New Engld.
Navigacon not promoted nor increased by ye By Boat men.

Adjd till Monday.

Lune 3 die Aprilis 1699.

The Commee met and sevll merchts attended, and it was moved,
That the orriginall Charter be laid before the Commee.
The cop. of the Patent read once over and then paragraph by paragraph.
1st Clause.
If any man shall kill another or if any shall steal[b] the goods of any other to ye value of 40s, the offender shall be brought into England & tryed in any County[c] as his Maty shall direct.
A Clause that there shall be be 2 green men for one boat.
That one to be a man that has been but one year at sea & the other that has[d] never been at sea.
Sevll persons for ye Bill & alleadged that the Mercht Adventurers to Newfoundland have been of great advantage to Engld by increasing the number of seamen by their imploying yearly great numbers of landmen in their fishing voyages there, wch hath produced a continuall succession of marriners for ye comon service of this nation.
That the said trade hath been further advantagious to this nation in that it hath caused a consumption of great quantityes of provisions, manufactures & other produccons of the nation & constantly hath imployed great numbers of poor artificers and tradesmen in ye carrying on thereof & that the effects thereof (by the returnes made thereby from sevll foreign parts to England) have highly advanced his Mats Customes.

[a] *Error for* 1699.
[b] *Followed by* from *erased.*
[c] *Followed by* shall direct *erased.*
[d] *Followed by* been 2 years at sea *erased.*

---

[1] Continued from fo. 63v. None of this evidence was reported to the House; it is reflected in several clauses of the Act.

[fo. 64v.]
That the said trade at present doth and for some yeares last past hath lain under great discouragem^ts from ye ill practices of a sort of interlopeing traders comonly called By Boat Keepers, whose method is to carry from England to Newfoundland only the best and most experienced fishermen, confineing their service purely to their own private interest, and employ three such able fishermen in one boat who cannot kill in a day more fish than such boat can carry, whereas were these three dispersed by the merchants that send fishing ships thither in three severall boats togeather wth some less experienced men to make up a due complement, their influence would be so diffusive as to occasion the takeing more then double the quantity of fish (by instructing the said less experienced fishermen) above what is possible for the said three men togeather to take, and would propagate a constant supply of fit men for that imploym^t and be a setled nursery for seamen in generall.

That of late yeares the trade is soe much reduced and ye number of skillfull fishermen so [a] decreased that not half ye quantity of fish caught now as formerly.

That such ports as have formerly sent 50 sail of ships to Newfoundland.

If care be not taken, the trade will be totally lost & the subjects ruined in their trade and the King lose a great income.

That the nation is soe farr from haveing any [b] benefit from those irregular traders either by consumpc͞on of its provisions or propagateing of seamen as that they are for ye most part supplyed wth provisions from foreign plantations, and breed up noe seamen, but they themselves either stay in Newfoundland and absent themselves from the nation's service or else transport themselves to other foreign parts where they live & dye.

If they were totally restrained from By Boat keeping, they would be of advantage as well to the nation as to the merch^ts, which would naturally produce the good effects aforesaid.

Adj^d to Thursday morning next.[1]

[fo. 65r.] [c]
At ye Comm^ee to whome the Bill to Enable Sam^ll Wake als Jones to sell Lands to pay debts & to purchase other Lands adjoyning to & formerly parcell of his Mannor of Waltham als Waltham Holy Cross in ye County of Essex to be setled to ye same uses.[2] [d]

Jovis 13° Aprilis 1699.

The Comm^ee met and adj^d till tomorrow morning.

[a] *Followed by* much *erased.*
[b] *Written above* the *erased.*
[c] *At the head of the folio* Jovis 6° die Aprilis 1699. The Comm^ee met and adj^d till Tuesday morning *erased.*
[d] *Followed by some illegible words erased.*

[1] There is no entry of any meeting on this date; the proceedings are continued on fo. 67r. under date 15 April.

[2] Wake's Estate Bill came down from the Lords on 3 April (630) and on 12 April (639) it was read a second time and committed to a committee of 32 to meet at 5 in the Speaker's Chamber. On 14 April (641) Mr. Conyers reported the bill without amendment.

Veneris 14° die Aprilis 1699.

Mr Conyers in ye Chair.

The Commee met and went thro' the Bill.

[fo. 65v.]

At ye Commee to whome the Bill to Enable Tho. Bide Esqr. an Inft wth ye consent of his Guardians & next Relations to make a Contract for ye buying in his Mother's Joynture & to sell a small Estate in Great Amwell in ye County of Hertford & for ye secureing & raiseing a pencõn for Barbara Bide his Sister.[1]

Jovis 13° die Apr. 1699.

The Commee met and adjd till till tomorrow morning.

Veneris 14° die Apr. 1699.

Mr Brotherton in ye Chair.

The Comee met and the Bill read over and ye Deeds exm̃ed, viz. the Marriage Settlemt dat 25th May 1677 read.

The Ld Grandison signifyed his consent und hand & seal, as also Sr Tho. Bide und hand and seale.

Dugall Campbell Esq.
Mary his wife
Mr Villars
Tho. Bide Esq.
} all psonally consented.

The Bill ordered to be reported wth out any amendmts.

[fo. 66r.]

At ye Commee to whom the Peticõn of ye Patentees, Assignees & others who are interested in Annuall Sum̃es payable out of ye Hereditary Excise is referred.[2]

Jovis 23° die Martij 1698.

The Commee met and adjd till tomorrow morning.

Veneris 24° die Martij 1698.

The Commee met and adjd till tomorrow morning.

[1] Byde's Estate Bill came down from the Lords on 24 March (612) and on 4 April (631) it was read a second time and committed to a committee of 29 nominated members and those for Essex and Herts, to meet at 5 in the Speaker's Chamber. On 15 April Mr. Brotherton reported the bill without amendment (644).

[2] Hereditary Excise Patentees. On 23 March (611) the petition of patentees, assignees and other persons interested in annual sums payable out of the hereditary excise was presented and read. Its substance was that they had prompted the methodizing of a fund sufficient to answer the principal and interest due, without diminishing the revenue, and they prayed that the same might be applied to the payment of the said debt. It was at once referred to a committee of 57 to examine the matter and report their opinion, to meet at 5 in the Speaker's Chamber. On 31 March the petition of divers pewterers, the substance of which is blank in the Journal (625), was referred to the same committee, to whom power was granted to send for persons, papers and records. On 4 May (687) Sir Robert Napper reported the matter, the report was read and was then re-committed to the committee, and that was the end of the matter, since Parliament was prorogued the same day. Since the report is not set out in the Journal, Courthope's minutes, though incomplete, have a certain interest.

Sabti 25° Martij 1699.

The Comm[ee] met and adj[d] till Monday morning.

Lune 27° die Martij 1699.

The Comm[ee] met and adj[d] till tomorrow morning.

Martis 28° die Martij 1699.

The Comm[ee] met and adj[d] till tomorrow morning.

Mercurij 29° die Martij 1699.

The Comm[ee] mett and [a] the Peticon was read and M[r] M[r] Murray appeared on behalfe of the Pet[s] an delivered into the Comm[ee] a proposall in writeing w[ch] was also read. And the Pet[s] prayed, That the same may be applyed to the payment of the pet[s] debts.

And then adj[d] till Fryday morning next.

Veneris 31° die Martij 1699.

The Comm[ee] met and adj[d] till 5 a clock in y[e] afternoon.

Post Meridiem ejusdem diei.

The Comm[ee] met and the Peticon of the Pewterers was read.
Ordered, That the Pet[s] doe attend the said Com[ee] on Monday in y[e] afternoon at 5 a clock.
Ordered, That M[r] Williamson attend the Comm[ee] on Monday and give them an acco[t] what progress has been made in any of the Courts [b] at Westm[s] or elsewhere [c] in relacon to the Bankers' debt.
M[r] Murray delivered in a state of the debt to Lady Day 1699.

[fo. 66v.]
M[r] Murray's proposall was again read,[d] the substance of w[ch] is, That an exact Assize in all liquid measures amongst retaylers be enforced under severe penaltyes, and the surpluss of the duty ariseing thereby reserved by the late Act for setling 700000£ p. ann to y[e] King be appropriated to this end.
Ordered, That an acco[t] be laid before y[e] Com[ee] [e] of y[e] produce of y[e] Excise for these 5 yeares last past.[f]

Adj[d] till Monday 5 in y[e] afternoon.

Lune 3° Aprilis 1699.

The Comm[ee] met and adj[d] till tomorrow morning.

[a] *Followed by* M M *erased.*
[b] *Followed by* of *erased.*
[c] *Followed by* has been made *erased.*
[d] *Followed by* w[ch] *erased.*
[e] *Followed by an illegible word erased.*
[f] *Followed by three lines crossed out:* M[r] Broxby (?) a brewer appeared and offered to lay before the Comm[ee] the cheife cause of the great decay and fall of y[e] Revenue of Excise & how the same may be improved.

Martis 4° Aprilis 1699.

The Comm^{ee} met and adj^{d} to Thursday moring.

Jovis 13 Aprilis 1699.

The Comm^{ee} met and Mr Murray's proposall was again read.
And then adj^{d} till Saturday morning.[1]

[fo. 67r.]
Newfoundland Bill.[2]

Sabti 15° die Aprilis 1699.

The Comm^{ee} met and severall Clauses were offered to be added to the Bill.
Mr Nisbet objects ag^{t} y^{t} of goeing back to 1680,
Objects ag^{t} Vice-Admiralls being Judges.
Not to have ye stages [a] taken from ye planters who have built them.
Since 1680 great infringem^{ts} upon ye ships' room.[3]
Mr Holman & his son do attend on Monday morning next.
Adj^{d} till Monday morning.

Lune 17° die Aprilis 1699.

The Comm^{ee} met and proceeded upon the Bill.[4]

[fo. 67v.]
At ye Comm^{ee} to whome the Peticõn of Robt Barton, Master of a ship called ye Adventure, is referred.[5]

Mercurij 29° Martij 1699.

The Comm^{ee} met and adj^{d} till tomorrow morning.

[a] *Followed by* ag^{t} *imperfectly erased.*

---

[1] There is no further entry of any proceedings of this committee.

[2] Continued from fo. 64v.

[3] The force of Mr. Nisbet's objections can only be appreciated by reading certain sections of the act. The Vice-Admiral of a harbour or creek during a fishing season was the master of the second fishing ship to enter the harbour or creek during the season (s. 4). By s. 5 persons who since 1685 had detained any stage, cook-room or beach must relinquish the same to the public use of the ships: so Mr. Nisbet succeeded in reducing the retrospective period.

[4] Continued on fo. 68v.

[5] Forestallers, etc., of Corn. On 29 March (620) the petition of Robert Barton against John Lofton, Peter Kesterman, Thomas Merritt and Dinah Mason, forestallers, etc., of corn, was read. It complained that the petitioner, being freighted with corn at Plymouth, brought it to London; and because he would not, contrary to the act of Parliament, carry it to Rotterdam, Ostend or Dunkirk, they refused to pay him his freight; and prayed that he might have liberty to come and give information of their notorious practices. A committee of 36 was nominated to examine the matter, to meet at 5 in the Speaker's Chamber, and to have power to send for persons, papers and records. On 24 April Mr. Offley, presumably chairman of the committee, reported the matter and his report is set out in full in the Journal (662). It was resolved that the complaint was malicious, vexatious and groundless.

Jovis 30 Martij 1699.

The Comm^ee met and adj^d till Saturday morning.

Sabti 1° Apr. 1699.

The Comm^ee met and adj^d till Monday morning.

Veneris 14° Apr. 1699.

The Comm^ee met and ordered, That

Mr John Lofton in Bow Church Yard
Mr Tho. Merrit in Harp Lane
Mr Peter Kesterman, Lawrence Poultney Lane
M^s Dinah Mason in Breadstreet
Mr Carter } partners
Mr Book }
Mr Lord doe all attend the said Com^ee on Monday morning next.

[fo. 68r.] Lune 17° die Aprilis 1699.

Mr Barton appeared & said he is charged at Kesterman's suit for 18^£.
That M Lofton freighted his ship with corn and sold ye corn to Kesterman.
Mr Kesterman produced a Charty party dat^d 29th Nov. 1698 made between him and Lofton whereby he was obliged to take in corn at Falmouth & Plymouth.
He also produced the Bill of Ladeing.
Tho. Beckly lives at Mr Williams' in Cha. Street, Westm^r.
That Mr Lofton told Ld Mayor that he had two attachm^ts ag^t Barton & that Ld Mayor sent to both ye Coumpters & none was found there.
Mr Hen. Book, That he made an attachm^t in his name in Mr Lofting's hands for 30^£ for money lent Barton upon Bottom Ree.
Mr Barton, That he complained to Ld Mayor before his ship was seized.
That it appeared to the Comm^ee to be frivolous & groundless an vexatious.
Adj^d till tomorrow morning.[1]

[fo. 68v.] Martis 18° die Aprilis 1699.[2]

Fol. 6. L. 6. The Clause conc. By Boat Keepers postponed.
Clause, That there shall be one man that has not been at sea more then once & one that has never been at sea before.
By [a] Boat Keepers not to take up ships' room.
mem^d ye Collecto^r of ye port to take bond that ye By Boat men shall carry 2 green

[a] *Preceded on line above by* 2 green men *erased.*

[1] There is no further entry relating to this committee.
[2] The committee on the Newfoundland Trade Bill, continued from fo. 67r. Clauses to the effect of those here entered were inserted in the bill and are to be seen in the act.

men in every six, one that has not been at sea more then once & one that has never been at sea before.
Likewise that the Masters of ships shall have one green man in every five.
Adj^d till tomorrow morning.

Mercurij 19° die Apr. 1699.

A Clause to restraine the planters.
Another Clause that in case difference arises ab^t the stages & shipps [a] the Comander of any of his Ma^tys Ships of Warr there present shall determine the right.
Adj^d to Fryday morning next.[1]

[fo. 69r.]
The Engrossed Bill for ye Enabling Cyriack Westlyd Esq^e. to sell some part of his Estate wch by Articles upon his Marriage was agreed to be setled upon his wife & children & for setling other part of his Estate to ye same uses.[2]

Jovis 20 die Aprilis 1699.

The Comm^ee met and proceeded upon the Bill and examined the Deeds, and it appeared to the Comm^ee that the lands to be setled for the same uses as the lands agreed to be sold to Mr Moor are of greater value the [b] the said lands to be sold.
Mr Westlyd [c]} consented
M^s Westlyd }
Sr Wm Massingbeard} Trustees consented.
Mr Prideaux }
Ordered, That the Bill be reported.

[fo. 69v.] Veneris 21° die Aprilis 1699.[3]

Incouragem^t to ye Inhitants.
That ye planters may have ye liberty of men y^t have been in ye Sack ships & those that have been formerly in Newfoundland and as many green men as they please wch is liberty enough & will [d] sufficiently supply the planters.
Adj^d till tomorrow morning.

Sabti 22° die Aprilis 1699.

[a] *Written above* the Comodore shall *erased*.
[b] *Obvious error for* then.
[c] *Followed by* con *erased*.
[d] *Preceded by* th *erased*.

---

[1] Continued on fo. 69v.
[2] Westlyd's Estate Bill came down from the Lords on 6 April (634), and on 17 April (645) was read a second time and committed to a committee of 41 nominated members and those for Lincolnshire, to meet at 5 in the Speaker's Chamber. Mr. Dormer, presumably chairman, reported the bill without amendment on 22 April (659).
[3] The committee on the Newfoundland Trade Bill, continued from fo. 68v. No clause of this kind is to be found in the Act.

Sev^{ll} Clauses were offered to the Bill.[a]
Ordered, That the Bill wth the amendm^{ts} be reported to the House.

[fo. 70r.]
Press 2. Leave out (concerning) & insert (commencing).
Press 3. L. 2. After (trusts) add (disposicons limitacons & appointm^{ts}).[1]
4. L.

[fo. 70v. blank.]

[fo. 71r.]
Com^{ee} to draw up Reasons conc. y^{e} L$^{ds.}$ Amendm^{t} to y^{e} Paper Bill.[2]

Mercurij 3° die Maij 1699.

Mr Harcourt in y^{e} Chair.
The Comm^{ee} mett and agreed upon these Reasons foll. viz.

Reasons to be given to the Lords at a Conference ag^{t} their Amendm^{t} to the Bill for laying a Duty upon paper parchm^{t} vellum and pastboard for the purposes therein mencōned.

That all Ayds which are granted in Parliam^{t} are the Sole and Entire Guift Grant and present of the Commons in Parliament, And that it is the undoubted Right and Priviledge of the Commons that such Ayds are to be raised by such Methods and with such provisions as the Commons only think proper, And that yo^{e} Lordpps by the Antient Law and Constitution of Parliam^{ts} are not to alter any such Guift or Grant or the Methods or provisions for Collecting Raiseing or Enforceing the paym^{t} thereof.
Ordered, That Mr Harcourt do report these Reasons to the House.

[fos. 71v. to 86v. blank.]

[fo. 87r.]

Wooll

Sir ff. Mr Ingram.[3]

[fos. 87v. to 92r. blank.]

[a] *Followed by* viz. A Clause *erased.*

---

[1] These entries must refer to a committee on some ingrossed bill sent down by the Lords, but there is no clue to its title.

[2] The Lords amendments to the Supply Bill, Duty on Paper, were considered on 3 May, and the motion that the House doth agree, etc., was negatived *nem. con.* It was ordered that a conference be desired, and also that a committee of 21 nominated members or any 3 of them should draw up reasons for disagreeing and withdraw to the Speaker's Chamber for that purpose. Mr. Harcourt reported as here set out the same day (683). The prorogation on 4 May prevented any further proceeding in the matter. This assertion of the Commons' right had already been made in 1671 and 1678, see Erskine May (15th ed.), p. 780. This re-statement of 1699 is not mentioned in May: its wording is that of 1678 (9 C.J. 509).

[3] There is little clue to these isolated jottings.

[fo. 92v.]

An Abstract of the Arreare due to the Land Forces Guards & Garrisons.[1]

To clear ye Arreares of Pay from 1st Apr. 92 to 31 Dec. 1697	1275054. 16. 3
To clear ye Arrear of Subsistance to yt time . . .	741753. 9

[*Rest of folio blank.*]

[fos. 93r. to 94v. blank.]

On inside of back cover.[2]

	0.	3.	4
	0.	13.	4
	0.	2.	6
	0.	7.	6
		6.	8
	1.	3.	4
for Ordᵍ	0.	6.	8
for Reading . .	0.	2.	0
for Attendance . .	0.	13.	4
	1.	2.	0

[1] See p. 1, n. 2, above for the relation of these figures to the accounts referred to the Select Committee on Estimates and Accounts in December 1697.

[2] These are obviously calculations by Courthope of the fees due to him for attendance on committees on private bills, the total of the first sum being incorrect. They tally with the fees payable to the clerks without doors for attendance on such committees as set out in the Table of Fees of 1700 (13 C.J. 356–7). We know that there was a table of fees agreed to by the House in 1695, though it was not entered in the Journal, and that it was very similar to that of 1700. The first of the two sums could be itemized as follows: for attending to adjourn the committee 3*s.* 4*d.*, for attendance on two days at 6*s.* 8*d.* a day 13*s.* 4*d.*, for summoning a witness 2*s.* 6*d.*, for taking three consents 7*s.* 6*d.*, for drawing and transcribing the report 6*s.* 8*d.*

INDEX